THE

PUBLICATIONS

OF THE

Lincoln Record Society

FOUNDED IN THE YEAR

1910

VOLUME 95

ISSN 0267–2634

'GRATEFULL TO PROVIDENCE'

THE DIARY AND ACCOUNTS OF
MATTHEW FLINDERS
SURGEON, APOTHECARY AND MAN-MIDWIFE
1775–1802

VOLUME I · 1775–1784

EDITED BY

MARTYN BEARDSLEY and NICHOLAS BENNETT

The Lincoln Record Society

The Boydell Press

First published 2007

A Lincoln Record Society Publication
published by The Boydell Press
an imprint of Boydell & Brewer Ltd
PO Box 9, Woodbridge, Suffolk IP12 3DF, UK
and of Boydell & Brewer Inc.
668 Mt Hope Avenue, Rochester, NY 14620, USA
website: www.boydellandbrewer.com

ISBN 978–0–901503–59–6

A catalogue record for this book is available
from the British Library

Details of other Lincoln Record Society volumes are available
from Boydell & Brewer Ltd

This publication is printed on acid-free paper

Typeset by Pru Harrison, Hacheston, Suffolk
Printed in Great Britain by
Anthony Rowe Ltd, Chippenham, Wiltshire

CONTENTS

ILLUSTRATIONS

The plates appear between pages 102 and 103.

ACKNOWLEDGEMENTS

The thanks of the Lincoln Record Society are due to Robert and Ursula Perry, the owners of the Flinders diaries, for allowing them to be published. The staff of the Lincolnshire Archives, where the Flinders Papers are deposited, have been most helpful throughout the project. The editors also wish to thank: Flinders descendants Witgar Hitchcock and Lisette Flinders Petrie; Miriam Estensen of Queensland, Australia, author of an excellent biography of Matthew Flinders the son; Keith Flinders for his very helpful genealogical advice; the staff at the Donington and Lincoln Central Libraries; Dr Katherine Webb of the University of York's Borthwick Institute for Archives, and Miss Pearl Wheatley of the Society for Lincolnshire History and Archaeology.

For permission to reproduce photographs Lincoln Cathedral Library, Lincolnshire County Council, and the Wellcome Library, London, are gratefully acknowledged.

ACKNOWLEDGEMENTS

EDITORS' NOTE

This volume comprises an edition of the first of the two memorandum and account books kept by Matthew Flinders, apothecary of Donington. The other book, covering the years from 1785 until Flinders's death in 1802, will be published as Volume II of the edition; it will also include appendices and an index to the whole work.

The work of transcribing the memoranda has been undertaken by Martyn Beardsley, who has also contributed the Introduction to the work. The text of the memoranda has been revised by Nicholas Bennett, who has also transcribed the accounts.

We have endeavoured as far as possible to preserve the general layout of the entries and present them in the order in which they appear in the Diary. This means, however, that in a few cases entries may not be strictly chronological.

The Diary was written at a time when conventions relating to spelling and punctuation in the English language were still more fluid than they are today. On the whole, Flinders's spelling is consistent and his meaning clear, and it has been reproduced here as it stands in the original. In the small number of places where it has been necessary to correct minor errors, the original version is given in a footnote. Flinders's use of capitals has been retained where possible. Punctuation has been modernised.

Martyn Beardsley
Nicholas Bennett

ABBREVIATIONS

Allen   Thomas Allen, *The History of the County of Lincoln* (2 vols, London, 1833–4)

Bryant   Joseph Bryant, *Captain Matthew Flinders RN: his voyages, discoveries and fortunes* (London, 1928)

Burnby   'The Flinders family of Donington: medical practice and family life in an eighteenth century fenland town', *LHA* 23 (1988), 51–58

ESTC   English Short-Title Catalogue, The British Library

LAO   Lincolnshire Archives Office

LAR   *Lincolnshire Archives Office, Archivists' Reports*

LHA   *Lincolnshire History and Archaeology*

Lincolnshire   A. R. Maddison (ed.), *Lincolnshire Pedigrees*, 4 vols, Harleian
Pedigrees   Society 50–52, 55 (1902–6)

Mills   Dennis R. Mills, 'A "directory" of Lincolnshire medical men in the late eighteenth century', *LHA* 23 (1988), 59–62

ODNB   *Oxford Dictionary of National Biography*

OED   *Oxford English Dictionary*

Plomer   H. R. Plomer et al., *A Dictionary of the Printers and Booksellers who were at work in England, Scotland and Ireland from 1726 to 1775* (Oxford, 1932)

PRO   Public Record Office (now The National Archives)

Supplement Samuel Frederick Gray, *A Supplement to the Pharmacopoeia* (London, 1821)

FLINDERS FAMILY TREE

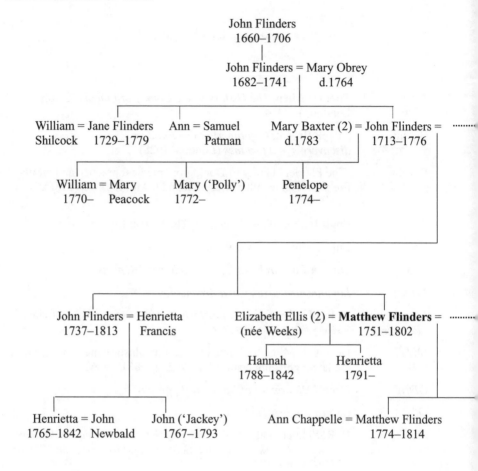

John Flinders
1660–1706

John Flinders = Mary Obrey
1682–1741   d.1764

William = Jane Flinders   Ann = Samuel   Mary Baxter (2) = John Flinders = ·········
Shilcock   1729–1779   Patman   d.1783   1713–1776

William = Mary   Mary ('Polly')   Penelope
1770–   Peacock   1772–   1774–

John Flinders = Henrietta   Elizabeth Ellis (2) = **Matthew Flinders** = ·········
1737–1813   Francis   (née Weeks)   1751–1802

Hannah   Henrietta
1788–1842   1791–

Henrietta = John   John ('Jackey')   Ann Chappelle = Matthew Flinders
1765–1842 Newbald   1767–1793   1774–1814

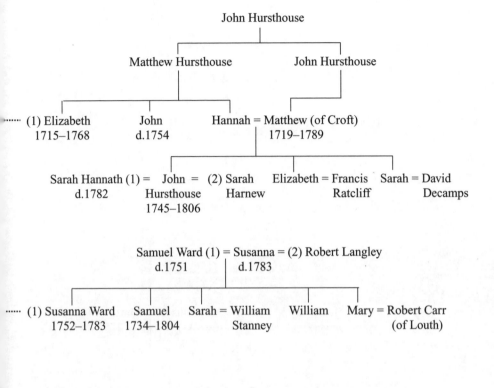

John Hursthouse

Matthew Hursthouse   John Hursthouse

(1) Elizabeth   John   Hannah = Matthew (of Croft)
1715–1768   d.1754   1719–1789

Sarah Hannath (1) =   John   =   (2) Sarah   Elizabeth = Francis   Sarah = David
d.1782   Hursthouse   Harnew   Ratcliff   Decamps
              1745–1806

Samuel Ward (1) = Susanna = (2) Robert Langley
d.1751   d.1783

(1) Susanna Ward   Samuel   Sarah = William   William   Mary = Robert Carr
1752–1783   1734–1804   Stanney   (of Louth)

Elizabeth ('Betsey') = James   Susanna = George   John   Samuel Ward = Mary Ann
1775–1799   Harvey   1779–1827 Pearson   1781–1834   1782–1834   Bolton

INTRODUCTION

In the late 1990s I was carrying out the research for *Deadly Winter*, a biography of the Arctic explorer Sir John Franklin. He being a Spilsby man, my enquiries took me to the offices of the Lincolnshire Archives. I knew there were ties between the Franklin and the Flinders families, and at one point I was seeking a single brief quote regarding a visit Franklin made as a teenager to the Flinders house in Donington before embarking on his new naval career. I was presented with two old leather bound volumes from the Flinders Collection. At first sight they appeared to be accounts ledgers kept by Captain Flinders's father (also named Matthew), but on closer inspection it became apparent that they were part ledger, part diary or journal.[1] As I scrutinised the entries looking for the quote I wanted, I became more and more drawn into the eighteenth century world of the person who had written them. I made a mental note that it might one day be worth going back to those volumes and transcribing everything, in the hope that other people might also find them fascinating. This book is the result.

THE DIARY

The Diary consists of two foolscap volumes of similar thickness.[2] They have hard covers, apparently made from stout card bound in what might be calfskin; Volume I has a further outer layer of thick paper glued onto the leather binding. The covers of both volumes show the expected signs of age, being stained and frayed at the edges, but the inner pages are in a remarkably good state of preservation for the most part and are generally easily readable. The pages were originally blank, and Flinders has added neat margins and extra columns on right-hand pages for his accounts.

The Diary changes format over the years – and in fact it is certainly not a diary in the modern sense: a printed book with neatly divided spaces and dates.[3] It is, first and foremost, a home-made cash ledger, with accounting entries on the right-hand page of the open book and personal and professional comments on the left-hand side. Flinders's initial motivation for making the diary entries may have been to record brief medical notes concerning his patients, particularly his "man

---

[1] To avoid confusion between Matthew Flinders the author of the Diary and his explorer son of the same name, I have unless otherwise stated referred to the father as "Flinders" and the son as "Matthew" throughout.

[2] For an account of the Flinders archive, see *LAR* 17 (1965–66), 28–30.

[3] Flinders does not give a daily record of events and the Diary does not provide the detailed account of his world that can be found in those of his contemporaries William Cole and James Woodforde (see F. G. Stokes (ed.), *The Blecheley Diary of the Rev. William Cole, 1765–1767* (London, 1931); John Beresford (ed.), *The Diary of a Country Parson* (5v., Oxford, 1924–31). Like theirs, however, Flinders's diary entries reveal a good deal about his personality; his concern over the way posterity might view his remarriage (Diary, f.66) is particularly striking.

midwife" visits. However, by the second volume references to specific medical cases no longer feature; all entries now relate to family and financial matters – particularly the latter towards the end of the Diary. As his family grew (and grew up), and his health gradually became a cause for concern, the impression grows of a man preparing for the future financial stability and security of those who would be left behind when he was gone. The last quarter of the Diary is dominated by various financial investments and the buying and selling of land. Flinders was still practising at this time, and it seems almost certain that he was by then recording the medical information elsewhere. (From quite an early date he must have been recording the labours he attended separately: when his wife gave birth to still-born twins in July 1777 he wrote ". . . the particulars of the Labour I have noted in my Midwifry Cases".)[4]

Another motive for his later wheeling and dealing is given on 20 August 1796: ". . . if I have any prospect of being freed from the fatigues of Business selling my Land begs fairest for it . . ." And, writing of his business at the conclusion of that year, he says, "I find it heavier upon me every Year." His health seems no worse than usual at this point, however, so it can only be assumed that after twenty-six years of doling out potions and being on call for women in labour night and day, even to the point of being called home early from pleasure trips or missing out on them entirely, he was beginning to feel that he had simply had enough.

On Flinders's death, the Diary passed to his wife Elizabeth, to whom he had bequeathed most of his personal belongings in his Will.[5] Elizabeth added her own comments in the Diary shortly after her husband's death, and again a year later. On 30 June 1829, as the opening inscription in Volume I records, the book was given to Lieutenant Samuel Flinders RN by his step-mother Elizabeth. This introduction was probably written by Samuel, though it is signed by Elizabeth herself, in a very unsteady hand.

FLINDERS THE MAN

Although it seems Flinders never sat for a sketch or portrait, we are fortunate in having had a description of him – and other members of the family – recorded by a niece of his daughter Susanna.[6] We are told that Flinders was short, clean shaven, with brown hair and grey eyes. He was "active", and assiduous in his professional life. He was fond of reading, as we can tell from the Diary, but we learn that he had a hobby which he never mentions there – etching with pen and ink. He is reported as being religious ("established church"), affectionate, and generous to his relatives; but words like "exact" and even "rather stern" are also applied to him. Certainly, little humour is evident in the Diary; but it would be unfair to conclude from this that Flinders was completely lacking in that quality. Although one does get the sense of a practical, methodical, perhaps even rather dour pillar of the community, it is clear that he enjoyed socialising and entertainments, and appreciated satirical works such as *Churchill's Poems* (February 1780)

---

4 Diary, f.23.
5 The Will of Matthew Flinders will be printed as an Appendix in Volume II of this edition.
6 Francis Galton, *Record of Family Faculties* (London, 1884). Galton was a cousin of Charles Darwin, who made a study of heredity and intelligence.

and the *Critical Review* (May 1782). It is not too hard to imagine this intelligent and knowledgeable man displaying a quiet wit at dinner parties or sessions at the Bull among friends and colleagues. The Diary, consisting of brief notes relating to the principal events of Flinders's daily life, and largely written for his own eyes, was never a ready vehicle for whatever sense of humour he possessed. The relative's description concludes by informing us that Flinders suffered from "ague fever" every autumn, and died of a stomach disease.

Like his own father, Flinders married twice and had a large family, but there is some confusion surrounding the earlier generations of the Flinders and their arrival in Donington, Lincolnshire.[7] Part of the problem is that stories relating to the earliest known generations of the family, apparently current at least as far back as the time of Matthew the explorer, do not quite tie in with documentary evidence. For example, most of Matthew's biographers speculate that the origin of both the family and its name lies in Flanders. While this may be true of the Flinders surname in general, genealogical investigation has uncovered no specific evidence of this for the branch of the family in which we are interested. Flinders's grandfather John (I) almost certainly came to Lincolnshire from neighbouring Nottinghamshire, where the trail much further back soon turns cold.

Then there is the mystery concerning John Flinders (I) himself. After arriving back in England on being released from captivity in Mauritius, Matthew sent to the Parish of Ruddington in Nottinghamshire for information relating to his great-grandfather. It is perhaps telling that his request was passed on to the parish of Gedling, because, while genealogists have failed to find any trace of this John or his family in Ruddington, one who fits the bill has been found in the Gedling area. Yet Matthew left money in his will for memorial tablets dedicated to his father, grandfather, great-grandfather and himself to be erected in the local church in Donington (where they can still be seen) and the inscription for John Flinders (I) has him as a "farmer and grazier formerly of Ruddington". So, despite Matthew's request for information being forwarded from Ruddington to Gedling, and the fact that the birth and death dates of the inscription (1682–1714) are those of the Gedling John, the family chose for some reason to stick with Ruddington. It could be that he lived for some time in that parish between leaving Gedling and arriving in Donington. Or it could simply be that the family got it wrong. Anyone who has traced their family tree will know that this is a surprisingly common occurrence: anecdotal evidence relating to even fairly recent generations can and does become radically distorted. The Ruddington Flinders could have been someone other than John; Matthew may have drawn a blank there, but his family, while recalling his initial belief in the veracity of this connection, might not have been aware of this and so perpetuated the notion.

John Flinders (I) is also usually said by biographers to have been an apothecary, which again contradicts Matthew's memorial tablet. Some have asserted that he switched from farming to medical work after moving to Donington. One suggestion[8] is that John became so successful at treating his own and his neighbours' sick animals that he branched out into the treatment of humans. Perhaps

---

7 For an account of the origins of the family and an outline family tree, see J. G. L. Burnby, 'The Flinders family of Donington: medical practice and family life in an eighteenth century fenland town', *LHA* 23 (1988), 51–52. See also the family tree printed above, pp. xii–xiii.

8 Made by descendant Witgar Hitchcock.

part of the problem lies with the actual term "apothecary". There were numerous "freelancers" practising a form of unofficial medicine at this time, and perhaps this is a skill John practised as a sideline to his farming. A complete career change seems unlikely. Bona fide apothecaries served an apprenticeship, and in common with other trades this was almost invariably undertaken in the trainee's early teens. Besides which, if John had ended his life as a fully fledged apothecary, this would surely have been noted on the tablet.

John married a Mary Obrey, and among their children they had a son, also called John, born in 1713. This was John Flinders (II), our Diarist's father. He was certainly an apothecary, though little is known about his practice. He served as a churchwarden in Donington, and is said to have been an acquaintance of Thomas Secker, Archbishop of Canterbury between 1758 and 1768. Secker was born in Nottinghamshire and had earlier qualified as a doctor, which is presumably how his path crossed with that of John Flinders.[9] Two of the sons of John Flinders (II) were to follow in his footsteps as apothecaries. A third John, born in 1737, set up in practice in Spalding. Numerous Diary entries show that John was nothing like as shrewd or successful as his younger brother Matthew, and a rash move to Odiham in Hampshire, followed by an attempt to set up a school in Greenwich with his wife, both backfired, leading to a somewhat ignominious return to Spalding.[10]

Our Matthew Flinders stayed in Donington and lived in a reasonably sized brick-built house in the centre of the town, fronting onto the market place. At least one Diary entry seems to indicate that he had purchased it from his father (see June 1776). A photograph taken before it was demolished some time in the early twentieth century shows a two-storey building, with dormer windows providing evidence that the attic was also used as living space; his apothecary's shop, a small, single-floored building, abutted one end of the house. It is said that Flinders used to have a slate hanging on the inside of the door of his shop on which he chalked appointments and other reminders for himself. (It is even said that Matthew junior, unable to bring himself to tell his father of his intention of going to sea, informed Flinders by writing an explanatory note on that slate.)[11] We know from the Diary that he made numerous improvements and alterations to the building over time: sometimes in response to an increase in the size of his family, sometimes (e.g. the bricking up of windows) as a way of lowering his tax bill. It must have stood in a sizeable area of land – Flinders records growing a wide variety of crops and the keeping of a horse and cow – and there were various outbuildings: a coalhouse, brewhouse and barn are all mentioned.

Apart from his growing family, there would have been at least two servants in the house: a maid and a boy. One entry stating the size of his "family" (25 June

---

9 Burnby, 'Flinders family', 52. For Secker, see *ODNB*.
10 Diary, ff.60v, 64, 70, 73v. Brother John and his family recur at regular intervals in the Diary. His son, another John (Jackey) was sent away to school at Guilsborough in Northamptonshire; Flinders's journey there in June 1778 to bring him home is recorded in great detail (Diary, ff.32v–33). Flinders followed with interest Jackey's later career in the Navy. Jackey's sister Henrietta (Henny) also features frequently in the Diary, visiting at Donington and keeping house for Flinders after the death of his first wife in 1783.
11 Sir Ernest Scott, *The Life of Captain Matthew Flinders RN* (Sydney, 1914: reprinted 2004), 29.

1782) seems to indicate the possibility of a third servant, but this is at odds with the impression given throughout the rest of the Diary. Thirteen children were fathered by Flinders in total: ten by his first wife and three by his second. This is not an unusually large number for the times, and it does include two sets of twins – to which the Flinders line seemed to be predisposed: his father's first marriage also produced a set of twins. And, of course, this was still a time of very high infant mortality.

The modern reader might be somewhat shocked and dismayed by Flinders's apparent attitude to infant death in his own family. When his third child died in November 1776 at the age of around two months, Flinders wrote: "we ought to account of this a mercifull Dispensation in that Providence made choice of the Youngest; to have parted with either of the other two would have afflicted us much more; and as we have nought in a natural sense, but my industry in Business to depend on we ought to think the non increase of our Family a blessing". There are other, similar entries.

To ascribe such a loss to Providence or the will of God is something we can still just about identify with even in this increasingly secular age, but the concept of the death of a newborn as a blessing for financial reasons jars on the modern sensibility. Yet, as the Diary progresses and the reader begins to develop a better understanding of Flinders and his world, it becomes easier to place oneself in his shoes. He was comfortably off, but not so much so that he did not have to count the pennies. Financial disaster could strike anyone – occasionally even the fabulously rich, though usually through their own foolishness – at any time. There is a strong sense that an individual had much less of a sense of control over his life or destiny then, be it financial, medical or otherwise, and a much keener feeling of being at the mercy of forces beyond his control. To us a financial calamity might mean embarrassment, perhaps a lower standard of living and accommodation than we are used to, and having to rely on state benefits. In Flinders's world things could rapidly spiral downwards towards the horrors of homelessness, hunger, lack of money for medical care, and, when food was scarce and prices high, even starvation.

Perhaps we should leave the last word on Flinders as a person to Elizabeth, his wife, who added her own poignant note at the end of the Diary. To her, he was "one of the Best of Men".

THE MEDICAL CONTEXT

In advertising the sale of his business a few weeks before he died, Flinders described himself as a "surgeon, apothecary and man-midwife". In many biographical accounts, Flinders is referred to as a doctor, and as "Dr Flinders" – sometimes from the understandable motive of wishing to avoid confusion with his sailor son. It must be emphasised that this nomenclature is simply wrong, and can lead to confusion of a different type. There was a very clear and important difference between a surgeon-apothecary and a doctor, much as there is today between, say, a General Practitioner and a pharmacist.

In Flinders's day, doctors trained at one of a very few medical schools, such as the highly respected establishment in Edinburgh, and were admitted as Fellows of the Royal College of Physicians, entry to which a required a degree from Oxford,

Cambridge or Dublin.[12] Apothecaries, however, undertook apprenticeships under experienced masters in the trade, and the better and more conscientious ones, like Flinders, kept abreast of developments in the medical world through contact with others in their field and by subscribing to medical journals.[13] It may seem that the apothecary was very much a second best option for the sick of the eighteenth century – but much of the theory about the causes and curing of disease that the physicians were learning in their elite colleges is now known to be nonsense, and many of their "cures" were as unpleasant as, if not worse than, the illness being treated. Apothecaries at least learned what did or did not work "in the field" as it were, from others who had done the same for generation after generation; they were also less likely to turn their noses up at the idea of using medicinal herbs, which even today many see as a perfectly valid form of treatment. So it is not too surprising to hear William Cole say in 1766, "I ever thought a good honest apothecary a much safer person to apply to than half the physicians and surgeons in the kingdom."[14]

Apothecaries had originally been purely sellers of drugs, but where physicians were either too expensive or simply unavailable – particularly in more isolated areas – it is understandable that their role began to expand. Modern pharmacists are often able informally to pass on practical advice as well as dispensing medicines, and it is easy to imagine that given the opportunity they could, and there have been indications in recent years that they would like to, make more of this side of their work much as their professional forebears did. The apothecary is often lumped together with the quack and the charlatan in general medical histories. Some undoubtedly did fall into this category, though it would be interesting to know whether the number of ineffective practitioners was proportionately any higher among apothecaries than physicians. The worst charlatans tended to crop up in larger towns and cities; someone like Flinders could probably never have survived financially (let alone have thrived, as he did) in a relatively small and close-knit community like Donington, without having established a solid reputation.

There could be antagonism between the different branches of the medical profession. It has been said that, "Physicians looked down on surgeons, but surgeons looked down on apothecaries."[15] But this perhaps overstates the situation, and certainly does not appear to apply in Flinders's case. Physicians readily offered him an opinion in difficult cases (and generally seemed to agree with his course of treatment) and he belonged to a local medical society consisting of six surgeon-apothecaries and two physicians (1 September1796).[16] Things became a little more formalised after Flinders's death with the Apothecaries Act of 1815, under which those setting themselves up as apothecaries had to be licensed – although the Act, a watered down version of what had been envisaged, still

---

[12] Roy Porter, *English Society in the Eighteenth Century* (London, 1982), 75.

[13] Flinders subscribed to the *Medical Magazine* until late 1777 when he switched to the *Medical Commentaries* (Diary, f.26v).

[14] Dorothy George, *Hogarth to Cruikshank: Social Change in Graphic Satire* (London, 1967), 95.

[15] Porter, *English Society in the Eighteenth Century*, 49.

[16] Physicians consulted by Flinders included William Hairby of Spilsby (during his first wife's final illness), Drs Knowlton and Beston of Boston, and Edward Blythe of Spalding. See D.R. Mills, 'A directory of Lincolnshire medical men in the late eighteenth century', *LHA* 23 (1988), 59–62.

allowed "irregulars" who did not term themselves apothecaries to continue to practise unlicensed.[17]

In the eighteenth century, neither apothecaries nor physicians understood what caused most illnesses – particularly serious ones – nor knew how to cure them. The main pathological model was based on "humours" within the body, such as blood and bile, which when out of balance caused illness. Roy Porter has suggested that, "Virtually all theorizing about the mechanisms of disease before 1800 was like a castle built in the air. It had little empirical foundation and was completely false in modern scientific terms. Therapies derived from these humoural theories were almost without exception injurious to the patient."[18] Death rates were high. It has been estimated that a fifth of babies died before their first birthday, and up to a third before the age of five.[19] Add to that the number of women like Susannah, Flinders's first wife, dying during or soon after childbirth, and the perusal of parish registers of the time can make for depressing reading. On finding an entry under "Baptisms", one's eye eventually tends automatically to seek out the same name a few days later under "Burials".

But surprisingly, things were already improving. The population was steadily growing, and the death rate declined sharply during the period covered by the Diary. This has been ascribed to a growing awareness of the importance of hygiene and cleanliness, and, despite the "humours", the slow but inexorable forward march of medical knowledge.[20] These advances were no doubt one of the reasons that led to women increasingly placing themselves in the hands of trained male practitioners, as opposed to experienced female relatives and acquaintances, to assist them in bringing their babies into the world. It may come as a surprise to learn that not only was Flinders a "man-midwife", but that male midwifery was common by this time. Judging from the earlier years of the Diary, at least, attending to women in labour seemed to take up a great deal of Flinders's time. Dr Burnby has pointed out that Flinders attended 43 births in the first year of the Diary (including that of his own daughter Elizabeth); all the mothers survived, and only one child died (although there was also one miscarriage which occurred before his arrival).[21] Even though we don't know how many died in the subsequent weeks and months, this still seems a remarkable success rate for the period.

We know from the Diary that Flinders served his apprenticeship as an apothecary in London. On a trip to London in October 1796 he mentions revisiting his old master, Richard Grindall FRS (who was by then "nearly worn out" and did not recognise his former pupil). And in 1770 he attended lectures on midwifery given at St Saviour's, Southwark, by David Orme.[22]

There can be no doubt that in terms of income and social standing, as an apothecary Flinders ranked alongside his friend Mr Gleed the attorney (another profession into which entry was by way of apprenticeship), among what we now call the middle-class. At that time it was still a fairly new category, and society in general seemed not quite sure what to make of it.

17 W. F. Bynum and Roy Porter (eds), *Medical Fringe & Medical Orthodoxy 1750–1850* (London, 1987), 119.
18 Roy Porter (ed.), *Cambridge Illustrated History of Medicine* (Cambridge, 1996), 123.
19 Porter, *English Society in the Eighteenth Century*, 13.
20 Pauline Gregg, *Social and Economic History of Britain* (London, 1971), 63.
21 Burnby, 'Flinders family', 53.
22 Burnby, 'Flinders family', 52.

THE FAMILY AFTER FLINDERS

Flinders's estate has been valued at upwards of £6,000.[23] Roy Porter suggests that by multiplying eighteenth-century monetary amounts by between 60 and 80 times it is possible to achieve a very rough modern equivalent. Any such comparisons must be treated with caution, but this would mean that even at a conservative estimate Flinders was worth £360,000 at the time of his death.

Flinders outlived most of his children. Of those by Susannah Ward, the "unfortunate son John", whose mental deterioration is painfully recorded by Flinders in the Diary, was admitted to the York Asylum in March 1801, aged 20, and spent the rest of his life there. He died in 1834 at the age of 53. Samuel (also known as Samuel Ward), who had followed his older brother Matthew into the Royal Navy, died in 1834 at the age of 52.[24] Matthew we shall come to later. The first of the three girls from his second marriage, to Elizabeth Weeks, died at birth. The next, Hannah, died in 1847 aged 58, and Henrietta died at the age of 47 in 1838.

Flinders's very first child and namesake, Matthew, is the most famous of them all and one of the most celebrated sons of Lincolnshire. The Diary shows how he thwarted his father's wishes of his continuing the family tradition and becoming an apothecary, and instead joined the Royal Navy. He quickly made a name for himself, learning his trade under the brilliant and unjustly maligned Captain William Bligh, and established a reputation as an intrepid but methodical and accurate navigator and hydrographer, despite the fact that his career was a tragically short one.

Matthew's greatest achievement was his charting of the Australian coastline, but his mission was dogged by a series of less than seaworthy vessels. His original craft for the mission was the *Investigator*, which had leaked from the moment it left port, but, with a great deal of pumping, had been manageable enough to complete most of the work intended for it. Eventually his carpenters were so alarmed by the state of the ship's timbers that he had to return to Port Jackson (now Sydney Harbour), where the ship was officially declared unsafe and beyond repair. The only ship available to him was the *Porpoise*, on which he was to return to England. But this small vessel struck rocks on the journey north from Port Jackson, leaving the crew stranded on a small island.

With a small hand-picked crew, Matthew sailed a cutter (which they christened *Hope*) salvaged from the *Porpoise*, on a perilous 750 mile journey back to Port Jackson for help. He arrived back at the little island six weeks later, just as the shipwrecked men were beginning to fear the worst. Now, in command of the schooner *Cumberland*, he attempted to resume his homeward journey – but this ship appeared to be in no better state than any of the others, and he was forced to

---

[23] James Mack, *Matthew Flinders 1774–1814* (Melbourne, 1966), 4.

[24] Samuel (born 3 November 1782) was the last of Flinders's children by Susannah; she died on 23 March 1783. Her other surviving children were Matthew (born 16 March 1774), Elizabeth or Betsey, born 24 September 1775, Susannah (born 22 May 1779) and John (born 5 April 1781). The Diary contains frequent references to the schooling and clothing of the children. The younger children were put out to nurse in Donington, a practice also used in the Austen family (Irene Collins, *Jane Austen, The Parson's Daughter* (London, 1998), 17–19).

put into Mauritius for urgent repairs. The island was then under French control and known as Ile de France, and worse still, Matthew did not know that England and France were at war again after a brief period of peace.

Before leaving England, Matthew had been issued with a "passport" giving him, as an explorer, immunity from arrest, under a reciprocal arrangement between Britain and France. However, the document was made out to him as commander of the *Investigator*, which was now rotting away in Port Jackson; and the island happened to be under the governorship of a rather paranoid, totally unsympathetic, and at times spiteful French army officer. Matthew was arrested as a spy. Although the conditions of his imprisonment gradually improved, and he was eventually under a kind of house arrest with a fair amount of freedom to move around and socialise, it was six-and-a-half miserable years of letter writing, petitioning and bickering with the haughty governor before he was released – and even then only when a British attack on the island (which proved successful) was imminent.

Matthew arrived in England in 1810, having been away for just over nine years in total. During his imprisonment, he had been allowed to correspond with family and friends, and knew about the death of his father. In London he was reunited with his wife Ann – with whom he had spent less than two months of married life in 1801 before sailing. (The marriage had been a matter of discord between father and son, as the Diary relates: the ceremony having been conducted in haste before Matthew sailed and Flinders being informed only after the event.)

He set to work on preparing for publication his account of his Australian discoveries and his time at Ile de France. In 1812 he and Ann had a daughter, Anne – their only child. Matthew's health was declining steadily, and it is a great tribute to his fortitude that he not only produced the mammoth, three volume *A Voyage to Terra Australis*[25] (he is generally given the credit for the change of name from New Holland to Australia) but he also carried out ground-breaking research into discrepancies in compass readings at sea caused by iron on board ship, and his solution to the problem came to be universally adopted.

Sadly, Matthew did not live to see the publication of his *Voyage to Terra Australis*. In the summer of 1814 his first lieutenant from the *Investigator*, Robert Fowler, wrote to John Franklin, who had sailed with them as a midshipman, to say that he had seen Flinders in May, ". . . looking miserable. I don't think long for this world." It is said that he was lying in bed unconscious when the three volumes, fresh off the press, were placed beside him and his hand laid on top of them. Matthew died the next day, probably of a kidney related illness.

Ann, his wife, lived on in difficult financial circumstances until 1852. Their daughter Anne had married William Petrie; she gave birth to a son the year after her mother's death. The child was William Matthew Flinders Petrie, who became an eminent scholar and renowned archaeologist and Egyptologist.[26]

---

25 *A Voyage to Terra Australis, undertaken for the purpose of completing the discovery of that vast country, and prosecuted in the years 1801, 1802 and 1803, in His Majesty's Ship the Investigator, and subsequently in the . . . Porpoise and Cumberland schooner. With an account of the shipwreck of the Porpoise, arrival of the Cumberland at Mauritius, and imprisonment of the commander . . . in that island.* (3v., London, 1814).

26 Anne Petrie (1812–1892) was herself a linguist and Egyptologist (*ODNB*).

DONINGTON AND THE LINCOLNSHIRE FENS

The England that Flinders knew was of course very different to the one we know today; but the fenlands of Lincolnshire were different again – even as regarded by the rest of eighteenth-century England. The county at that time has been described as "remote, little known and unfashionable".[27] The vast, flat and comparatively featureless landscape may possess a starkly unique beauty, but it is not everyone's cup of tea and has always been less likely to inspire poets and artists in the way that, say, the rugged coastlines and quaint fishing ports of the south-west have. George Byng, later Viscount Torrington, touring the county in 1791, found it uninspiring. Few of the inhabitants seemed to be aware of the richness of its past; the inns were mostly dirty and uncomfortable, and there was little in the way of society. "Not only gentility have fled the county, but the race of yeomanry is extinguished." His visit to Donington was uneventful, however: "a small market-town, where I dined, comfortably, on a shoulder of lamb, peas and tart".[28]

There were some significant changes happening in Flinders's lifetime. Enclosure – the fencing off and parcelling up of previously common land – was being implemented nationwide. An equally dramatic transformation was brought about locally by the drainage of wetlands. Drainage on a small scale had been going at least since Roman times, but was begun in earnest in the seventeenth century by the Earl of Bedford, who brought over skilled men from Holland.[29] Over centuries, the people of the area had evolved the know-how and skills necessary to eke out a living in their unique environment; then, like the spinners and weavers in other parts of the country affected by the mechanisation and industrialisation of their cottage trades, the fowlers and fishermen of the fens saw their traditional way of life being annihilated. There were sporadic outbreaks of violence against those involved in drainage work, and full-scale rioting between 1768 and 1773, just before the Diary period.[30] The reclaimed land was used for the growing of crops such as flax and hemp, the latter being woven into rope.

Donington itself was a small market town with a population of probably just over one thousand people. In 1842 it was reported that the town formerly had a large Saturday market, but that "it sunk into insignificance many years ago".[31] The communities within towns like Donington and Boston, and even cities like Lincoln and London, differed significantly from their modern counterparts in that the centre of town was a place to both live and work for all but the landed gentry. Flinders was typical in having his shop attached to his house. People actually lived right in the centre of town: "The poor were not relegated to slums and the rich had not yet migrated to the suburbs," as Reed succinctly puts it.[32]

---

[27] Neil Wright, *Lincolnshire Towns and Industry 1700–1914* (History of Lincolnshire XI, 1982), 3.
[28] C. B. Andrews (ed.), *The Torrington Diaries* (4v., London, 1934–36), ii. 360, 371; R. J. Olney, *Rural Society and County Government in Nineteenth-Century Lincolnshire* (History of Lincolnshire X, 1979), 1.
[29] Joseph Bryant, *Captain Matthew Flinders RN, His Voyages, Discoveries, & Fortunes* (London, 1928), 15.
[30] Michael Reed, *The Georgian Triumph 1730–1830* (London, 1983), 69.
[31] William White, *History, Gazetteer and Directory of Lincolnshire* (Sheffield, 1842), 193.
[32] Reed, *Georgian Triumph*, 106.

The typical kind of dwelling that Flinders would have visited during the course of his midwifery and other work would probably have been a "mud and stud" cottage: that is, timber framed with a mixture of mud and straw applied.[33] Many such homes would have had no floor boarding – just bare earth underfoot with perhaps a covering of straw, and most would have had a thatched roof. The one thing they would have had in common with the houses of the better off folk like Flinders, and those of an even higher social standing, was lighting. Candles provided the only form of artificial light.[34]

Travelling had been made easier during Flinders's time by the growth of Turnpike Trusts which took responsibility for the upkeep of stretches of road, the cost of which was borne by travellers paying tolls. Because of these improvements, most of the Diary period falls in what is known as the golden age of coaching, from around 1780 until the advent of rail travel in the 1830s.[35]

The hardships experienced in Donington as recorded in the Diary are a microcosm of those being experienced throughout the nation. A combination of bad weather and poor harvests, combined with wars with America, Holland and France, led to food shortages and inflation. The poorest sections of society in Donington and elsewhere, with no savings or food stocks of their own to fall back on, were very vulnerable at these times. In periods of greatest desperation the poor relied solely upon the benevolence of people like Flinders, and there are mentions of the raising of charitable subscriptions in the Diary.

The author of the entry in White's Directory quoted above might recognise some parallels today. Although by no means shabby, like many modern rural towns and villages it shows some signs of having seen better, more prosperous days – perhaps best represented by the boarded up and sorry-looking Red Cow, where Flinders attended meetings of the local medical society.[36] But it is a friendly and pleasant enough place, and there are still many old houses and buildings left among the modern developments that Flinders would recognise, not least of which is the impressive and, for the size of the town, surprisingly huge thirteenth-century church of St Mary and the Holy Rood. The Peacock, where Flinders attended a book auction,[37] is no longer an inn, although a plaque on the wall of the building commemorates its passing. The Black Bull thrives, and is presumably the same pub – though not then Black – as another of Flinders's haunts, being virtually next door. His own house, once on the western edge of the market place, is sadly long gone. A blue plaque marks the spot where it stood.

---

33 Wright, *Lincolnshire Towns and Industry*, 15.
34 Porter, *English Society*, 215.
35 For the establishment of turnpike trusts in south-east Lincolnshire, see Wright, *Lincolnshire Towns and Industry*, 37–9.
36 The Cow was also the venue for the display given in May 1778 by Mr Powell the Fire-Eater (Diary, f.30v). Flinders also attended the exhibition and lectures given by Mr Lowe in March 1779, and the plays performed by a group of travelling comedians in the autumn of 1784 (Diary, ff.36v, 73v).
37 Diary, f.73. Flinders was a frequent buyer of books, making regular purchases from John Albin, the principal bookseller in Spalding. His interests included literature, travel and the law. He bought a Latin grammar in January 1781 in order to give lessons to Matthew; it seems likely, however, that the purchase of a two-volume edition of *Robinson Crusoe* in April 1782 had a more lasting impact on the boy (Diary, ff.50v, 58; see also Scott, *Life of Captain Matthew Flinders*, 27).

THE DIARY AND ACCOUNTS OF
MATTHEW FLINDERS

1775–1802

[f.1]

This MS book given by Mrs Flinders senior to Lieutenant S.W. Flinders 30 June 1829 as containing the remainder of the events relating to his mother's life.
    [signed] Eliz[th] Flinders[1]

[f.1v]
January 1775: 1st Month, 31 Days
Sunday 1. Mr Pakey & Family got tea here. Thaw but froze at night.
2. Sharp frost.
3. Ditto. Dined at Mr Gleed's.
4. Fine thaw.
5. Went at night to G. West.
6. Mr Whitehead & Family got tea here &c.
8. Called at Bicker to Mrs F., Gosberton. My Father & Family got tea here. Mr G's child's head.
12. Finished transcribing Letters.
13. We got tea and supped at Mr Pakey's: home by 12.
16. Priestley's Institutes. British Biography.
19. At 2 in the morning called to S. Rudham: home by 3. Mr Green's Daughters came and staid 2 days.
21. Miss Baxter and Shepherd got tea here.
25. Extremely cold. Windy and frost.
26. Snow and Frost.
27. In the afternoon at D. called to Mrs Godley B.G. – home by 8, nothing done. At 9 called to Mrs Northern B.G. – home by 2 in mane.[2] Supped at my Father's.
29. Got tea at Mr Shepherd's.
31. We got tea and supped at Mr Ward's Drapers. We got home by 11½.

Midwifry
No 1. 5th. Called at night to one Mrs Fairbanks Gosberton West. She had had a violent cholic for some days, but nought as to Labour. By exhibiting large doses of Opiates the pain was somewhat appeased & as expected she had a very expeditious Labour the 8th in mane, insomuch that I was not in time for any part of the Business.
No 2. 19th. Early in the morn called to S. Rudham, excellent Labour and home by 3. This woman had been much disordered long time but recovers tolerable.[3]
No 3. 27th. At 9 in the Evening called to Mrs Northern, Bicker Gauntlet.[4] A good natural Labour, and I got home by 2 in the Morn. 'Tis the 2d Child I have attended her.

---

1 The signature is in very shaky handwriting, quite different to that of the inscription.
2 'In mane': in the morning.
3 On 19 January 1775 Martha, daughter of Sarah and John Rudham, was baptised in Donington; she died aged 2 in January 1777 (Donington Parish Register).
4 Three miles north-east of Donington.

Surgery

I have to note a remarkable particular concerning Mr Gleed's[5] child's head: the scalp was pretty much tumified[6] at delivery, but not at all uncommonly. I saw it no more the 5th or 6th day. When not settling they were uneasy & desired me to inspect it. I found a considerable large tumour on the left side near the Lambdoidal[7] suture with evident fluctuation.[8] I was afraid of an Internal communication, and that it was serous or bloody, from some of the sinus's. The child was well in other respects, and on touching gave no sign of pain. I was timorous of opening, & we deferred to consult Dr Blithe,[9] who advised a small puncture. This was done and about 2 spoonfulls of fluid black blood was discharged. By a small dozil[10] of lint, and a spirituous Embrocation to corrugate the scalp, it cleaned and healed very fast, and is now together with the child quite well.

Books

12th. I note that I finished transcribing the letters that passed betwixt myself and wife. I have been long about them, and am pleased they are done. They are a decent collection & fill about 4/5th of the book.[11]

16th. I got from Mrs Worley Dr Priestley's Institutes. Vol. 3d.[12] I cannot speak too much in praise of this excellent work. I ordered it bound, which I find a much cheaper way, than buying in sheets & then binding.

Same day I got No 1 the British Biography,[13] to come monthly in place of the Univ. Magazine which I now give up, as the other is[14] far more valuable for preservation than the confused jumble of Magazines.

Visiters

1st. Mr and Mrs Pakey got tea here, also Mr and Miss Golding but did not stay supper.

6. Mr Whitehead and wife & Mr Dawnay: ditto.

8. My Father[15] and family, & staid supper.

19. Mr Green's 2 eldest daughters came & staid with us two days agreably.

21. Miss Baxter of Helpringham[16] & Miss Betsy Shepherd got tea, and staid a rubber at whist: the former sings very agreable.

---

5   Flinders's attorney and family friend, whose name crops up on numerous occasions in handling Flinders's legal and financial affairs later in the Diary.

6   Tumified: swollen/inflated.

7   Lambdoidal suture: connecting the parietal and occiptal bones at the rear of the skull.

8   MS 'fluctuation'. The undulation of fluid in a tumour (*OED*).

9   Edward Blythe of Spalding was an ex-army surgeon (Mills, 62). After his death, Flinders's brother John would move in to his house (see 8 Aug. 1787).

10   Dozil or dossil: a plug of lint or rag for stopping a wound (*OED*).

11   Sadly, this book of letters does not appear to have survived.

12   Joseph Priestly (1733–1804): political theorist, clergyman and chemist; he had discovered oxygen the previous year and was in the process of publishing numerous volumes on his observations and experiments (*ODNB*).

13   Possibly *British Biography: or, an Accurate and impartial account of the lives and writings of eminent persons . . .* by Joseph Towers. Published in seven volumes between 1766 and 1772, and reissued 1773–80.

14   MS 'in'.

15   John Flinders also of Donington.

16   Eight miles north-west of Donington.

[f.2]

January 1775		Received		Paid	
1st	Retail and small bills	8s	6d		
	House bill this week			13s	2½d
6	Of Mr Reckaby, by bill	11s	6d		
7	House bill last week			9s	6d
	Retail and small bills	17s			
	Boots mending by P. Moor				4d
9	Of Mr Fairbanks, Gosberton, by bill	15s			
	Of Mr Cole, Wheelwright, by bill	13s			
	Of Molly Foster at Wm Coles, by bill	£1 16s			
	Of Benjamin Upton, by bill	11s	4d		
	One Medical Magazine No 13: 1s; & Un. Mag.				
	December, 6d			1s	6d
	Gave the Ringers 6d; the Plowmen 3d				9d
11	A Pint 2s 6d and tunnel 6d of Mr Beesly			3s	
	Received of him for old Pewter		11d		
14	Carriage of Druggs from Robinson			4s	6d
	Of Mr Marsh, Quadring, by bill	5s	6d		
	Of Mr Thomas Tenny, by bill	£1 2s			
	Of John Thomson, by bill	10s	6d		
15	Retail &c.	9s			
	House bill last week			3s	3d
	Lost at Cards at Mr Pakeys the 15th				6d
16	Pair of Kitchen Tongs of Mr Bycroft, Boston			2s	4d
	Lindsey's Liturgy[17] Binding 1s 8d; -do- Life of			2s	5d
	Cyrus 9d				
	Priestley Institutes 3rd Vol. 3s;				
	Brit. Biograph. No 1, 6d			3s	6d
20	Of Mr Day Junior, Swineshead, by bill	7s	9d		
21	Housebill this week			14s	10¾d
	Retail and small bills	14s	9d		
	To the Newsman for Carriage				2d
	Black studds of Mr Tory				2½d
24	Of Mr Cew, by bill	10s			
26	Of Mr Burr, by bill	6s			
	Of Mrs Maples, by bill	8s	3d		
28	A Pruning knife of Mr Tory			1s	2d
	House bill this week			18s	7½d
	Retail and small bills	10s	6d		
31	Limon Juice 1¼ Pint of J. Orry			1s	3d
	Of The Rev. Mr Trimnel,[18] Bicker, by bill	£4 18s			
	Presented me by that generous man over and				
	above my Bill	£1 8s			
	21 Turnpikes in January			2s	7½d
	Lost at Cards at Mr Ward's, Draper				6d
Carried over		**£17 3s**	**6d**	**£5 4s**	**2¾d**

[17] Perhaps Theophilus Lindsey (1723–1808), *A sermon preached at the opening of the chapel in Essex-House, Essex-Street, in the Strand, on Sunday, April 17, 1774. To which is added, A summary account of the reformed liturgy, on the plan of the late Dr. Samuel Clarke*. Printed in London, 1774 (ESTC).

[18] Revd Charles Trimnell MA, Vicar of Bicker 1750–1776.

Visits

3d. I dined at Mr Gleed's.

13. We drank tea & had an agreable Evening at Mr Pakey's. Mr Whiteh[ead's] Family there. Home 12.

27. We drank tea & supped at my Father's: called away.

29. We got tea at Mr Shepherd's.

31. Wonderfull: was invited to Mr William Ward's,[19] amongst others. We got home by 11½. I wish this movement for a reconciliation may be sincere. February 8.

[f.2v]

February 1775: 2nd Month, 28 Days

7. We had company to tea & sup. They staid till 12. Accidently Mr S. W. came. Fine weather.

9. We had the Remainder of our Company.

11. Memorandum: attended Mrs Ward.

Th. 16.

Fr. 17. My Birthday. My Father & Mrs F. dined here. Mr Birks got tea.

Sat. 18. Sowed Pease.

21. Remarkable Aurora Borealis.

Wed. 22. Sowed Lettice & Parsley.

Th. 23. Nonsuch Apples.

Fri. 24. Sowed Carrot.

Mon. 27. Hedge Plashing.

Business

Saturday 11. I was called to attend Mrs Ward, being ill. I was somewhat surprized at this, but am pleased that this reconciliation was of their bringing about, and that it seems sincere. The case has proved Icteric,[20] I imagine from Concretions,[21] but she is now greatly better.

Company

7. We had a party to tea and supper. Viz: Mrs Shilcock,[22] Mr & Mrs Ward, Mr Gleed, Miss Dawson, Mrs Maples, and by accident Mr S. Ward of B——. We had an agreable Evening. They left us about 12. Some others did not come.

9. We had the remainder of our company, viz. Mrs Pakey, Miss Golding, Mr and Mrs Whitehead, Mr Dawnay, Miss E. Shepherd, and Miss Shilcock.

Birth Day

Friday 17. I compleated my 25th Year. My Father & Mrs F.[23] dined with us, and accidently Mr Birks[24] came in the afternoon. I renew my gratitude to divine

---

[19] Matthew's wife was Susannah, daughter of Samuel Ward, and William was her brother. What led to the need for a reconciliation is unclear from the Diary.

[20] Relating to jaundice.

[21] Gallstones formed in the gallbladder or bile duct.

[22] Flinders's aunt Jane had married into the Shilcock family.

[23] This is probably his father's second wife, Mary Baxter.

[24] Anthony and John Birks were the authors of *Arithmetical Collections and Improvements* (1766) and were masters at Donington's Free Writing School (Burnby, 52).

mercy, in that I have been protected, bountifully supplied, and kept in Being the 4th of a Century.

Gardening
Saturday 18. I have lately taken much pleasure in my Garden; and the fineness of the season has induced [me] to plant and sow. This day I sowed 2 Rows of early Peas.

Wednesday 22. I sowed a small Bed of Lettice and also 2 trenches of Parsley.

Thursday 23. I had 4 Nonsuch Apples planted, these were recommended to me as excellent fruit, good bearers and proper for Espaliers.[25] I had them from Grimbald at Swineshead.[26] I had removed 4 of my old trees (worth nothing) to make room for them.

Friday 24. I sowed a Bed of Carrots.

Monday 27. James Bucknel begun to Plash[27] my Garden Hedge, it being too thin, & this is exteemed an excellent method to thicken & amend it: he finished it in two days.

I have further to remark that in January I pruned all my espalier hedge, wither properly or not experience will inform me. Also the begining of this month, I dressed up my Apricot tree and Vine, pruning and nailing them up, having had Instructions from Mr Burr.

Aurora Borealis
21. In the Evening we observed a remarkably splendid Aurora Borealis, extending a great way, and possessing uncommon and extensively waving motions towards the center. [f.3] I remember to have seen one some years ago nearly similar to this – tho' I think not quite so splendid, moving and extensive, seeming as if the atmosphere was in violent lucid agitations or convulsions.

Visits
About the middle of this month visited Mrs Maples, the party was agreable & we staid the Evening.

February 1775		Received			Paid		
Brought		£17	3s	6d	£5	4s	2¾d
1	Of Mr Stimson, Bicker, by bill	£1					
	Of Mr Flint, Barber, by bill		11s				
	To Him, for one year's shaving and Hair dressing, due January 28					12s	
3	Of William Morris, Blacksmith, by bill		7s	9d			
	Paid to him by bill					3s	11d
4	To Edward Laykins, by bill					15s	
	House bill this week					9s	3d
	Retail and small bills	£1	0s	6d			
6	Medical Magazine No 14					1s	
9	Lost at Cards 1s. Do the 7th 6d.					1s	6d
	To Ed: Gibson, by bill					8s	

25 Lattice or frame for training branches of trees or shrubs.
26 Swineshead, 4 miles north-east of Donington.
27 Plash: to bend and interweave twigs, branches etc. to form a hedge.

February 1775 (cont.)	Received		Paid		
11 Bees wax 2¼lb of Michael Moor at 1s 6d				3s	4½d
Of Mr Jarvis, Bicker	£1	1s			
House bill this week			£1	13s	10d
Retail and small bills		17s	6d		
To my wife £1 12s 6d: but 19s 6d being deducted					
on account to Mr Pakey reduces it to				13s	
13 To Mr Parker, by bill				7s	8d
Of him, by bills	£1	7s	2d		
14 White Arsenic 7lb of Mr Ward at 4d				2s	4d
The late Jos: Selby's bill		11s	6d		
15 Of Thomas Boots, by bill		11s			
16 Of Mr Jackson Junr, Bicker, by bill		6s	6d		
18 House bill this week			£1	2s	7¾d
Retail and small bills	£1	1s	6d		
22 Of Mr Northern, Bicker Gauntlet	£1	1s			
23 Carriage of a Box from Barrit & Co				1s	10d
One Chaldron of Coals from Boston			£1	2s	
Porterage &c of Do					11d
25 Of Samuel Bacchus, by bill		10s	6d		
Of Sarah Yates, by bill		5s	6d		
House bill this week				13s	8d
Retail and small bills		9s	6d		
27 Lemon juice of Orry 12oz					9d
British Biography No 2					6d
Coals half a Chaldron at 22s				11s	
Expences of -do-				1s	
Carried over	**£28**	**5s**	**5d**	**£14**	**9s**	**5d**

[f.3v]

March 1775: 3rd Month, 31 Days

Wed. 1. Finished plashing.

Th. 2. Sowed Onions.

Fr. 3. Planted Cabages.

Sat. 4. Was the Bull sale in the Evening.

Mond. 6. Dug up Potatoes.

Tues. 7. Planted Cauliflowers.

Wed. 8. Sowed Celery. Memorandum: Disorder, took Ext. Cath.[28] the 7th.

Th. 9. Dined at Mr Trimnel's.

Fr. 10. Sowed 3 Rows Peas. Went at night to a fractured Arm. Mr Fish & Son, Swineshead.

15. At 5 in the afternoon called to Mrs Clark, home by 6. Mrs Gleed got tea here.

Th. 16. Matthew's Birthday. New Book Case.

Fr. 17. At 2 in morning called to Mrs Godley, home by 7. After Breakfast went to Spalding, staid the day, got home by 8. Went immediately to Mrs Cottam, Swineshead Fen Houses, staid the night & day following. Forceps case.

Sat. 18. Home by 5.

Tu. 21. At 10 in the Evening called to Mrs Garner, home by 4 in mane.

Th. 23. Planted Hollys and Asparagus.

---

[28] Probably a cathartic.

Wed. 29. The 3 preceding days sharp weather. Frost & some snow. Paid J. Wells.
Fr. 31. In the afternoon called to William Buthy's wife, got home by 12 in the Night.

Midwifry

No 4. Wednesday 15. Called to Mrs Clark (Glover) at 5 in the afternoon, excellent labour. Home by 6.

No 5. At 2 in the Morn Friday 17th, called to Mrs Godley, Bicker G. I got home by 7. Natural Labour.

No 6. At 8 in the evening same day, called to one Mrs Cottam, Swineshead Fen-house,[29] an unexpected Labour – a very lingering one. A midwife had been with her 2 days, but though she had pains she was not in labour till the following morning; the pains insufficient and obliged to use the forceps,[30] which after several slippings at last proved effectual. She has done very well. This is the first Case I have had in that end, and 'tis likely to produce me some others. I did not get home till 5 in the afternoon the 18: much fatigued, as I had not been in bed or my boots off for 40 hours.

No 7. Tuesday 21st. At 10 in the Evening called to Mrs Garner – tolerable labour. Home by 4 in the Morn.

No 8. Friday 31. At 4 in the afternoon called to William Buthy's wife (Woadman) in Bicker Fen. I got home by 12 at night, which was a reasonable time compared with the last tedious hours I waited on this woman in a former labour, the pains were only just sufficient. She goes on well. The credit of these people being bad, I demand pay 'ere I go, though on very low terms.

Gardening

Th. 2. Sowed a large Bed of Onions, for the first time.

Fr. 3. Planted 20 Cabbages round the Onion Bed.

Mon 6. The Boy begun to dig up the Remaining Potatoes & continued till he finished them. I believe we shall have sufficient for family use, and also to set the ground anew. This article has saved me I may say 18s or 20s.

Tu. 7. I planted 10 Cauliflowers on a separate[31] Bed.

Wed. 8. Sowed a small Bed of Celery.

Friday 10. I sowed 3 Rows of later pease.

Th. 23. I had 3 Gardeners to work. Mr Grimbald from Swineshead who brought me 100 Holly's & planted them. From the sharp and dry weather since, I doubt many of them will not prosper. I thought a holly hedge betwixt my Fathers green & my Garden would make a good fence, and compensate the length of time it takes in getting up. John Lammin making an Asparagus Bed, and Thomas Hillyard removing flowers. Mr Grimbald since has brought me some quick sets

---

[29] Swineshead Fenhouses, 5 miles north-east of Donington.

[30] Obstetric forceps were invented in the seventeenth century by the Chamberlen family. The device consisted of two curved, hollow metal blades that were clamped around the baby's head to aid delivery. The Chamberlen family were very secretive about the invention, and it was not until the early eighteenth century that usage become widespread (M. J. O'Dowd, *The History of Obstetrics and Gynaecology* (Carnforth, 2000), 146–147).

[31] MS 'seperate'.

(200) and planted them at the bottom of the garden, perswading me they would be much better than the Elders before planted there.

Various
Sat. 4. Was at the Bull sale in the Evening, little or no Business done.
[f.4] Wed. 8. Felt some ill effects from my disorder; much alarmed at it, took some Ext. Cath., and with my wife contrived a bandage which I intend constantly to use, as I bless God I find it of use.
16. My Boys Birth day,[32] I bless God the child is better[33] in his health, than for some time past.
I have got from Parker a New Book case for my desk, 'tis a neat piece[34] of furniture and will be very usefull.
17. I paid my Friends at Spalding[35] a Visit, & returned in the Evening. For some days the latter end of the Month, we had remarkable sharp frosts. April 4.

March 1775 Brought over		Received			Paid		
		£28	5s	5d	£14	9s	5d
1	To J. Bucknel for 2 days Plashing					2s	
	Of a Stranger from Fleet		6s				
	6 Turnpikes in February						9d
4	Carriage of a Letter from Spalding						1d
	Spent at the Bull in the Evening					1s	
	House bill this week					19s	0¾d
	Retail and small bills		11s	6d			
5	Spent at the Cow with Mr Banks						6d
6	Medical Magazine No 15; Brit. Biography No 3					1s	6d
9	Of Edward Seymour, Bicker, by bill		5s				
11	House bill this week					9s	7d
	Retail and small bills		14s				
13	Of Mr Gainsborough, Swineshead, by bill		10s	6d			
14	Of William Wheatly, by bill		9s	6d			
17	A Bath Stove of Mr Jennings, Spalding				£2		
	Black Lead ½lb. for -do-						6d
	Paid to my Brother on the last Lottery account				£3	9s	3d
	Cheese of Mr Morgan, Spalding					8s	3d
	Hord. Perl.[36] 4lb: 1s 2d. Jallap[37] 1lb: 3s 4d. Corks 9d.					5s	3d
	Of My Brother for Lint 1lb: 7s. Bark 1½lb: 11s 3d.		18s	3d			
	Garden Shears of Mr Jennings, 3s 6d. Carriage 2d					3s	8d
18	House bill this week					9s	4¾d
	Retail and small bills		15s				
20	Of Mr Cottam, Swineshead Fen-houses	£1	1s	0d			
22	Of Mr Sargent at Mr Pakeys, by bill	£1	5s				

32 This refers to Matthew, their first child, who would go on to become a famous sailor and explorer. This was his first birthday.
33 MS 'is my better'.
34 MS 'peice'.
35 Market town approximately 10 miles south of Donington.
36 *Hordeum perlatum* (pearl barley).
37 Jalap: a purgative drug derived from the tuberous roots of some climbing plants (*OED*).

March 1775 (cont.)	Received			Paid		
23 To Mr Grimbald, Swineshead, for 4 Nonsuch						
Apples					4s	
To -do- for 100 of small Holly's					4s	
To -do- for a days work					1s	6d
To J. Lammin for a days work					1s	6d
Deals from Boston for Washboarding &c.					13s	
25 House bill this week					14s	6½d
Retail and small bills	£1	0s	6d			
27 Of Mr Thomas Pyke, by bill	£3	1s				
29 To Mr Wells, Mason, by bill				£1	5s	
Received of -do- by bill		3s	9d			
30 To Mr Strapps, by bill					3s	9d
Received of -do- by bill		3s	6d			
31 Of William Butthy, Woadman		10s	6d			
Turnpikes in March, 13					1s	7½d
Carried over	**£40**	**0s**	**5d**	**£26**	**9s**	**1½d**

[f.4v]
April 1775: 4th Month, 30 Days
Saturday 1. Fine day.
Wednesday 5. Mr Lynch.
Sunday 9. Was at B. Ch. Dined at Mr G's.
Tuesday 11. Was at Mr Hanleys, Swineshead.
Friday 14. Mr S. Ward.
Sunday 16. With Dr Thor.
Thursday 20. Dined at Swineshead.
Sunday 23. Was at B. Ch: dined at Mr T. Mrs Foggin.
Monday 24. Window Money.

Midwifry
No 9. Saturday 8. Attended Mrs Taylor in the N. Ing – with at 5 in the afternoon tolerable Labour. Home by 1 in the night.
No 10. Thursday 13. At 6½ in the Morn went to Mrs Morris at Bicker Marsh Mill (my third Attendance on her). Excellent time, home by 9.
No 11. At 7 in the Morn, Monday 17th, went to Mrs West, Swineshead North End; lingering but Natural. Got home at 2 the following Morn. NB the child by (I imagine) some natural defect, has one ankle remarkable flexile. I have applied a rowler,[38] to preserve the proper position, I hope to some advantage.
No 12. Tuesday 18. Went to Mrs Lee at 8 in the Evening. It proved a forceps case, I believe from wrong situation with respect to the ischiatic[39] spines. I managed, but after 3 or 4 Trials. I wish I could remember always to turn the head with the forceps 'ere extracting, as I think it would be accomplished easier. The child's head proved to have a tumor similar to that mentioned in January, which I opened with the same success & is now well. I got home by 2 the following Morn.
No 13. At 3 in the afternoon, called from Mr Trimnel's, Bicker, to attend Mrs Holmes at the Gantlet. Excellent Labour, tho' Twins, the last directly followed the

---

[38] Roller: a long bandage formed in a roll (*OED*).
[39] Relating to the pelvis.

first, footling, prior to the first Placenta. All do well. Went at 3 in the afternoon and got home by 5.

Gardening
Tuesday 4. I had Thomas Hilyard to set Potatoes.
Saturday 22. An Itinerant Gardener sowed me some curious purple Brocoli; and also some Speckled Dwarf Kidney beans, and 2 rows of Marrow Peas.

Purchase
Monday 3. I procured the £80 of Mr Gleed and signed the bond for the same. My Brother is so kind as to bind himself with me for it, the Money is one Thomas Beets of Wigtoft,[40] at £5 per Cent.
Wednesday 5. I got my Money of Mr Ward who has called in the bond I had against him &c, and made the remaining payment for this house &c. to Mr Bankes at the Bull, viz. £228. He has give me a surrender which cost me £1 1s 0d which I am to deliver into the Wikes[41] Court sometime in October, when I pay the fine and fees there due. Mrs Dunster sent a letter of Attorney to Mr Bankes to sign the surrender. I thank God that this capital affair is so far compleated.

Horse Dealing
Thursday 6. I sold my Mare to Mr Bennit, Apothecary to the Duke of Ancaster, for 12 Guineas, a sum much less than I expected, & the same day bought one of Edward Laykins for £14.14s.

Tidd Journey[42]
Tuesday 25. At 3 in the afternoon we went double on the new Mare to Spalding, staid the night, at 6 in the Morn, my Brother, Sister, and wife in a chaise,[43] myself on my Mare, went to Tidd. Got there by [f.5] Breakfast, but first was disgusted at meeting Mr H.[44] going to Lincoln Fair, and obliged to go, we were as happy as we could be, without him! Had some agreable walks & view of a delightfull garden of the Parsons, Mr Stephens, apparently a worthy old Gentleman, we returned to Spalding in the Evening & I came home the next, my wife not till Saturday night. I unfortunately missed a Labour viz. Mrs Jackson, Bicker; great alloy to an agreable visit. My Uncle H[ursthouse] has lately been depressed with the loss of two Daughters, viz. his Eldest Mrs Radclif & her child, also Hannah a younger, & his remaining two are in poor health.[45]

---

40 Five miles east of Donington.
41 The manor of Wikes in Donington, of which a moiety belonged to the Trustees of Cowley's Charity. The records of the manor include a letter written by Matthew Flinders Junior in 1811, concerning the copyhold property of his stepmother (*LAR* 13 (1961–62), 33).
42 Tydd St Mary, about 24 miles south-east of Donington, the home of Flinders's cousin John Hursthouse.
43 A horse-drawn carriage, often uncovered – as Flinders's use of the word "on" rather than "in" suggests in this case (*OED*).
44 Hursthouse – his mother's family.
45 Matthew Hursthouse's eldest daughter Elizabeth married F. Ratcliffe; she died in 1774. Matthew's younger daughters Hannah and Abigail both died in 1775 (*Lincolnshire Pedigrees*, 1265).

April 1775		Received			Paid		
	Brought over	£40	0s	5d	£26	9s	1½d
1	Housebill					10s	8½d
	Retail and small bills		18s	6d			
4	Of Mr Ingal, Swineshead, a bill on the parish		14s	4d			
	Cost me at Swineshead today & last week						7d
	To Thomas Hillyard 1s.6d; paid to him 1s.6d		1s	6d		1s	6d
	Gave to a Woman in Charity last week						3d
5	The late Mr Thomas Cole's bill	£9	11s				
	Interest from Mr William Ward	£1	17s				
	Spent at the Cow 6d; at the Bull 1s					1s	6d
6	Sold my Mare to Mr Bennit of Grimsthorpe	£12	11s				
	Bought one of Edward Laykins				£14	14s	
	Spent at the Bull					1s	
8	Housebill					12s	4½d
	Of John Seymour, Bicker		7s				
	Retail and small bills		16s	6d			
10	Of J. Garner, by bill		16s	6d			
11	Gave Mr Hanley's man						6d
15	The late William Watson's account, Gosberton	£1	10s				
	House bill this week				£1	1s	7¼d
	Retail and small bills	£1	3s	3d			
17	Of Thomas West, Swineshead North End	£1	1s				
18	To Thomas Barton, one Year's wages				£1	10s	
	What he lost in the Street					10s	6d
	Of Mr Dickinson, Swineshead Fen Houses		6s				
	Of Mr Taylor, in the North Ing		16s				
19	Of J. Howit's brother, Bicker		13s				
	Of Benjamin Baumford, Bicker		6s	6d			
20	Of Mr J. Birks, by bill	£5	11s				
	Thomas Kent's bill, Swineshead, by Mr Ingal	£2	4s	6d			
	Cost me at Mr Ingals, Swineshead					2s	10d
21	Of Mr Harrison, Quadring Fen Side	£1					
	Of Mr Henry Thorold, by bill	£1	11s	6d			
23	Retail and small bills		18s	6d			
	To a Gardener the 22d					1s	
	House bill this week					11s	5d
24	To Mr Dixon, half-year's Window Money					10s	2d
27	Expences to Spalding and Tidd					12s	1½d
30	Retail and small bills		15s	6d			
	House bill this week					15s	1d
	A Present to my Neice at Spalding					4s	
	Turnpikes in April, 8					1s	
	[Carried over]	£85	10s	6d	£48	11s	3¼d

[f.5v]

May 1775: 5th Month, 31 Days

Th. 4. Quick sets.

Wed. 10. Supped at Mr Shilcock's.

Th. 11. We dined at Mr Gleeds.

Fri. 26.[46] The fair. Called in the night to Mr Trimnel's sister, Bicker. Home 3.

---

[46] MS '25'.

Monday 29. Supped at Mr Trimnels.

Midwifry
No 14. Tuesday 30. At 2 in the Morn went to Mrs Asplin, Swineshead Fen Houses. Good Labour.

Surgery
1st in the Evening went to a Compound fractured Arm at Bicker G.[47] a girl of Wm Story's about 7 years of age. Done by a leap, and fall. The Ulna and Radius both fractured, and a portion of one of them pierced the integuments, but I found the bones very little displaced; a little plight[48] gentle bandage & the volatile Spirituous Embrocation, did well, relieved the pain, settled the tumification, and when the wound admitted, strict bandage with splints compleated the cure, towards the end of which I discovered that the head of the Radius was somewhat thrown from its situation towards the bend of the arm but was no impediment to the flexion of the joint, I have used compress with advantage.

Gardening
Monday 1st. I sow'd 2 Rows of late Pease.

Death
Mr Allen of Boston, Organist, died: and with great regret I have to note the death of Miss A. Shepherd on the 22d. I attended the funeral on the 25th.

Swineshead Society
Th. 4. I entered my self a member at the Swineshead Society, one similar to that established in this Parish.

Servants
May 13. Our servant maid Rebecca Knights left us, my wife thinking the Wages too much, and also that some things were not so agreable in her, as she cou'd wish; and the 14th our new one came, in company with her mother (my wife's Sister). She is young, and I am afraid will be scarce strong enough for the work, that upon the whole I almost wish we had not parted with the first. Mrs Stanny my Wife's Sister staid with us till the 17th.

Sundries
15th. I reckoned with my Father, paid him a year's Rent, and for sundry other particulars. I have mentioned to him that in future he must allow me £5 per annum for the 2 Ing[49] pasture, the barn, yard &c., which he has not said much against.
I have to note that the season has been remarkably dry a long time, the showers [f.6] being small, and but seldom occurring; every vegetable at present seems

[47] Bicker Gauntlet.
[48] MS 'pligit'.
[49] Meadow land (*OED*).

much in wants of that benign moisture, which makes the valleys "laugh and sing".

23d. We dined at Mr Gee's, Swineshead, and supped with Mr Birks, going purposely to visit them. Mrs F. senior was with us.

May 1775		Received			Paid		
Brought over		**£85**	**10s**	**6d**	**£48**	**11s**	**3¼d**
1	Easter offerings to Mr Powell						6d
2	Of Mr Pillings, Bicker Gauntlet	£1					
	Of Mr Cresswell at Mr Pakeys		12s	3d			
	Of Mr J. Pakey		15s	10d			
	To him a bill				£3	4s	7d
3	Of a stranger		6s	6d			
	Carriage of druggs from Swineshead last week					1s	
4	To Mr Grimbald for 200 quick sets					1s	
	Entrance at the Swineshead Society					1s	10d
7	Housebill					16s	9½d
	Retail &c.		16s				
	To my wife				£1	12s	6d
	Medical Mag. No 16, 17; Brit. Biography No 4, 5					3s	
11	Of Mr Richd Clay, Swineshead, by bill	£1	13s	6d			
13	To Rebecca Knight one year's wages				£3	13s	
	Gave the servant at Mr Gleed's the 11th					1s	
	House bill this week					12s	
	Retail and small bills	£1	1s				
15	To my Father for 2 Quarters of Oats				£1	6s	6d
	To -ditto- for half a Hogshead of Ale				£1	4s	6d
	To -ditto- for 5 stone 12 pound of Pork at 4s 3d				£1	5s	
	Small Beer 2s 8d. Pearl Barley 2s 11d					5s	7d
	Received of my Father		7s	3d			
	To him one year's Rent due Ap. 5. 75				£7	10s	
17	Of Mr Holmes, Bicker	£1	3s				
19	Lemon Juice of J. Orry sometime ago					5s	
20	Of Mrs Clifton, by bill	£1	6s				
	Retail, &c.	£1	16s	6d			
	Housebill					12s	
	Earnest money to our new Maid					2s	6d
23	Of Mr Hanley's Man, Swineshead, by bill		5s				
	Gave Mr Gee's Maid, 1s. Ditto Mr Hanley's Man, 6d.					1s	6d
25	To Mr Parker, for a Book Case				£1	10s	
	Of Mr Harnis, Ball-hall, by bill	£2	11s	6d			
26	Of Mr Torks, Swineshead, by bill		15s				
27	Of Mr Mackriss of Frampton, by bill	£1	16s				
	Second hand Books the 25th, viz. Tale of a Tub, 10d.[50] On Light & colours, 1s 0d[51] & Dryden's Poems, 10d					2s	8d
	John Wells, labourer, by bill		5s	6d			
	Housebill this week					13s	9d
	Retail and small bills	£1	11s	6d			

[50] Jonathan Swift (1667–1745), *A tale of a tub*.
[51] Probably Francesco Algarotti (1712–1764), *The philosophy of Sir Isaac Newton explained, in six dialogues, on light and colours*.

May 1775 (cont.)	Received	Paid	
30 To J. Newton for a pair of Boots		18s	
Received of him by bill	10s 6d		
31 Ten Toll barrs in the month of May		1s	3d
Trifles in the Month			3d
[Carried over]	**£104 3s 4d**	**£74 3s**	**4¾d**

[f.6v]
June 1775: 6th Month, 30 Days
Midwifry

No 15. Sund. 4th. At 2 in the Morn went to Mrs Pullin's sister, Northorp.[52] I got home by noon, the Labour Natural, and as easy as we usually expect the first.

No 16. Wed. 7th. At 6 in the Evening I went to Mrs Dickenson, Bicker. Got home by midnight.

No 17. Frid. 9. At 11 in the Forenoon went to Mrs Lammin. I got home by dinner, I think this is my 4th attendance on her, and she never has a natural Birth, this time it was a breech case, and passed well and soon.

No 18. Sat. 10. At 2 in the Morn, called to Mrs Grimes, Bicker Gantlet, my 2d attendance. This (as the last) was a lingering case, & the pains proving insufficient, I used the forceps more to my satisfaction & advantage than I remember ever to have done before. I got home by 3 in the afternoon.

No 19 Sund. 25. I was with Mrs Gibson various times being lingering. I got home early on the Monday Morn.

No 20. Mond. 26. At 2 in the afternoon went to Mrs Clark, Swineshead Fen houses. I got home by 6 in the Evening.

House Improvements

About the middle of this month I had the Carpenters, washboarding the Staircase & chambers compleat, this is[53] a very necessary improvement, and I wonder was omitted at the building of the house; I had my deals from Boston sometime ago. They have also made us a very convenient closet in our lodging room; these jobs have cost near 50s. I have since painted the Washboards brown and intend to have the closet & that room white.

Bicker Feast

The 22 and 23d I passed agreably at Bicker principally at Mr Jarvis's, but the latter day I dined at Mr Green's. We broke up both nights and got home in good time – my wife was there only the first day, at Mr Green's; I have for several years passed these days agreably among my friends at Bicker.

Books

I have lately perused Dr Garth's Dispensary, a Poem wrote the begining of the present century, lent me by the Revd Mr Trimnel. There is much pointed satire and good poetry in this peice, and as the blanks were filled, I read it with more information & pleasure than I otherwise should.[54]

---

[52] About 1 mile north of Donington.
[53] MS 'it'.
[54] Sir Samuel Garth (1661–1719), physician and poet. *The Dispensary* (1699) was a witty satire

The same Gentleman has also lent me Dean Swift's[55] Miscellany 3 Vol. 8vo.

[f.7]

Gardening

At the latter end of this month I transplanted out some of the purple Brocoli – the seed I had of an Itinerant Gardener.

June 1775		Received			Paid		
Brought over		**£104**	**3s**	**4d**	**£74**	**3s**	**4¾d**
3	Retail and small bills	£1	9s				
	3 Lancets grinding and carriage from Stamford					1s	3d
	Postage of a Letter from Robinson						3d
	Housebill					14s	5½d
	Saddle and Bridle mending						8d
5	Medical Magazine No 18					1s	
	Windows mending					2s	9d
7	Paid to Barrit and Robinson, in full				£7	2s	
	To him a bill				£3	4s	7d
9	The salary for Wigtoft Poor	£4	4s				
	Of Mr B. Pakey, Wigtoft, by bill	£1	15s				
10	Housebill					13s	5d
	Retail and small bills	£2					
	A pair of Shoes of John Hayes					6s	
12	Of Mrs Day at Mr Pullin's, Northorp		15s				
	Of Mr Pullin, Northorp, by bill	£2	2s				
16	Of Mrs Bradley, by bill		6s	6d			
	To my Father for keeping my Mare one year, due last Old Lady Day				£5	0s	0d
	Received of him for attending Mrs F.	£1	1s				
	Spent at the Cow in the Morning						6d
17	Retail and small bills	£1	16s	6d			
	House bill				£1	2s	4d
	To Mr Dalton for carriage						4d
	Church Assessment £4 at 5½d due last Easter					1s	10d
	Of Mr Pepper, Quadring, by bill	£1	9s	6d			
18	Of J. Dickenson, Bicker, by bill	£1	1s				
	Of Mr Trimnel's man, by bill	£1	7s				
20	Of Mr Crowder, by bill		14s				
21	Spent at Swineshead						3d
23	Cost me at Bicker						6d
24	Oak Posts 10. 6 feets, at 1s each					10s	
	Ditto 7. 4 feets, at 4d each					2s	4d
	House bill					17s	8d
	Retail and small bills	£1	8s				
27	One Chaldron & ½ of Coals, at 23s				£1	14s	6d
	Turnpike 1s 6d, Porterage 11d and Ale 4d					2s	9d
	Man's Expences 1s. Corn for the Horses 16d.					2s	4d
	12 Battens, at 11d each					11s	

inspired by a heated conflict which had broken out between the Society of Apothecaries and the College of Physicians (*ODNB*).

55　Jonathan Swift (1667–1745), author of *Gulliver's Travels*.

June 1775 (cont.)	Received		Paid		
6 Dales, at 1s 7d each				9s	6d
Of Mr William Gee, Swineshead, by bill	£4	19s			
28 Of Edward Gibson, by bill	10s	6d			
29 To Rich. Jackson, a bill			£1	16s	
Carriage of a Box from London				3s	4½d
Turnpikes in June, No 10				1s	3d
[Carried over]	**£131**	**1s**	**4d**	**£96**	**1s 7¾d**

[f.7v]

July 1775: 7th Month, 31 Days

Tu. 18. We dined at Mr Ward's.

Memd. Insurance. Mr Hall.

Midwifery

No 21. Mond. 3. At 6 in the Morn called to Mrs P. Moor, I got home by 9. The labour was natural but sharp. The child died the same day. She is well recovered. No 22. Sat. 15. At 5 in the Evening went to Mrs Bacchus, home by 7. Excellent Labour. This is my 3d attendance on her.

Gardening

About the middle of this month I planted 20 common Brocoli plants. They[56] were large but seem to thrive. Towards the latter end I had Thomas Hilyard, who transplanted me some curious purple Brocoli I raised from seed. He also transplanted me some celery to be fit for trenching in October, and planted me a 2d bed of pepper mint and layered my Pinks.

Fencing

I have this month put down a new post and rail fence between my house and garden, in place of the old pails; I hope this will stand firm a number of years. I find this mode of fence very expensive, this length costing me above 40s.

Land Tax

Frid. 21. I paid Mr Pakey 2s 6d being a quarter's Tax for my house and land, our separate quotas[57] are not absolutely fixed, but the assessors are to do it against the next quarter day. At present 'tis above my share.

Journey to Boston[58]

Wed. 26th. I went to Boston, in order to insure my house and outbuildings. I was in hopes the old bond would have done, but find I must be at the expence of a new one. I insure for £200 more on account of the house & in all £400.

I bought at Boston some grates &c. for a stove & furnace pan of Mr Bycroft. By chance had information my old acquaintance Mr Hall was at Boston, I found him at his Brother Baileys, drank tea with him, and was with him most of the after-

---

[56] MS 'there'.

[57] MS 'quota's'.

[58] The main town in the region, Boston and its port had experienced a boom following the drainage of the Holland Fen. It served as a major distribution point for the arable crops now being grown (Wright, *Lincolnshire Towns and Industry*, 61).

noon. He is come[59] into the country for the Benifit of his health: he will be here to see me, before he returns.

[f.8]
N.B. My Neice Henny Flinders[60] came to visit us on Thursday[61] the 27 meerly by chance, she returned on the Saturday in Mr Dalton's vehicle.

July 1775		Received			Paid		
Brought over		**£131**	**1s**	**4d**	**£96**	**1s**	**7¾d**
1	Of Mr Bonner, Bicker, by bill	£3	6s				
	Housebill this week					16s	9d
	Retail and small bills		18s				
4	A Painting Brush of Mr Ward						4d
7	Of Mrs Pell's man, Bicker, by bill		5s	6d			
	To J. Orry for Lemon juice, 1lb					1s	
	Housebill this week					18s	2d
	Retail and small bills	£1	7s	6d			
	Shoes soling & mending by Hayes					2s	1d
10	Of Robert Butcher, Hoflit,[62] by bill		15s	6d			
12	Of Mr Asplin, Swineshead Fen Houses	£1	3s	6d			
14	To Mr Beedezly, brazier, a bill					16s	
	Cera flava[63] 3lb, at 1s 6d lb, of J. Wells					4s	6d
15	Retail and small bills	£1	8s	6d			
	House bill					19s	0¾d
19	Of John Wells, shoemaker, by bill		10s	6d			
	Of Molly Foster at William Coles		6s				
21	For Land Tax, to Mr J. Pakey					2s	6d
	17 Pound of Honey at 5d., of J. Wells					7s	1d
22	House bill				£1	1s	
	Retail and small bills	£1	0s	6d			
26	Medical Magazine No 19					1s	
	British Biography No 6						6d
	Dinner at the White Hart Boston					1s	3d
	Mare at -ditto-						7d
	One year's Insurance to Mr Waite					5s	
	Brass handles of Mr Bycroft					1s	1d
27	Nails for the Paling						11¼d
	To Thomas Hilyard for half a day						6d
29	House bill					17s	3¾d
	Retail and small bills	£1	7s	0d			
	Of Mr Holbourn, Hoflit		6s				
31	Turnpikes in July, No 9					1s	1½d
	A Hat dressing &c.					1s	
[Carried over]		**£143**	**15s**	**10d**	**£103**	**0s**	**5d**

---

59 MS 'comed'.
60 Henrietta (1765–1842), the daughter of Flinders's brother John and wife Henrietta (Burnby, 51).
61 MS 'Thurday'.
62 Hoffleet or Hoflit: a hamlet in the parish of Wigtoft.
63 Yellow wax.

[f.8v]
August 1775: 8th Month, 31[64] Days
Mond. 21. Memd. Insurance.
Th. 31. New Sadle.

Midwifery
No 23. Th. 18. Called to Mrs Mitchel at 3 in the Morning. The labour was Natural. I got home by 10. This woman has done very poorly, but I hope is somewhat mending.
No 24. Sat. 26. About midnight called to Mrs Grant. Tolerable labour and not very tedious. She has done well. My 3d attendance.

Visitors &c.
My mother Langley[65] came the begining of August and is yet with us, and waits my wife's labour.
Mond. 21. Mr Hall came over to see me, he did not stay the night but went after tea.
Sat. 19. I dined and passed the Evening agreably with Mr Stukeley,[66] the company Mr Calthorp, Mr Theophilus Buckworth & wife;[67] we had a fine Haunch of Venison & were elegantly treated.
Th. 18. I supped (along with other company) with Mr Dawnay at the Cow – he is now commenced a man of great fortune. We got home by 11.

Illness
At the beginning of this Month I was much indisposed with I believe the common Illness of the country,[68] but I thank God am quite reestablished. I had fever with debility and pain, with chilness. I took 3 of Dr James's Analeptic Pills,[69] which procures about 6 motions, and each time seemed to much relieve me of that anxiety attendant on these fevers. The following day the chilness and fever returned, worse, upon which I took Tart. Emet. 1 gm;[70] this vomited me many times and I got rid of great quantities of Bile, some of it particularly glutinous; I

---

64 MS '30'.
65 His wife's mother, who had presumably re-married, since his wife's maiden name was Ward.
66 William Stukeley, esquire, of Quadring. Stukeley stood sponsor to Flinders's daughter Betsey (see below, 9 November 1775) and in the same month Flinders witnessed Stukeley's will (PRO, PROB 11/1071).
67 Theophilus Buckworth of Spalding (d.1803) and his wife Elizabeth (d.1793). See *Lincolnshire Pedigrees*, 203.
68 The symptoms he goes on to list indicate that he is talking about a general fever, the bacterial and viral causes of which were many years away from being discovered.
69 See *Supplement*, 394. These pills "For the Rheumatisms and colds" were advertised in the *Lincoln, Rutland & Stamford Mercury*: "Their peculiar Tendency to promote Perspiration, and all the natural Secretions, will account for their singular Virtues in these complaints of our Climate. They are admirably calculated for Disorders of the Stomach and Bowels." Just for good measure, they were also effective in cases of "headaches occasioned by Indigestion . . . removing the bad effects of free living . . . preventing Palsies and Apoplexies". That an intelligent and shrewd man like Flinders should resort to such an unlikely cure-all treatment as this – probably little more than a crude laxative – illustrates the timeless human tendency, as common now as then, to clutch at any hope of relief from suffering, however improbable.
70 *Tartarum emeticum*, or emetic tartar. It included antimony (*Supplement*, 280–1).

did not drink much. I found this operation excessively fatiguing, but I experienced the greatest benefit from it as the fever never returned, and I daily mended.

Surgery
Wed. 30. Mr Trimnel's Servant Boy fractured the tibia and fibula, about 2 or 3 Inches from the ankle. I reduced it much to my satisfaction, by the help of two assistants extending and counter extending, and used the side position. He is doing as well as I think possible, not the least fever or tumification[71] [f.9] coming on; which I attribute in great measure to his not being permitted the least Animal diet, not even yet.

House Improvements
Wed. 23. & Th. 24. We had the Mason setting us a furnace Pan & also erecting us an Heter Stove, usefull necessaries I suppose in every family

Insurance
Mond. 21. I got my Insurance bond and Policy from Boston. I have now 9s. annually to pay – 4s. every Midsummer & 5s. each Michaelmas. I wish they had been dated from one time.

August 1775	Received			Paid		
[Brought over]	£143	15s	10d	£103	0s	5d
1 To my wife, a bill for various					10s	7½d
2 Of Mr Lee, by bill		10s	6d			
5 Of Mr Dixon, by bill		9s	9d			
Retail and small bills		12s	6d			
House bill					13s	0½d
7 Medical Mag. No 20. Brit. Biog. No 7					1s	6d
8 Of Mrs P. Moor		10s	6d			
12 House bill					16s	11¾d
Retail and small bills	£1	11s	6d			
14 To Mr J. Ashworth, for Meat				£2	5s	
Of him, by bill	£1	3s	9d			
16 Of Mr Johnson, at the Wikes		5s	3d			
Of Mr Barnet, bricklayer, by bill		16s				
Paid to him by bill					5s	
19 House bill				£1	6s	2d
Retail and small bills		19s				
21 Of Mr Morris, Bicker, by bill	£1	7s				
Bicker Parish bill, by Mr Morris	£1	15s				
To Mr Bycroft of Boston, a bill					18s	6d
The Bond for Insuring my house					8s	6d
One Year's Insurance of Ditto for £200, at 2s[72] per						
Cent. to Midsummer '76					4s	
Carriage from London and to Donington					1s	2d
24 Of Mr Ekins, Swineshead, by bill		9s				
Of Widow Capondale, ditto, by bill		6s	6d			
Lost at Cards at Mr Stukeley's, Sat. 19th					2s	

[71] Swelling.
[72] MS '£2'.

August 1775 (cont.)	Received		Paid		
Pule.[73] C. P. 4oz of Mr Lane, Boston				2s	6d
25 Writing paper 7d. Bees Wax 1½lb 2s 3d				2s	10d
Retail and small bills	£1	6s			
House bills			£1	3s	8½d
31 To J. Strapps, balance between my old and a New					
Sadle			£1	5s	6d
To him, a bill for Sundries				6s	
Of him a bill		6s 3d			
15 Toll Barrs this Month				1s	10½d
[Carried over]	£156	4s 4d	£113	15s	3¾d

[f.9v]
September 1775: 9th Month, 30 Days
Midwifry
No 25. Frid. 7. At 4½ in the Morning called to Edward Ashton's wife, excellent quick Labour. Home by 5½.

No 26. At 6 in the Morn Mond. 11, called to Mrs Cook Junior. Tolerable labour. I got home by 9.

No 27. Sund. 17. In the Morn called to a Mrs Alvey. The child was delivered just before I went, it appeared a Miscarriage at about 7 months. I delivered the placenta; the woman has done well, the foetus lived a few hours.

No 28. Sund. 24. About 2 in the Morn my wife was delivered of a fine girl,[74] and both I thank God are doing very well: the labour was rather difficult, but by suddenly turning over, an immediate good alteration ensued, and the delivery was quickly accomplished.

A Mare
Mond. 4. I had a little Mare came from Mr Wm Dodd of Fulbeck on trial, an exceeding pleasant going thing, but after some days I found her lame, so sent her on the 19th to Mr Dadd's at Burton.

Money
Sat. 9. My Brother requesting of me a loan of £20, on account of his Son going to School, he this day sent me a Note for it with Interest, with promise to repay me by Lady Day Next, when I shall certainly want it.

Gardening
Mond. 11. I had Thos Hilyard to plant me 60 Hollies to fill up the vacancies of those that died. I had them as before of Grimbald and paid him 1s 6d for them, they all look healthy. I find this a much better Season, to transplant trees or shrubs than the Spring, though it ought to be considered that the dryness of the late Spring was much against them; so that not above 40 survived out of the hundred – and also that the late continued moisture much favoured those now planted.

---

73   *Pulegium* (pennyroyal).
74   This was Elizabeth (Betsey), their second child (after Matthew).

[f.10]
Weather
The begining of this month proved wet, and injurious to the harvests, but the latter part has been very fine and so continues.

Sundries
Sat. 2. My Nephew Jackey[75] came from Spalding to take his leave of us, being to set forwards for a School in Northamptonshire on the Monday.
Mon. 4. Was the smallest fair.
Sund. 24. Mr S. Ward[76] dined with us and left us in the afternoon.

September 1775	Received			Paid		
Brought over	**£156**	**4s**	**4d**	**£113**	**15s**	**3¾d**
1 To Mr Wm Ward, in full				£10		
Of -ditto- by bill, in full	£5	7s				
2 Retail and small bills	£1	9s				
House bill				£1	6s	2¼d
A Present to my Nephew					2s	6d
3 Of Edward Wakefield, Swineshead, by bill		11s	6d			
4 British Biog. No 8, 6d. Medical Mag. No 21, 1s.					1s	6d
5 To J. Strapps, balance between a new and old bridle					3s	6d
6 Of Mr Pycroft, by bill	£1	2s				
7 Of John Morley, Swineshead, by bill		8s	6d			
Of Edward Ashton in part		5s				
9 Retail and small bills	£1	12s				
Housebill this week					18s	8d
10 Wax 4 Pound 3oz, at 1s 6d. of Geo. Bufham					5s	7d
12 Of John Lammin, by bill		10s	6d			
A Currying Comb, 10d. A Brush, 1s.					1s	10d
13 To Wilson and Ferneyhough in full				£3	10s	6d
16 Retail and small bills		19s				
Housebill					16s	9¾d
To my wife, due August 6th				£1	12s	6d
19 Of Mr Wilkinson's Housekeeper	£1	5s	6d			
Lemons ½ a dozen of J. Orry						9d
23 To Richard Jackson in full				£1	4s	
Of Mrs Orme at Quadring		5s	6d			
Of Mr Bennit, Bicker		7s				
Retail and small bills	£1	3s	6d			
House bill				£1	1s	8¼d
26 To Mr Dan. Lynch in full				£5	14s	
29 To P. Moor, for mending Boots					1s	
30 Writing Paper						7d
Thirty Turnpikes in September					3s	9d
Retail and small bills	£1	0s	6d			
Housebill this week				£1	4s	
[Carried over]	**£172**	**11s**	**4d**	**£142**	**4s**	**8d**

75 Probably John Flinders, baptised 7 January 1767, son of John and Henrietta, Spalding.
76 Either his father- or brother-in-law, both of whom were called Samuel.

[f.10v]
October 1775: 10th Month, 31 Days
Tu. 17. The Fair.
Frid. 20. The Stamford Paper.

Midwifry
No 29. Tues. 10th. At 4 in the Morn went to Mrs Wright. Excellent quick Labour, got home by 6. This is my 2d Attendance on her.
No 30. Wed. 18. At 11 in the forenoon went to Mrs Lowe. Home by 12½. My 2d Attendance on her.

Gardening
I had Thos Hillyard 3 Days the beginning of this month planting Box, adown all the borders that any way seemed to require it. It looks neatly, and I think will be a considerable improvement. He has also contrived me an[77] Arbour in part in the old place, planting some Roman Willows, Honeysuckles and Roses. We were supplied with Dwarf Box in part by an old bed we took up and replanted, and partly by favour of Mr Thorold from his Garden.

Wikes Court
Wed. 11. I attended at the Wikes Court at the Cow in order to deliver in my surrender and take up my house, and pastures. I dined there and paid some small fees to the Bailiff and Jury, but shall not have to pay my fine and for my Copies till some time hereafter, of which Mr Smith[78] the Steward will give me timely notice: am afraid the expence of the Copies will be encreased on account of their deeming the 2 pastures, and house, 3 seperate things.

The Fair[79]
Tues. 17. Was the fair. I had not near so good fair in regard to receipts as last year.

Stamford Paper
Frid. 20. I began to take in the Stamford News & think it the most impartial paper, so have omitted joining with my Father for the Cambridge Paper, which is very barren of entertainment, and partial on the furious and patriotic side.

[f.11]

October 1775	Received			Paid		
Brought over	**£172**	**11s**	**4d**	**£142**	**4s**	**8d**
5 3 Stone 1 Pound of Com. Cheese, at 3s					9s	2½d
1 Stone 8½ Pound of New Milk -ditto-, at 4s					6s	4½d
2 Quarts of Rum of Mr Harvey					5s	3d
10 Gallons of Small Beer of -ditto -					2s	1d

---

[77] MS 'a'.

[78] For Benjamin Smith & Co., Solicitors of Horbling and Donington, see Albert Schmidt, 'Partners and their times: the Smith firm in history', *LHA* 37 (2002), 34–43.

[79] Donington had 4 annual fairs: cattle, sheep, horses and flax according to Bryant. The Diary clearly indicates a May and an October – or Autumn – Fair, with possibly a Christmas Fair in December. There is also a mention of the "smallest Fair" in the month previous to this. In the 1830s there were 'three large fairs' on 26 May, 6 Sept. and 17 Oct., with a horse fair on 17 Aug. (Allen, 342).

October 1775 (cont.)		Received			Paid		
	Received of him by bill	£1	3s	6d			
	Of Mr Clark, Glover, by bill		13s				
	Paid him					4s	
	Of Isaac Injelaw, by bill		15s				
	16 Yards of sheeting cloth at 1s 6d per yard					17s	4d
6	A Gimblet 2d. A Pitcher of Leaches 2d.						4d
	Of Thos Bee, Bicker		5s				
	Retail and small bills	£1	3s	6d			
	Housebill this week					18s	9¾d
	Seventeen Leaches					1s	5d
9	Medical Mag. No 22, 1s. Brit. Biog. No 9, 6d.					1s	6d
10	To Mr Barnet, a bill					15s	
	To Mr Grimbald, Swineshead, for 60 Hollies					1s	6d
11	The News, 2½d. Gave my Barber 6d.						8½d
	To the Bailiff of the Wikes Court					3s	
	To the Jury of -ditto-					1s	
12	Of Mr Wires, Swineshead Fen Houses		8s	6d			
13	Of Mrs Vessey, Gosberton, by bill		8s				
	To Miss Ward, Horncastle, for Teas				£2	8s	9d
	Of -ditto- for Druggs	£1	14s	9d			
	Flannel &c. for a Waistcoat lining						11d
14	½ Dozen Lemons 9d. Sugar for Shop use 10½d.					1s	7½d
	House bill this week				£1	1s	5d
	Retail and small bills	£1	7s	6d			
17	Of Mr Kennywell, Swineshead, by bill		12s				
	Of Mr Jackson, Bicker, by bill	£1	10s	6d			
	Of Mr Jackson Junior, Bicker		6s				
18	Eight oz. of Worstead for Stockings					2s	
19	To the Overseers of the High Ways, 1 Day						6d
20	The Stamford News						2½d
21	Housebill this week					18s	11d
	Retail and small bills	£1	16s	6d			
22	Of Eliz. Symons by bill		8s	6d			
	Of Mr Whitehead by bill	£1	9s				
	To Frances Ingerson for Nursing					15s	
	3 Lancets Grinding and Carriage					1s	2d
23	Of Joseph Kircum by bill		5s	6d			
	Of Thomas Foster, Gosberton, by bill		8s				
	To Thos Hillyard for Gardening					1s	6d
24	Window Money 10s 2d. Land Tax 2s 6d.					12s	8d
25	A Blanket for Matthew's Bed					2s	3d
	Stuff for a Quilt for -ditto-					2s	6d
	Hardon[80] for a Close Bag 2 Yards & ¾						10d
27	Sugar for Shop use 1s 1½d. Ferrit[81] 6d.					1s	7½d
	Carriage from Ferneyhough & Wilson					4s	6d
[Carried over]		**£187**	**6s**	**1d**	**£153**	**8s**	**6¾d**

---

[80] Harden or hardon: a coarse fabric made from the hards of flax or hemp (*OED*).
[81] A tape or ribbon (*OED*).

[f.11v]
November 1775: 11th Month, 30 Days
Mon. Oct. 30. Mrs Dodds' Account.

Midwifry
No 31. Wed. 1. At 4 in the Morn, attended J. Berry's wife. I had been several times before, the Case being lingering but ended Naturally. I got home by 7 in the Morning.
No 32. Th. 2. Attended Mrs Birks at times most of the day. Home by 6 in the Evening. 2d Attendance.
No 33. At 8 in the Evening, Frid. 3, went to Mrs Allen at Swineshead. I got home by 4½ in the Morn. 2d attendance
No 34. Sund. 5. At 3 in the morn went to Wm Hall's wife.[82] Got home by 5, excellent labour.
No 35. Same Evening went to Wm Swallow's wife. Got home at 1½ in the Night.
No 36. Th. 9. At 2 in the afternoon went to J. Thomson's wife (Ostler); got home by 4.
No 37. Sund. 12. Attended J. Orry's wife all this night and at times all day the 13th. I got home by 9 in the Evening. This case proved remarkably lingering, and I never met with so great want of pain, when delivery was so far advanced, continuing all day without any pain (of consequence) tho' the head was far advanced. I was obliged to use the forceps, the pains not being sufficient when they did come on. I managed exceeding well with them.
No 38. Mond. 20. At 4 in the morn went to Mrs Garner, Donington Fen. I much feared this case as I was obliged to use the Crochet[83] before; it, however proved very lingering and the pains inadequate till the next Evening when the birth proved Natural & I got home by 8. 2d Attendance.
No 39. Frid. 24. At noon went to Mrs Brumpton, Bicker. Finished by 5 o'clock.
No 40. Sund. 26. At 1 in the Morn went to Mrs Everit Junior. The case somewhat lingering, got home by 8 to Breakfast. 4th Attendance.

Christening
Th. 9. We made our Daughter a Christian: the Sponsors were Wm Stukeley Esq., Miss Shepherd, Mr Wm Ward and Mrs Flinders, Spalding. We went to Church in the afternoon and had a very snug agreable party, besides the Sponsors, we had Mr Thorold, Mr Powel,[84] my Brother[85] and Henny, my Father and wife, the 2 Miss Greens. My Brother's Family left us that night, being in a chaise. Mr Powell made it 6 o' clock the following morn 'ere he left us, quite happy. We had a neat supper, and I hope the whole was conducted to satisfaction.

Gardening
Early in this month I got my potatoes covered well from the frost with straw, and

---

[82] William Hall is listed as a bricklayer of West Street, Donington, in White's *Directory of Lincolnshire* (1816).
[83] An implement related to the obstetric forceps. It seems clear from this and subsequent references that its use was often a painful experience for the patient and that it was turned to only as a last resort.
[84] Lewis Powell, Vicar of Donington 1772–1794.
[85] John.

also my Asparagus and Mercury[86] Bed, with manure. [f.12] Towards the end of the Month Thos Hillyard planted me 200 Quicksets which I had of Grimbald to make a cross hedge at the upper end of the Garden and Mr Grimbald planted me 2 Orleans and one Green Gage Plum at the lower end of the Garden.

Newspaper
Sat 4. I begun to take the Hartford Paper. I do not like it so well as the Stamford.

Servant
Sat 25. We got our New Maid Servant viz Mary Goodyear. I hope she is like to suit us very well.

November 1775		Received			Paid		
Brought over		**£187**	**6s**	**1d**	**£153**	**8s**	**6¾d**
Oct							
27	Of Mr Coggles, Hoflit, in part		10s	6d			
28	Of Mr Oliver Shepherd by bill	£4	10s				
	Of the Parish of Quadring by bill		8s	6d			
	A Chair for Matthew, 1s 6d. Writing Paper 7d.					2s	1d
	Retail and small bills		17s	6d			
	House bill this week				£1	14s	11¾d
30	Of Mrs Dodds	£1	1s				
Nov							
1	Of Mr Akeland, Swineshead, by bill		19s	6d			
	To Jonathan Warriner, Taylor				£1	6s	6d
	Of -ditto- by bill		12s				
	Turnpikes in October, No 34					4s	3d
	Trifles in October						6d
2	Of Mr Turfit, Schoolmaster, Swineshead		5s				
4	News 2½d. A Letter 1d. Housebill 19s.					19s	3½d
	Retail and small bills		16s	6d			
	Of Wm Swallow in part		6s				
7	One pair of Gloves of Mr Clark					1s	6d
8	Of J. Hunt at J. Joy's, Swineshead		10s	6d			
	Of Mr J. Ward by bill		17s				
10	Of Mr Grant, Baker, by bill		14s	6d			
	Of Mr Audis, Swineshead, by bill		7s	6d			
	Of Mr Hewison, Bicker, by bill		6s				
	Of Mr Holmes, -ditto- , by bill		6s				
	House bill this week				£1	9s	0¼d
	Retail and small bills		12s	6d			
13	To Mr Wm Ward for Sundries					8s	
	Of Mr Thos Jarvis, Bicker, by bill		12s	6d			
	Medical Mag. No 23. British Biography					1s	6d
18	House bill £1 7s 2¼d. Retail 14s 6d		14s	6d	£1	7s	2¼d
19	Of J. Alvey, Donington, by bill		8s				
20	To my Wife £1 12s 6d. Of Mr Cook 12s 6d.		12s	6d	£1	12s	6d
	Of Mrs Maples £1 3s 0d. Best Brandy 1lb	£1	3s			2s	
	Sugar for Shop use 21d. Of my Father's Maid		8s	6d		1s	9d

---

[86] Probably Dog's Mercury, but its mention in this context is curious since it is now considered a wild flower – little more than a weed if appearing in the garden.

November 1775 (cont.)	Received		Paid	
23 To Polly Stanny ½ a Year's Wages			£1 5s	
6 Limons 9d. A Letter 1d. News & Paper 6d.			1s	4d
Housebill 16s. Retail 13s 6d	13s	6d	16s	
27 To Mr Robinson, Druggist			£4 12s	6d
An 8th of a Lottery Ticket			£1 15s	
Rum 2s 7½d. Earnest Money to our Servant 1s.			3s	7½d
30 Nineteen Turnpikes in November			2s	4½d
Writing Paper				7d
[Carried over]	**£205 19s**	**1d**	**£171 16s**	**0½d**

[f.12v]

December 1775: 12th Month, 31 Days

Friday 15. Being my Father's Birth Day we dined &c. and Brother came.
Monday 18. Trees Cutting.
Tuesday 19. Supped at Mr J. Ward's. Home by 11½.
25. At 6 in the Morn went to Mrs Cam, confined the whole day.

Midwifry

No 41. Mond. 4. At noon went to Mrs Wires Junior, Swineshead Fen Houses. Got at liberty by 7 in the Evening. The Labour was natural, but lingering, from the very slow dilation of the os Uteri, whence I broke the Membranes early which sometimes I find a good way. Also very great obstruction from the external parts, being the 1st Labour.

No 42. Sat. 9. At 10 in the Evening went to Sarah Yates. Got home by 3 in the Morning. Difficult natural, found the upright posture usefull.

No 43. Th. 14. At 3 in the afternoon went to Mrs Tenant, Bicker Gantlet. Good Labour, home by 6½. 1st Attendance.

Gardening

Monday 18. I had Mr Grimbald from Swineshead to cut my Fruit trees, who I believe has done them very well. He also advised me to strew saw-dust round the young hollies to prevent the frost injuring them, which we have done; also to put manure amongst the earth about the young Quicks.

Conclusion of the Year

On casting up my accounts I find I have gained £40 this Year, which is beyond my expectations, and will be exceeding usefull to pay off part of the £80 I was obliged to take up, the half of which I mean to pay if possible at Lady Day[87] next. In my Five Years of Business, it seems I have saved near £250 clear, which to be sure is a very happy circumstance. I have had overtures made me to take an apprentice, a Mr Dawson's Son at Horncastle; I ask a premium of 80 Guineas, but have not had an answer.[88] If I take him I intend to have some form of writing to prevent his fixing over near me: I am humbly gratefull to Providence for the blessings that continue to attend me, and my Family: must acknowledge my own demerit, and entreat the continuance of the Mercies I enjoy. January 2 1776.

---

[87] 25 March – until 1752 the official start of the new year, and continued to be used as a date for the payment of bills and taxes, along with other Quarter Days such as Michaelmas (29 September).
[88] Presumably, no more was heard from Mr Dawson – Flinders never did take on an apprentice.

[f.13]

	[December 1775]	Received			Paid		
	[Brought over]	£205	19s	1d	£171	16s	0½d
2	Check 10d for the House. The News 2½d.					1s	0½d
	To Thos Hillyard for Gardening					1s	
	1½ Chaldron of Coals, £1 13s. Expences -do- 3s 9d.				£1	16s	9d
	Housebill this week 16s 6½d. Retail £1 1s 6d.	£1	1s	6d		16s	6½d
	Of Mr Godley, Bicker Gauntlet, by bill	£1	8s				
3	Remainder of Ed Ashton's bill		5s	6d			
5	Sugar for Shop use, 1s. Of Joseph Wright Junior		10s	6d		1s	
6	Of Mr Clark, Swineshead Fen Houses	£1	1s				
8	Lemons 1s. To Mr Beedezley, a bill, 14s.					15s	
9	To T. Hillyard, 1s. An Almanack, 9d. News, 2½d.					1s	11½d
	House bill 12s 4d. Retail this week 18s 6d.		18s	6d		12s	4d
	2 Iron Candlesticks, 2s. Cloth for Pillows, 3s 2d.					5s	2d
12	Of Mr Garner, Donington Fenn, by bill	£1	13s	6d			
	Of Sarah Yates in part, 6s. The News, 2½d.		6s				2½d
14	Carriage of Goods from Barrit & Co					9s	2d
16	Of Mr Tenant, Bicker Gantlet	£1	1s				
	Of George Grimes, Bicker		14s				
	Of John Berry, 11s 6d. B. Brand, Wigtoft, 17s.	£1	8s	6d			
	House bill 17s 5¼d. Retail 15s		15s			17s	5¼d
17	Of Mr Cook's Man, Hoflit		7s	9d			
18	To Mr Grimbald, for Tree & Work					6s	9d
	A Letter from Robinson						7d
20	Large Corks, 1 grose, 13d. Best Paper, 1 quire, 10d					1s	11d
	Of S. Garner, by bill		8s	6d			
	12 Pounds of Flax of -ditto- at 9d					9s	
	Of Mr Passmoor, Quadring, by bill		15s				
	To Edward Laykins, by bill					9s	6d
22	Of J. Orry by bill, 12s 6d. R. Hubbard, 13s.	£1	5s	6d			
	Medical Magazine 1s., No 24. Biography, 6d.					1s	6d
23	Retail, &c. 18s 6d. Housebill £1 7s 4½d.						
	News, 2½d.		18s	6d	£1	7s	7d
27	Worstead 1s 5d. Cloth for the Shop 1s. Vinegar 1d.					2s	6d
29	Christmas Boxes 4d. Lemons 9d. A Letter 7d.					1s	8d
30	Of Mr Northern, Bicker Gauntlet		7s	6d			
	Of J. Thomson, Ostler at the Bull		12s	6d			
	Retail &c. 11s 6d. Housebill 15s 7¾d.		11s	6d		15s	7¾d
		£222	8s	10d	£181	10s	3½d

Received in 1771	£72 0s 7d	Paid	£58 16s 0d
Received in 1772	£154 4s 8d	Paid	£95 3s 5d
Received in 1773	£224 15s 5½d	Paid	£124 15s 1d
Received in 1774	£182 5s 1d	Paid	£145 19s 3d
Received in 1775	£222 8s 10d	Paid	£181 10s 3½d
Total Received	£855 14s 7½d	Paid	£606 4s 0½d
Total Gained	£249 10s 7d	in 5 Years	

[f.13v]
January 1776

Date		Received	Paid
2	Gave the Ringers 6d. The News 2½d.		8½d
	Turnpikes last Month No 23		2s 10½d
4	Of Mr Parker's Servant Maid	8s 6d	
6	Housebill 15s 0¼d. News 2½d. A Letter 1d		15s 3¾d
	Retail &c. 10s. Gave some distressed Players 3s	10s	3s
8	The Biography and Medical Magazine		1s 6d
10	Of John Daff by bill	8s	
	Christmas Gifts 8d. Two Pd Stuff Spining 1s 6d		2s 2d
13	House bill £1 2s 0½d. Retail 10s	10s	£1 2s 0½d
20	Remainder of Sarah Yates's bill	5s	
	Retail 9s. Housebill £1.	9s	£1
	To my Father for Corn &c. in full		£2 4s
	A Pair of Spurrs Rowling[89]		4d
24	To Mr Lane, Druggist, Boston		6s
	Cost me at Boston		1s 9d
	Gave to Mary Twell		6d
25	Of Mr Jackson Junior, Bicker	6s 6d	
	Carriage of Druggs from London		3s 4d
27	Roger Bates's account of Mr Pakey	£1 2s 3d	
	Of Mr J. Pakey by bill	14s 8d	
	Of Miss Eliz. Golding by bill	11s	
	To Mr J. Pakey in full		£2 5s 8d
	Writing Paper 7d. Carriage to Spalding 3d.		10d
	Housebill 14s 6½d. Retail 10s 6d.	10s 6d	14s 6½d
29	Of Benjamin Blackwell by bill	10s	
	Of J. Kendall 6s 6d. Lemons ½ doz. 9d	6s 6d	9d
	Land Tax 2s 6d. Paid Ann Kendall 1s.		3s 6d
31	15 Turnpikes in Jan. 1s 10½d. Lemons 5d		2s 3½d
[Carried forward]		**£6 11s 11d**	**£9 11s 1¼d**

We have had a most severe frost which continued a Month and broke up the beginning of February. I never remember it so severely sharp and cold as it was.[90] The last week of it, it froze amazing keen: the Ice being near a foot thick, I skated on January 24 in Company with the Mr Trimnels to Boston, but we found it very indifferent on account of the snow which fell previous to the frost. I was much wearied with this expedition;[91] some of the days were so cold that I could not stand the shop above 10 minutes at a time in making up Medicines.

---

89 Rowelling.
90 The extreme cold this month was also noted by James Woodforde in Oxford: 'Scarce ever was known so deep a snow as at present' (John Beresford (ed.), *The diary of a country parson* (London, 1926), 173).
91 It is difficult to ascertain how this journey was accomplished as there is no single continuous waterway between Donington and Boston, but possibly surrounding land was also iced over. This is a trip of around 10 miles even as the crow flies!

[f.14]
February 1776

		Received			Paid		
Brought over		**£6**	**11s**	**11d**	**£9**	**11s**	**1¼d**
2	Two Chaldron of Coales				£2	4s	
	Expences of Do					4s	4d
	Shoes mending 6d. A Rough Mat 6d.					1s	
3	Retail 12s. Housebill 15s 3½d.		12s			15s	3½d
5	Med. Magazine 1s. Bladders 4d. News 2½d					1s	6½d
8	Of Wm Story, Bicker Gantlet		15s				
9	1 Pint of Pease 3d. For Setting to T.H.[92] 3d						6d
	Retail &c. 10s 6d. Housebill 19s		10s	6d		19s	
12	Of Mr Gleed's Man by bill		8s				
14	Of Mr Lowe, Baker, by bill		16s				
16	Of Mr Terry, Glazier, by bill		6s	6d			
	To -ditto- a bill					8s	6d
	To Molly Asthton for 6 Days					2s	
	Of Mr Johnson's Man by bill		14s				
17	Of Mr Willoughby by bill	£1	12s				
	Two Quire of Cappaper[93]						7d
	Retail £1. Housebill 19s 3d	£1				19s	3d
	Four Pounds of Stuff Spining					3s	
19	Cost me at Spalding					1s	3d
	To Mr Wm Ward for Sundries					4s	7½d
24	Of Mr Carnal, Swineshead, by bill	£4	9s				
	Retail &c. 11s. Housebill 12s 5¼d.		11s			12s	5¼d
	1 Night Candlestick from Boston					1s	6d
	Rum 1 Quart 2s 7½d. The News 2½d.					2s	10d
26	Of Mr Caswell, Quadring, by bill	£1	16s				
	Of Mrs Spencer by bill		7s				
29	Of Mr Joys, Swineshead, by bill		12s	6d			
	Turnpikes in February No 14					1s	9d
[Carried over]		**£21**	**1s**	**5d**	**£16**	**14s**	**6d**

Sat. April 6. 76. This day I took in the Bond Mr Beet of Wigtoft had against me for £80 when I purchased this House &c. From my first having it I intended to pay him a part at this time. I had intended £30, then £40, but at length I mustered up £50, which I bless God was a great part of it to discharge in one Year; but upon application to Mr Beet he was not willing to take a part, but I must either keep the whole, or pay it. Therefore I thought it the best way to pay the whole, accordingly my Brother Mr W. Ward[94] let me have £30 on my Note – and therefore have got rid of the whole Bond. I also paid the £4 interest.

May 12th. 76. I parted with my servant Thomas Barton who has lived with me 2 Years, he growing careless saucy & very ill behaved. I have got one J. Harmston who has lived some time at Mr Warrintons, & the lad seems obliging and assid-

---

92 Thomas Hilyard.
93 Cappaper was a type of wrapping paper (*OED*).
94 Strictly his brother-in-law, but it was usual at this time to refer to in-laws in this way.

uous & I hope will suit. I give £1 15s Wages and the 1s Earnest Money.[95] May 16. 76.

[f.14v]
March 1776

		Received			Paid		
Brought over		**£21**	**1s**	**5d**	**£16**	**14s**	**6d**
1	Of J. Mapletoft for bills on the Parish	£2	2s	0¼d			
	To -do- for Poor Assessment and Window Money				£1	3s	10d
	Of David Reed, Swineshead, by bill		8s	6d			
	To my wife Feb. 6.				£1	17s	
2	Housebill £1 3s 10d. Retail &c.		18s	6d	£1	3s	10d
	Of Mr Johnson's Man by bill		5s	6d			
	Stockings knitting 2s. Gardening 1s. News 2½d.					3s	2½d
3	Lemons 9d. Of J. Stephenson, Swineshead Fen		17s				9d
6	Sugar for Shop use 1s 9d					1s	9d
7	Of Mr Hinting, Swineshead, by bill		19s	6d			
9	Stuff Spining 4 Pound 3s. 2 Bread Tins 4s.					7s	
	Hog's Lard 8d. The News 2½d.						10½d
	Retail 17s. Housebill 18s.		17s			18s	
	Postage of a Letter from Wilson						3d
11	Of Mr B. Bowers, White House		9s	6d			
	One Beast's Heart of Wilkinson						10d
	Medical Magazine & Biography					1s	6d
15	Sugar for Shop use					1s	
16	Gave Mr Gleed's Servant (at Christening) the 14th					1s	6d
	One Pair of Ivory Studds of Mr Torry						4d
	Housebill 18s. Retail &c. 18s 6d.		18s	6d		18s	
	Of Mr Jackson, Asperton,[96] by bill	£1	6s	6d			
	Saddle mending 4d. The News 2½d.						6½d
	To the Cambridge Newsman						6d
18	Paid for sundry things at Goodyear's Sale					3s	
19	A Letter from Mr Lynch						3d
	Of Mrs Matson, Swineshead		6s				
22	½ dozen Lemons 9d. The News 2½d.						11½d
23	Of John Orry by bill		5s				
	Housebill 18s. Retail £1 0s 0d	£1				18s	
	Of Mr Southern, Swineshead, by bill		10s				
	Spining 4 Pound 2s 10d. Nails &c. 1s 2d.					4s	
25	Of J. Damms, Swineshead Fen Houses, in part		10s	6d			
26	Of J. Brown, by bills		14s	6d			
29	Of Mr Mason, Swineshead, by bills		11s	6d			
	1½ Yard of Muslin for 3 Neckcloths of -ditto-					7s	6d
30	Writing Paper 7d. News 2½d. Trifles 4d.					1s	1½d
	Housebill 18s. Retail &c. £1 1s 0d.	£1	1s			18s	
	Paid to Mr Grimbald for Trees &c.					6s	6d
	Turnpikes in March, No 18					2s	3d
[Carried over]		**£35**	**2s**	**9d**	**£26**	**16s**	**9½d**

---

95 A token payment to confirm the "contract".
96 A hamlet in the parish of Wigtoft.

May 23d. 76. I was obliged to take up £20 of Mr Gleed as Mr Wm & Mr Samuel Ward want the £30 they let me have, and with this sum I hope I shall be able to manage as bills have come[97] in very well this month. I intend to pay it off as soon as I can, but possibly it will not be within this year, as there is the fine to pay Mr Smith and heavy accounts with Druggists, however I thank God that I have been able to rub off £60 of the £80 in the Course of little more than one Year.

[f.15]
April 1776

		Received			Paid		
Brought over		**£35**	**2s**	**9d**	**£26**	**16s**	**9½d**
2	Of Mr John Birks	£1	1s				
	Spent at the Cow					1s	
	A Letter 1d. Rudd 1d. Wine at Swineshead 3d.						5d
4	To Mr Morris, Blacksmith, a bill					5s	
	Of Mr Ashworth, Gosberton, for self 4s. Poor 9s.		13s				
5	Cloth for Shop use					1s	3½d
6	Of Mr Barber, Gosberton, by bill	£4	9s				
	The Salary for Wigtoft Poor	£4	4s				
	Retail and small bills		18s				
	Housebill this week					18s	
	The News 2½d. A Knife Grinding 1d.						3½d
8	Biography 6 Nos 3s. Medical Mag. 1s.					4s	
	Stuff Spining 3 Pound at 8d.					2s	
	An Halter 3d. Phial Corks 5 Gr. 1s 3d.					1s	6d
10	Of Valentine Bucknel, Bicker		17s				
	Of Mrs Merril, Bicker		7s	6d			
12	Carriage of Druggs 2s 3d. Gardening 1s 6d					3s	9d
	Gave to Joseph Hayes 3d. Thread for the Shop 4d.						7d
13	Of Mr Jarvis's Man by bill		7s				
	Retail 18s. Housebills 18s.		18s			18s	
	Of a Man at Mrs Clifton's		5s				
18	Of Mr Dickenson, Swineshead Fen Houses	£1	1s				
20	Retail &c. 18s. Housebill 18s.		18s			18s	
	Bungs 1d. The News 2½d. Saddle mending 3d.						6½d
22	The Poor Assesment £4 at 16d					5s	4d
	Of Uriah Castor by bill		10s	6d			
23	Cappaper[98] 3½d. Mare at Swineshead 6d.						9½d
24	Easter offerings to Mr Powell						8d
25	Land Tax 2s 6d. Window Money 10s 2d.					12s	8d
27	Retail &c. 18s. Housebill 18s.		18s			18s	
	Carriage from Swineshead 4d. The News 2½d.						6½d
28	Lancets Grinding 6d						6d
29	One table 5s and Dish 1s at Mrs Brown's Sale					6s	
30	Of Henry Everit Junior by bill		13s				
	Toll Barrs No 18 in April					2s	3d
	2½ Pound of 9d Stuff and Spinning					3s	9d
[Carried over]		**£53**	**2s**	**9d**	**£33**	**1s**	**8d**

---

97 MS 'comed'.
98 See n.93 above.

June 4th 1776. I am sorry that there is a dispute between my Father and self about our Rent. I always expected that the part he occupied of my late purchase would fully satisfy him for keeping my mare, but on our accounting I find it very different, he being willing only to allow me £2 3s for my 5 Acres of Land & the use of my Green, Barn, Yard &c., making me pay as usual £7 10s for my House. We cannot help thinking this very exorbitant and cruel and we have had words about it; I believe it is principally through his Tyrannical Wife.[99] As we are to be thus shackled for 10 years, I have offered him £20 to give up my part of the lease, and he says he will consider of it.

[f.15v]
May 1776

		Received			Paid		
Brought forward		**£53**	**2s**	**9d**	**£33**	**1s**	**8d**
2	Of Mr Burton Swineshead by bill	£1	5s	6d			
	Of Widow Watson, Gosberton Risgate	£2	2s				
4	Retail &c. 18s. Housebill 18s.		18s			18s	
5	Of Mr J. Gleed by bill	£4	6s				
	Paid to him in full				£1	3s	
	The News 2½d. Lost at cards last M. 6d.						8½d
6	Med. Magazine 1s. B. Biography 6d.					1s	6d
10	To Edward Gibson, a bill					12s	6d
11	Retail &c. 18s. Housebill 18s.		18s			18s	
	Of Mr David Pike by bill	£3	1s				
	Of Mrs Buff by bill		5s				
	Black Ferrit[100] 1½ Yard 4½d.						4½d
12	To Thos Barton 1 Year's Wages				£1	12s	
	Of Michael Petchill's Daughter, Gosberton	£1	1s				
15	Cost me at the Wire dancing[101]					1s	3d
	7 Thorn Kidds for Quick fencing						10½d
	Stuff spinning 7d (Hemp)						7d
	Of Robert Winters, Swineshead North End		10s	6d			
	Matthew's Entrance at Mrs Moor's School					1s	
18	Retail &c. 18s. Housebill 18s.		18s			18s	
	Two News's 5d.						5d
	Half a Year's Wages to Mary Goodyear				£1	10s	
	Of Mr Burr by bill		13s	6d			
19	To Mr Harvey for 10 Gallons of Ale at 14d					11s	6d
	To -ditto- for 2 18 Gallons Porter Casks					13s	
	Of him by bill		8s				
21	Paid to my Brother for drugs &c.					17s	
	Received of him for -ditto-		12s				
	Our Journey to Spalding cost us					5s	
23	To Messrs Barrit and Robinson for 2 Parcels on account				£9	5s	

99 This is a reference to father John's second wife. The parish records show that Elizabeth Flinders, Matthew's mother, died in January 1768 aged 54. In July of the following year John (then aged 56) married Mary Baxter – it is clear from this and subsequent references that Matthew did not approve of this match.
100 See n.81 above.
101 The performance of acrobatic feats on a wire rope (*OED*).

May 1776 (cont.)		**Received**			**Paid**		
	To Mr Gleed for drawing a Bond					5s	
24	Three Lemons 6d. Gardening 6d.					1s	
	Of Mr Cam, Quadring Edike	£1	10s	6d			
25	Retail &c. 18s. Housebill &c. 18s.		18s			18s	
	Stuff Spining 2 Pounds & ¼ (Hemp 18½d)					1s	6½d
	Of J. Crampton, Donington Northorp	£1	4s				
	Cappaper[102] 3½d. The News 2½d.						6d
	Mr Gee's Bill (of Hale)	£4	16s				
	16 Yards of Hempen Cloth Bleaching					2s	4½d
	One Pound of Hemp Spining						7½d
27	Of Thomas Hackworth, Bicker		5s				
	Of Thomas Ledger, Swineshead Fen Houses		13s				
	Of John Day, Swineshead		10s				
	Of J. Brumpton, Bicker	£1	4s				
	Of J. Stimson, Bicker		6s				
	Of Mr Pillings, Bicker		8s				
	Of Mr Love, Swineshead	£6	16s	6d			
	Church Assessment for last year £4 at 3d					1s	
	Trifles at the Fair						7d
	3 Pints of Wine					3s	
[Carried over]		**£88**	**12s**	**3d**	**£54**	**5s**	**0d**

[f.16]							
[May–June 1776]		**Received**			**Paid**		
Brought over		**£88**	**12s**	**3d**	**£54**	**5s**	**0d**
[27]	China at Mr Pierrepont's Sale					7s	
	A Lantern 1s. and Teaboard at -ditto- 1s 2d					2s	2d
28	Sold half a dozen Chairs at Mr Coles's Sale		11s				
	Bought ½ dozen -ditto- at -ditto- for					18s	
	6 Coffee Cups 3s and a Bell 1s at -ditto-					4s	
	One Hat of Mr Wm Ward 10s 6d. Stock 3s 4d					13s	10d
29	To my Wife				£1	17s	6d
30	Carriage of Druggs from Barrit & Co.					5s	4d
	Of Wm Stukeley Esq., Quadring, in full	£12	1s	3d			
	Presented me above my Bill	£1	1s	9d			
31	Gave in Charity on account of a Fire						6d
(June)							
1	Retail &c. 18s. Housebill 18s. News 2½d.		18s			18s	2½d
	Of Mr Harness, Ball Hall		9s	6d			
	Hemp Spining 7½d. Gardening 6d.					1s	1½d
3	Nine Gallons of Ale of J. Lee					10s	6d
	To Richard Jackson a bill				£1	2s	10d
4	To one & half Chaldron of Coales at 22s				£1	13s	
	Expences of -ditto-					4s	5d
	One slit deal 2s 2d. Tin Pot mending 10d.					3s	
	To my Father a balance in full				£4	2s	6d
7	Of Mrs Wilton, Bicker, by bill		9s	6d			
8	Retail &c. 18s. Housebill 18s.		18s			18s	
	The News 2½d. Treacle 1½d. A Letter 6d.						10d
	Turnpikes No 16 in May					2s	

---

102 See n.93 above.

[May–June 1776] (cont.)	Received		Paid		
10 Magazine &c 2 Nos 2s. Writing Paper 7d.				2s	7d
13 Cost at Swineshead Fair				1s	6d
15 Retail &c. 18s. Housebill 18s. News 2½d.	18s			18s	2½d
Carriage to Dalton 5d. A Deal 2s 4d.				2s	9d
17 Of Widow Symons by bill		6s	6d		
Of Mr Tenny by bill	£1	8s			
19 To Mr J. Pakey in full			£1	2s	5d
Received of him by bill		9s	8d		
22 Retail &c. 18s. Housebill 18s. News.	18s			18s	2½d
Cotton Wool ½ a pound of Mr H., Swineshead				1s	3d
Shoes of Mr Hayes 6s. Recd. of him 4s 6d.		4s	6d	6s	
23 Insurance Money to Mr Waite, Boston				9s	
24 Gave Mr Green's Servant Maid					6d
28 Of John Damms, Swineshead Fen Houses		10s	6d		
Of Mr Fisher, Swineshead, by bill	£2	2s			
Paid to him a bill			£1	10s	6d
29 Retail &c. 18s. Housebill 18s.	18s			18s	
Of Mr D. Trimnell for a Man Servant	£1	6s			
26 Yards of Cloth Bleaching				3s	
Cloth for Shop use 1s. Thread 8d.				1s	8d
30 Of Wm Edinborough's wife, Donington		10s	6d		
16 Turnpikes in June				2s	
Sacrament Money last Sunday					6d
Gave the Newsman for Carriage 3d. Trifles 3d.					6d
[Carried over]	**£114**	**12s**	**11d**	**£75**	**8s**	**4d**

[f.16v]
July 1776

Brought forward	Received			Paid		
	£114	**12s**	**11d**	**£75**	**8s**	**4d**
1 To J. Strapps a bill in full					4s	8d
Cappaper[103] 3½						3½d
2 Of J. Elveson £4 4s in part of £6	£4	4s				
Of Mr Shepherd by bill	£1	5s	6d			
4 To Mary Twell for Quilting at 4d a day					2s	6d
6 Of Mr Marsh, Quadring, by bill	£1	3s				
Retail &c. 18s. Housebill 18s.	18s				18s	
8 Med. Mag. 1s. 8 No of Biography 4s.					5s	
9 To Mr Wm Ward in full				£5	12s	8d
Received of him by bill		12s	10d			
12 Matthew's Schooling 8 Weeks due the 9th					1s	4d
Retail &c. 18s. Housebill 18s. News 5d.	18s				18s	5d
14 Of John Mitchell by bill	£1	0s	6d			
Sugar for Shop use 10½d. The News 1½d.					1s	
18 Wine 1s. Black Currants & sugar 8½d.					1s	8½d
20 Buttons and Tape 5d. News 1½d.						6½d
Retail &c. 18s. Housebill 18s.	18s				18s	
27 Retail &c. 18s. Housebill 18s. News 1½.	18s				18s	1½d
Presents to my Brother's Children					5s	

---

103 See n.93 above.

July 1776 (cont.)	Received		Paid		
1½ Pound of 10d flax spinning				1s	3d
One quarter's Land Tax				3s	
Of Mr Edwards at the Toll Barr	£1	2s			
Carriage to Mr Dalton 6d. Trifles 6d.				1s	
30 Gardening 1s. 15 Turnpikes 1s 10½d.				2s	10½d
[Carried over]	**£127**	**12s**	**9d**	**£86 3s**	**9d**

Lunar Eclipse

Tuesday July 30. We sat up till something past midnight to observe the long expected Lunar Eclipse, the only one I suppose of the luminary that has been total for 26 Years. I cannot say that it exhibited the appearance that I expected it would. It is true that from a fine Moon light, it became a fine star light night, but as the change was very gradual it did not appear very striking. I sat up with Mr Birks and had the opportunity of observing it with his 18 Foot Telescope: the appearance before the eclipse begun was amazing grand and striking. Its[104] glob-ular appearance was evident together with its beautifull diversity of light and dark parts, with great reason said to be water and land. One peculiarly light circle near the upper part seemed as it were its Polar circle with bright radii as Meridians diverging from it. The eclipsed part appeared as a shadow gradually over-spreading the Moon's surface, but the body of the moon was perfectly visible when in the darkest, and no part of it I think appeared so dark as I have seen some other eclipses of this luminary: the reason of this I am no wise able to account for.

[f.17]
August 1776

Brought forwards	Received		Paid		
	£127 12s	**9d**	**£86 3s**		**9d**
1 Retail &c. 18s. Housebill 18s. News 1½d.	18s		18s		1½d
5 10 Nos of the British Biography			5s		
Medical Magazine No 32 July			1s		
Jack's Expences to Spalding twice			1s		
6 To my Wife			£1 17s		6d
8 Of Mr Samuel Pike by bill	£2 10s				
9 To the Bidder at Mrs Coles's Funeral					6d
Retail &c. 18s. Housebill 18s. News 1½d.	18s		18s		1½d
15 The Rent of the Spalding Barrs one Year			10s		6d
Carriage from Spalding 2d. A Letter 3d.					5d
17 Housebill 18s. News 1½d. Retail 18s.	18s		18s		1½d
Tape 3d. Nails 2d. the 20th					5d
Of Mr Stafford, Quadring, by bill	£1 3s				
18 Of Mrs Bacchus 10s 6d. Of Wm Swallow 4s 6d.	15s				
19 Cost me at Fosdike			2s		
22 Of the Parish of Bicker by bill	16s				
24 To Edward Laykins, a bill			14s		
Retail &c. 18s. Housebill 18s. News 1½d.	18s		18s		1½d
Trifles at Mr Wm Ward's			3s		0½d
Currant Wine (Sugar & Currants)			6s		5d
26 A Letter from Mr J. Hursthouse					6d

---

104   MS 'It'.

August 1776 (cont.)	Received			Paid		
Of Mr Grant, Baker, by bill		11s				
27 Of J. Allen, Shoemaker, Swineshead	£1	1s				
One Pound of Shop thread						8d
28 A Quire of Writing Paper						7d
Of Mr Harvey's Servant Maid		5s				
29 To Mr Wm Ward by bill					5s	11d
30 Of Mr Gee, Swineshead	£2	2s				
Of Mr Huddleston, Swineshead		13s	6d			
Of Mr Harmston, Bicker		9s	6d			
31 Housebill 18s. News 1½d. Retail 18s.		18s			18s	1½d
Two Pound of Bee's Wax of Mrs Pepper					3s	
To Mary Twell for 3 Days					1s	
Trifles this Month 6d. 16 Toll Barrs 2s.					2s	6d
[Carried over]	**£142**	**8s**	**9d**	**£95**	**10s**	**4d**

Birth of a Second Son

Friday September 28 1776. About ½ past 7 o' clock at night my wife was safely delivered of a Son. For 3 days and nights preceeding this day, she was much afflicted with a violent Fever, with very frequent returns of Shivering, several times a day – pulse generally very small and quick with violent thirst heat and head ach – insomuch that I apprehended symptoms of putridity would come on. I gave her a Mixture with a small proportion of Tart. Emet.,[105] Nitre &c., and it had some good effect – but two of the Pil. Anod. Sud.[106] procured the most apparent benefit, by mitigating the violence of the pain, procuring rest & free perspiration. The labour seemed faintly to come on in the night & continued very lingering the whole day, till about 6 in the evening when I broke the membrane which I believe hastened the Birth.

[f.17v]
September 1776

Brought forwards	Received			Paid		
	£142	**8s**	**9d**	**£95**	**10s**	**4d**
2 Of Mr Maples's Servant Maid by bill		14s				
Two Letters 10d. Cappaper[107] 3 ½ d. Lime 6d.					1s	7½d
7 Drill 4d. Reed 2d. The News 1½d.						7½d
Retail &c. 18s. Housebill &c. 18s.		18s			18s	
9 Mr Vicars's bill, Swineshead	£1	14s				
Mr Pakey's Servant Maid's bill		5s				
Medical Mag. No 33 1s. Bottle Brushes 6d.					1s	6d
10 Richard Lea's bill (late of Swineshead)		15s				
11 Of Mr Rickaby, Kirton Holme		14s				
To Mr William Ward for Sundries					4s	4½d
13 Of Charles Fever, Hoflit, by bill		5s	6d			
14 Retail &c. 18s. Housebill 18s. News 1½d.		18s			18s	1½d
Cloth for Shop use 1s. Ivory Black 2d.					1s	2d
To Messrs Ferneyhough and Wilson in full				£9	12s	

---

105 See n.70 above.
106 An anodyne pill (see *Supplement*, 393–394) with sudorific qualities.
107 See n.93 above.

September 1776 (cont.)

		Received	Paid
	Of Mr Northern, Bicker Gantlet	11s	
15	Of Molly Ablewight	11s	
19	Of a Man at Edmund Robinson's, Bicker	8s 6d	
	To Thos Hilyard for 5½ Days Gardening		5s 6d
	Stuff for Window Curtain &c 2s 7d		2s 7d
	Spent at the Cow 1s. The News 1½d.		1s 1½d
	Retail &c. 18s. Housebill 18s. Pears 8d.	18s	18s 8d
21	Of J. Clark Senior by bill	5s 6d	
	Of J. Tunnard by bill	8s	
	Of Mr Bonner, Bicker Gantlet	6s	
23	Sugar for Shop use		1s 5½d
20	One Horse Lock of Mr Weeks		8d
27	Of J. Beecroft Junior by bill	10s 6d	
28	Writing Paper 7d. Black Ferrit[108] 6d.		1s 1d
	Of Mr Millington for Mr Clay's Boy	7s	
	Housebill this week 18s. The News 1½d.		18s 1½d
	Retail &c. 18s.	18s	
29	Of Mr Jonathan Brown, Hoflit, by bill	£2 8s	
	13 Turnpikes 1s 7½d. Trifles 2d.		1s 9½d
[Carried over]		**£156 3s 9d**	**£109 18s 9d**

[f.18]

October 1776

		Received	Paid
Brought forwards		**£156 3s 9d**	**£109 18s 9d**
1	Of Codling, Kirton Holm	10s	
2	To Mr Daniel Lynch in full		£3 13s
3	Carriage of Druggs 1s 10d. Letter about -do- 7d.		2s 5d
4	Sugar 3 Pound for Shop use		1s 3d
	Retail &c. £1 3s. Housebill this week	£1 3s	£1 3s
6	Sugar 1s 9d. Med. Magazine No 34 1s.		2s 9d
8	Of Mr Dixon by bill	9s 6d	
9	Of Mr Pinion, Swineshead, by bill	£1 9s	
10	The Beauties of England Displayed[109] in 26 Numbers of Mr Albin, Spalding[110]		13s
11	One Year's Quit Rent & Receipt		8s 7d
	Retail &c. £1 3s. Housebill £1 3s	£1 3s	£1 3s
15	To the Overseer of the High Ways		2s 4d
16	To Mr Grimbald, Gardener, Swineshead		3s
	Of Mr Jackson, Donington North Ing	£1 6s 6d	
17	Of Thos Britain, Swineshead, by bill	6s 6d	
	Of George Brooks, Gosberton Risgate, by bill	6s 9d	
	Of Joshua Page, Gosberton Risgate, by bill	13s	
	Of Mr Fant, Swineshead, by bill	11s 6d	
	Of Mr Wires Junior, Swineshead	£1 4s 6d	
	A Letter 4d. Trifles to day 4½d.		8½d
18	Towards 2 large Silver Spoons		4s 6d

---

[108] See n.81 above.

[109] Probably *The beauties of England displayed . . . Exhibiting a view of whatever is curious, remarkable, or entertaining* (London, 1762, reprinted 1770) (ESTC).

[110] John Albin, printer, publisher and principal bookseller in Spalding, 1775–1800 (Plomer).

October 1776 (cont.)

		Received			Paid		
	One Japan Night Candlestick					1s	8d
19	Retail and small Bills	£1	9s	6d			
	Housebill				£1	9s	4½d
22	Of Mr Read, Swineshead, by bill		9s				
	A Mahogany Table 17s 6d. A Chamber Glass 3s 6d				£1	1s	
25	Carriage of Druggs from Swineshead					1s	6d
26	To Molly Ashton for 4 Weeks' Nursing					15s	6d
	Retail &c. £1 0s 0d. Housebill 19s 11½d.	£1				19s	11½d
27	Of a Labourer of Mr Trimnell's, Bicker		19s	6d			
	Of Mr Johnson's Man by bill		8s				
28	Land Tax and Window Money					13s	2d
	Of Mr Stephenson, Swineshead Fen Houses		5s	6d			
	Of Mr Lowe's Servant Maid		6s				
29	Of Mrs Codling by bill		11s				
	To -ditto- for 14 Pound of Honey					7s	
	7 Turnpikes in October						10½d
[Carried over]		**£170**	**15s**	**6d**	**£123**	**6s**	**4d**

[f.18v]

November 1776

		Received			Paid		
Brought over		**£170**	**15s**	**6d**	**£123**	**6s**	**4d**
2	Retail and small bills	£1	1s	6d			
	Housebill this week				£1	1s	6¾d
	Of R. Nicholls by bill		5s	6d			
	Of Charles Shepherd by bill		10s	6d			
4	Medical Magazine No 35					1s	
8	3 Yards of Harden[111] for Matthew's Bedd					2s	6d
9	Housebill. Retail &c.		13s	6d		13s	6d
10	Of William Hickabottom by bill		10s	6d			
11	Of Mr Gunthorp by bill		11s	9d			
	Of Mr Dunn, Quadring, by bill		16s	6d			
12	Of Richard Hudson, Swineshead, by bill		8s	6d			
14	27 Yards of Table Linnen Working					14s	6d
	Biscuits 1s 6d. Wine 1s. To Molly Ashton 1s 6d.					4s	
	To my Wife				£1	17s	6d
	To Mr Ward for Sundries at the Funeral					4s	9½d
	To Mr Powell for the Affidavit						6d
15	Bee's Wax 1 Pound 10 oz.					2s	6d
	One Quire of Common Writing Paper						7d
16	Of Mr Garner, Gosberton Risgate		10s				
	Retail and small bills	£1	6s				
	Housebill this week				£1	6s	1¼d
	Half a Chaldron of Coals					13s	
	Expences relating to -ditto-					1s	6d
17	To Messrs Barrit and Robinson in full				£5	13s	
21	Of Anthony Robinson, Swineshead, by bill	£1	3s				
22	Of Mrs Fox, Quadring		7s				
23	Retail &c. £1 3s 0d. Housebill £1 3s 0d	£1	3s		£1	3s	

111 See n.80 above.

November 1776 (cont.)	Received		Paid		
26 Of —— Grant, Donington	5s				
30 Of Mr J. Weeks, by bill	7s	6d			
Retail &c. 17s 6d. Housebill 17s 3¾d.	17s	6d		17s	3¾d
Turnpikes in November No 9				1s	1½d
[Carried over]	**£181**	**12s**	**9d**	**£138**	**4s**	**3¾d**

Death of our 2d Son

On Wed. Nov. 13th at 4 in the Morn, Death made his first approach in our little Family, by taking from us our second son – Jackey. He was very poorley for at least above a Month before and though an exceeding fine child born, gradually lost his flesh, and seldom retained his food. We ought to account of this a mercifull Dispensation in that Providence made choice of the Youngest; to have parted with either of the other two woud have afflicted us much more; and as we have nought in a natural sense, but my industry in Business to depend on, we ought to think the non increase of our Family a blessing.

[f.19]
December 1776

Brought over	Received			Paid		
	£181	12s	9d	£138	4s	3¾d
1 Of Thos West, Wigtoft, by bill	7s					
2 Of Samuel Ashton in part	10s	6d				
5 A Letter from Mr J. Hursthouse					7d	
[7] Carriage of Druggs from Barrit & Co				3s	6d	
Of Mr Bones, Bicker, by bill	11s	6d				
Retail and small bills 14s 6d. Housebill	14s	6d		14s	6d	
8 A Ladies Diary for 1777					8d	
9 Of John Orry's wife, by bill	6s					
Medical Magazine No 36				1s		
Gave Mr Johnson's Man last night					6d	
14 To Mr Lane, Druggist, Boston, in full				9s	9d	
One Slate paper book of Mrs Worley				1s	8d	
Four grose of Phial Corks				1s		
Expences at Boston				2s	1d	
To Mr Bartram, Carpenter, in full				£1	1s	6d
Received of him in full	£1	2s				
Retail & small bills 19s. Housebill	19s			19s	1½d	
15 Of Thos Moor, Northorp	15s					
18 Of Mr T. Sikes' Maid Servant	12s	6d				
Hog's Lard for Shop use					5d	
19 Of Stephen Dalton by bill	11s	6d				
20 Of Mr Foster, Dancing Master	5s					
21 Of Mr David Trimnell, Bicker, by various bills	£26	15s				
By retail and small bills	£1	7s	6d			
Housebill this week				£1	7s	8½d
27 To Mr Wm Ward in full				£10	2s	6d
Received of him by bill	9s	3d				
28 Retail &c. 18s. Housebill 18s 1d.	18s			18s	1d	
29 Lancets Grinding 10d. Lemons 9d.				1s	7d	
30 To Mr Gleed, Interest on a Bond				15s		
31 Turnpikes No 6. Trifles 2d.				11d		
[Carried over]	**£217**	**17s**	**0d**	**£155**	**6s**	**4½d**

Received and Paid in the last 5 Years   £855 14s 7½d   £606 4s 0½d
Receipts and Payments in 6 Years   £1073 11s 7½d   £761 10s 5d

Total Gained in 6 Years   £312 1s 2½d

December 31 1776. Through the gracious Providence that continues to attend me and my Family from year to year, I have this year been a gainer of something above £60 and in the whole of my six years' Business of £312 1s 2½d as per account appears, which sum is employed in my Purchase and Shop. How thankful ought I to be to the mercifull disposer of all events, who blesseth my poor endeavours with such unmerited success; may the same blessings continue to attend me, and may I learn to be more deserving.

[f.19v]
Death of My Father
I enter on the New Year with the affecting memorandum of my Father's death; he departed this existence for one I hope more perfect, on Thursday December 26th 1776 about 10 o' clock at night. He had been Anasarcous[112] for a considerable time past, sometimes better, sometimes worse, and had the assistance of Drs Beston and Knolton,[113] but all to no effectual purpose, for some days before his dissolution he became highly Asthmatic, I imagine from a translation of water to the lungs, all our efforts by expectorants, blisters &c. were vain, nay my Brother[114] ventured to take a few ounces of Blood away which seemed to give a little temporary ease, but of short duration as he died as above specified.

It is with pleasure that I note it, that he was sensible of his death, and to appearance resigned to the will of God, and expressed not the least regreat at leaving the world. He continued quite rational as long as he could speak, which was within half an hour of his death, after which he gradually sunk. I left him before expiration as the scene was too affecting, my Brother left us in the afternoon, which I was sorry for, but he apprehended[115] him somewhat better.

He was interred Sat. December 28. It was his desire that his funeral should be attended with as little expence as might be, so be it was decent, as he well knew poor man that he left a young family, and I fear in but scanty circumstances. We had the Will read over before my Brother left us, and (as we expected) found that every thing was left to his present Family. Indeed my Brother comes in for a very pretty estate that he could not deprive him off, but his 2d Marriage is peculiarly hard upon me. I don't blame his will; it is the Marriage I blame. I am much afraid when all is paid, there will be but a scant bringing up for them, therefore we could not expect any thing.

Money Matters
It is with pleasure that I note that on the 30th December I paid Mr Gleed £20 with Interest which I had on Bond, so I thank God I am clear in every respect as to my

---

112 Suffering from dropsy, or oedema: swelling caused by fluid retention.
113 Dr Beston (Cambridge) and Dr Knowlton (Edinburgh), physicians of Boston (Mills).
114 His elder brother John was also a surgeon-apothecary.
115 MS 'apprenhended'.

purchase except the Fine to Mr Benjamin Smith, and I have the Money by me whenever he pleases to call for it.

Payment of the Fine[116]

I have the additional satisfaction to note that on Saturday January 25 I paid the above Fine with the Fees to Mr Benjamin Smith. I found it somewhat more moderate than expected, the Fine being £9 9s 0d, but the Fees I thought high, viz. £2 17s 0d, so I praise God; all in respect to my purchase is now clear.

Visiters

Mr J.H.[117] and wife paid us an agreable visit: they came on Thursday Evening the 23d and left us the 25th in the Morn. This was a peculiar favour, and we shall gratefully esteem it as such.

[f.20]
January 1777

		Received			Paid		
	Of Mr R. Barber, Gosberton Risgate	£2	6s				
	Of Mr John Birks, Donington	£2	2s				
1	Of Mrs Jugg, Donington	£2	5s				
	Gave Stiles Mapletoft's children					1s	
2	Of Luke Tebb, Northorp (in part)		10s	6d			
3	Of John Alvey, Donington		12s				
	One Chaldron of Coals				£1	6s	
	Expences relating to -ditto-					2s	3d
4	Of John Wells, Shoemaker		10s	9d			
	Of Mr Thos Green Junior, Bicker		6s				
	By retail £1 0s 6d. Housebill £1 0s 3¾d	£1	0s	6d	£1	0s	3¾d
	Cloth 1 yard for Shop use					1s	
5	Shoes 6s. -ditto- mending 3d. Spent at						
	Swineshead 6d.					6s	9d
6	Red wine 1½ pint 1s 6d. Med. Mag. No 37, 1s.					2s	6d
10	Of Wm West, Donington	£1	0s	6d			
11	Of Mr Joseph Terry, Glaizer	£2	5s	4d			
	To him a bill in full				£1	10s	10d
	Of Mr Turfit, Schoolmaster, Swineshead		6s				
	Of Mr Holbourn, Hoflit	£1	11s				
	To -ditto- for 3 Posts					3s	4½d
	By retail and small bills		13s	6d			
	Housebill this week					13s	5d
13	Of Joseph Wright Junior		16s	6d			
	To -ditto- for Carriage of a Table and Glass					1s	
14	Of Peregrine Moor, Shoemaker		10s	10d			
	To -ditto- for 1½ Stone of Pork					6s	
	To his wife for Matt's Schooling 21 weeks					4s	
15	Of John Brown, Donington		11s				

---

[116] This would not be a fine in the modern sense, but was legal jargon for part of the payment involved in land or property transactions.
[117] Probably John Hursthouse, a cousin on his wife's side (see *Lincolnshire Pedigrees*, 1265, and n.42 above).

January 1777 (cont.)	Received			Paid		
16 Of Mr Dowse, Burtoft[118]		9s	6d			
To Mr Weeks for 12 Pound Candles at St Thomas					6s	6d
17 Writing Paper 7d. Mr Birk's Servant the 16th, 1s.					1s	7d
18 Retail &c. £1 0s 0d. Housebill £1 0s 0d.	£1			£1		
2 Pound Hemp 9d. One Pound Hemp Spining 8d.					1s	5d
19 To J. Warriner, Taylor, in full				£1	9s	6d
21 British Jewell 1s. Mr Whitehead's Servant 1s.					2s	
23 Lost at Cards 1s. Spent at the Bull the 20th, 1s.					2s	
25 Of Mr Morris, Bicker Mill	£1	7s				
Housebill £1 2s 11½d. Retail £1 3s.	£1	3s		£1	2s	11½d
Of Mr Lee, Donington		17s	6d			
26 Of John Philipps, Gosberton Risgate		5s				
27 Of Mrs Fendelaw, Donington		7s	9d			
29 Of Mr Berry, Donington		14s				
Towards the Act for recovery of small debts in the						
Hundred of Kirton[119]				£2	2s	
Hogg's Lard 1½ Pounds, 7½d.						7½d
30 Of Mr Elveson in full	£1	17s				
To him one quarter's Land Tax					3s	
6 Toll barrs 9d. Trifles this month 3d.					1s	
[Carried over]	**£25**	**8s**	**2d**	**£12**	**11s**	**0¼d**

[f.20v]

Crochet Case

Jan. 22. I was called to Lydia Horn at Donington Eadike,[120] about 2 in the Morn. I found the Membranes ruptured but the os Uteri but little dilated. I waited the remaining part of the night and the succeeding day – she had good pains but the dilation went on very slow, no impression was made on the Head, and it never compleatly entered the Pelvis, finding them quite ineffectual for delivery, I used the forceps twice but they were not well fixed, slipped, and I had no success with them. Hence obliged to use the crochet, with which I soon, and easily succeeded. I had the great satisfaction to believe that the child was dead previous to their application, the woman seems doing very well. Feb. 6. 77.

Laborious Case terminating Praeternaturally

Feb. 15. I was called to Wm Story's wife, Bicker G. I waited the whole night having no pains of any good effect. After 5 in the Morn I broke the membrane but, after waiting several hours, found not the least descent of the head into the Pelvis though the os Uteri was sufficiently dilated – nor was the Pelvis any ways strait, and her pains apparently strong. I determined to try an experiment which I never put into practice before, nor do I recollect ever to have heard of it (the head presenting), that is to endeavour to turn and deliver footling, the goodness of the pelvis determined me to this. I gradually insinuated my left hand above the head and directly found both arms, advancing almost to fundus Uteri. I obtained a leg and very slowly & somewhat difficultly turned the body and brought the leg into

---

118 A hamlet in the parish of Wigtoft.
119 See below under 27 June 1777.
120 A hamlet about 2 miles north-east of Donington.

the Pelvis, the head gradually turning upwards. I was a considerable time ere I brought the other into the Pelvis, but at last managed and difficultly delivered the body. The child was dead; the woman is doing well.

Birth Day
On Monday February 17 I compleated my 27th Year, and have all reason to praise God for his continued Mercies. My Brother, Sister & Daughter did us the favour of a visit and left us in the Evening. Mrs F.[121] also dined here.

My Wife's Journey
My Wife sometime ago designed to pay a visit among her relations, and as Mr Sam. Ward always attends our Easter Market, took the favourable opportunity of going behind him on the Sunday March 31. She proposes being out about a fortnight, first staying 2 or 3 days at Bolingbrook,[122] then Mr Ward is to take her to our Uncle H's[123] at Croft to continue with that worthy family a night or 2, and then Mr Ward or Mr H. to take her to her mother and sister at Louth to continue there till she returns home. She is to touch at Bolinbrook in her way home and Mr Ward has promised to come through with her. Ap. 2.
[f.21] I bless God she returned from her Journey in Good Health on Saturday Ap. 12.

February 1777

		Received			Paid		
Brought over		£25	8s	2d	£12	11s	0¼d
1	Retail &c. 16s 0d. Housebill 15s 10½d.		16s			15s	10½d
	One Japan Bread Baskett					3s	6d
2	Of Mr John Ward, Donington	£1	5s				
5	Of the Revd Mr Coats		7s				
6	To my Wife				£2		
7	Of Mr Boyfield, Quadring Eadike	£1	17s				
8	Of Mr John Harvey		17s				
	Paid to him in full					12s	3d
	Retail &c. £1 0s 6d. Housebill £1 0s 7d.	£1	0s	6d	£1	0s	7d
11	Of Mr Turpin at Mr Ward's		9s				
	Sugar for Shop use 3½ Pounds					1s	9d
14	One Pound of Fine Stuff Spining					1s	
15	Retail &c. £1 0s 0d. Housebill £1 0s 1¼d.	£1			£1	0s	1¼d
16	Medical Magazine No 38					1s	
	Of Mr Tenant, Bicker Gantlet	£1	1s				
17	Of Michael Grant, Baker, Donington		10s	6d			
18	Spent at Mrs Ingalls, Swineshead						6d
20	Mr Turner's Shepherd's bill, Wigtoft		16s				
	One Chaldron of Coals				£1	6s	
	Expences relating to -ditto-					2s	5d
	One Strong Padlock for the Coal house					1s	6d
22	Retail &c. 16s 6d. Housebill this week 16s 8½d.		16s	6d		16s	8½d
	Letter from J. Hursthouse the 20th						6d

---

[121] Presumably Mrs Flinders, his step-mother.
[122] Her place of birth, about 27 miles north-east of Donington.
[123] Matthew Hursthouse (see *Lincolnshire Pedigrees*, 1265).

February 1777 (cont.)	Received		Paid		
24 One large Salting Pot of Mr Hunt				3s	9d
25 Of Mr Clark, Glover, in full	15s	6d			
Paid to him in full				16s	6d
Various seeds for Gardening of J. Lammin					7½d
Of Mr Hill at Mr Ward's	7s	6d			
To Thos Hillyard for one day's Gardening				1s	
26 One hundred and a half of Pens				2s	
27 Of Thos Speed, Donington	10s	6d			
Money at the communion, Sunday 23d					6d
Turnpikes in February					9d
[Carried over]	£37 17s	2d	£21 19s	10d	

Servants

We have agreed with both our Servants to stay another Year. Our Maid Mary Goodyer is to have the same wages as before, viz. £3, with 3s for the Earnest money; she is to have the liberty of taking vails,[124] as they are called. My Servant Boy, John Harmston, I have been obliged to raise his wages to 50s, and 2s 6d Earnest money. I should not have done this, but the lad is ingenious and can do many things which other boys cannot, as jobs in carpentry and masonry, painting lettering bottles &c, by which he has and will save me the additional wages; nor are we fond of new faces, if we are any ways near well. April 22d.

[f.21v]
Remarkable Infant Head

May 12 in the Morning I was called out of Bed to a Mrs Grant in this town in Labour, but the child was delivered before I could possibly get there. She was not at full time, but between 7 and 8 months. The child was dead, but the reason that I make a Memorandum of this is a remarkable tumour on the child's head, about 2 thirds of the size of the whole head. It was situated on the lower part of the occiput, which bone I found was imperfect, having a circular hole at nearly the bottom part of it. The tumour itself was soft, and exactly resembled those termed Spina Bifida. I cut into it, but no blood or other fluid issued from it; it appeared a soft dark coloured substance. I could introduce a finger easily into the opening in the occiput; it undoubtedly had this imperfect conformation from its origin, and it was happy the child was not produced alive. The poor woman had been in a bad state of health some months before, and lived but a few weeks after delivery.

Mr H...........s[125] of Croft's Visit

My Uncle H. of Croft paid us a visit on May 24. We had some talk concerning how the estates at Maxey, Deeping, and Spalding devolve, according to Mr J. H.'s will. I had an equall share along with my Brother & 4 of Mr H.'s (Son & 3 Daughters) but by the will preceeding that, it seems that Mr J. H. had no right to dispose of the Spalding estate by will, consequently it goes to the 2 heirs at Law, Mr J. H. of Tidd[126] and my Brother; but £10 10s at Deeping Copyhold,[127] and

---

124 "Tips" in modern parlance.
125 Matthew Hursthouse.
126 Flinders's cousin, John Hursthouse (see n.42 above).
127 Land held by copy of the manorial court roll.

£10 Freehold at Maxey it seems go according to the will, so that when sold, I shall be entitled to something more than I expected, though I doubt it will not yet raise me £100. My Uncle left us the following Morning. Monday June 23. 77.

Journey to Spalding
On Monday June 16 I made a Journey to see my friends at Spalding, having not been there since last October. I thank God I found them all well, and passed an agreable day, returning in the Evening; was pleased to find my Brother acquiesced to the division of the Estate, as unfolded to us by our Uncle H. The old Lady they have as Boarder, I fancy will leave them when her year expires, though she pays well, they find great inconveniencies. (July 25. 77.)

[f.22]
March 1777

		Received			Paid		
Brought over		**£37**	**17s**	**2d**	**£21**	**19s**	**10d**
1	Retail &c. 18s 0d. Housebill 18s.		18s			18s	
2	To 21 Yards of Cloth, warping, weaving &c.					6s	6d
7	Of Mr Shepherd in full	£3	4s				
	Of Mr Gibson in full	£1	10s	6d			
	Paid to -ditto- in full					10s	6d
8	Housebill this week					12s	8d
	Retail and small bills		12s	6d			
	One Pillion and Cloth of Mr Bell, Spalding				£1	5s	
	Of Mr Jarvis, Bicker	£2	3s	6d			
10	Mr Cox by bill for the late Mr Edwards		15s				
	Of Mr Sewerds, Quadring, by bill		11s				
	Of Mr Tricket by bill		14s				
	Medical Magazine No 39					1s	
11	Of George Ingle, Donington Fenn, by bill		10s	6d			
	Of Mr James Shilcock by bill	£3	13s	6d			
	Black Ferrit[128] and Hair Pins					7s	2d
15	Carriage of Ol. Oliv. C. Cong. un. from Spalding [129]					3s	
	Retail and small bills this week		18s				
	Housebill this week					18s	
	Carriage of Druggs on the 13th					5s	3d
17	One Pair of Black Stockings					3s	4d
20	22 Yards of Shirting Cloth at 2s 1d				£2	5s	
21	5 Pounds Anex. Porcin.[130] at 5d.					2s	1d
22	Of Mr Marsh, Quadring, by bill	£1	4s	6d			
	Retail and small bills		18s				
	Housebill this week					18s	1¾d
23	Of Mr Whitehead various bills	£2	8s				
25	Of Mr Dowse, Wigtoft, by bill		15s	6d			
	Of -ditto- for Wigtoft Poor	£4	10s				
	Writing Paper 2 Quire					1s	6d
	To Thomas Hillyard for a day's Gardening					1s	

---

128 See n.81 above.
129 *Oleum olivarum*, or olive oil. A *Congius* was a gallon.
130 *Axungia porcina*, hog's lard. It was used in the making of ointments (*Supplement*, 226).

March 1777 (cont.)		Received			Paid		
28	Brandy 1 Pint for Shop use					2s	
	One dozen of Phials						6d
29	Of Mr Petchill, Gosberton, by bill	£1	1s				
	Of Mr Anderson, Gosberton, by bill		10s	0d			
	By retail and small bills	£1	0s	6d			
	Housebill this week				£1	0s	6½d
30	26 Nos of the British Biography					13s	
	My Mare cost me at Bicker						6d
31	Turnpikes this Month No 7						10½d
	Trifles during the Month						6d
[Carried over]		**£65**	**15s**	**2d**	**£32**	**14s**	**0¾d**

Bicker Feast June 23d

It has been remark't as somewhat odd, that Mr Jarvis did not invite his Donington neighbours this year as usual. We have been used to spend an agreable day at his house, and I dare say it was a great disapointment to several. I was at Mr Greens the latter day, and came home in good time. (July 25. 77.)

[f.22v]
April 1777

		Received			Paid		
Brought over		**£65**	**15s**	**2d**	**£32**	**14s**	**0¾d**
1	Of Mr Morris, Blacksmith, in full		5s	6d			
	Paid to -ditto- in full					5s	6d
2	Of Widow Robinson, Bicker, in full		15s				
4	To Mr Wm Ward in full				£7	17s	
	Of him in full		9s				
	Gave to Joseph Hayes						3d
5	Retail &c. 14s 6d. Housebill 14s 6d.		14s	6d		14s	6d
9	Of Mr Stains, Swineshead, in full	£1	1s				
	Of Mrs Warrington in full		10s				
11	Of Mr Warren, Butcher, Swineshead, by bill		12s				
	Of Mr Wm Morley, Bicker, by bill	£2	5s				
	To Mrs Mary Flinders in full, as by bill				£14	11s	8d
	Received of her for Rent	£9	13s				
	Received of her for Fencing		9s	6d			
12	By Retail &c. 15s. Housebill 14s 10¼d.		15s			14s	10¼d
14	Of Mr John Birks	£1	1s				
17	Carriage of Druggs and the Letter					4s	10d
18	Of John Kendall, Donington		11s	6d			
19	Medical Magazine No 40					1s	
	Retail and small bills	£1	5s	9½d			
	Housebill this week				£1	5s	9½d
20	Of Mrs Berry's Daughter, Donington		12s				
21	Easter dues to the Revd Mr Powell						8d
26	By Retail and small bills	£1	8s	3¾d			
	Housebill this week				£1	8s	3¾d
28	Half a Year's Window Money					10s	2d
	Land Tax ¼ Year, both to Mr Elveson					3s	
	1½ Chaldron of Coals at 24s				£1	16s	
	Porterage 11d. Ale 4d. Man 1s.					2s	3d
	Turnpike 1s 6d. A Dust Pan 10d.					2s	4d

April 1777 (cont.)		**Received**			**Paid**		
	One slit deal in 3 leaves					2s	6d
30	To Richard Jackson a bill in full					8s	6d
	Turnpikes No 10 in April					1s	3d
[Carried over]		**£88**	**3s**	**3¼d**	**£63**	**4s**	**5¼d**

Court of Requests, Friday June 27th[131]

I attended the first court (held at the School Chamber) being[132] one of the commissioners. This is an excellent act for our Hundred.[133] I do not in the least regret the money I subscribed towards obtaining the act, as it will soon repay me more. We had 12 Causes, which much entertained us; it will bring the never pay villains to a little sense of honesty. It has already brought me I belive more than one bill. I had no Causes the first Court, but have summonsed John Uffindale, to appear at the next Donington Court, August 8th.

My Wife's Fourth Labour

I have great reason to acknowledge the unmerited goodness of the Supreme, that my wife was safely delivered of two Daughters on Saturday July 19 1777.[134] They are both dead, being two months before [f.23] due time. The particulars of the Labour I have noted in my Midwifry Cases. How kind is the Providence of God[135] thus to free us from the expence and care of a numerous family, for had all our young ones lived with us, we should scarce [have] known what to have done with them. The two we have living, if agreable to divine Wisdom, I would gladly keep, but by no means wish an increase. However let that happen as it may; I hope we shall always acquiesce to the good will of God. I praise God my wife is well recovered. Aug. 12. 77.

May 1777

		Received			**Paid**		
Brought over		**£88**	**3s**	**3¼d**	**£63**	**4s**	**5¼d**
1	One Yard of Cloth for Shop use						11d
3	Of Mr Taylor, North Ing		15s				
	By Retail and small bills		12s	8¾d			
	Housebill this week					12s	8¾d
5	Of John Bettison, Donington		10s	6d			
6	Gave Mr Stukeley's Servant Man					1s	
8	A Letter 3d. Carriage 3d.						6d
	One Strike of Lime						6d
	To Mr Daniel Lynch in full				£7	9s	6d
10	Of Mr Houseley, Bicker Gantlet	£1	18s				
	By Retail and small bills		17s				
	Housebill this week					16s	11½d

---

131 The Court was established by Act of Parliament: *An Act for the more easy and speedy recovery of small debts, within the several parishes of Surfleet, Gosberton, Quadring, Donington, Bicker, Swineshead, Wigtoft, Sutterton, Algarkirk, Fosdike, Kirton, Frampton, Wiberton, and Brothertoft, within the Hundred of Kirton, in the parts of Holland, in the county of Lincoln* (1777).
132 MS 'been'.
133 An area of local government dating back to Saxon times.
134 One twin was named Susanna; the other does not seem to appear in the parish records as being baptised.
135 The section from here to the end of the paragraph is inserted at the foot of f.23v.

May 1777 (cont.)		Received		Paid		
12	Of Mrs Lowe by bill		14s 6d			
	Medical Magazine No 41				1s	
	Of Francis Horn by bill		16s			
13	Writing Paper 1 Quire					6d
14	1¼ Grose large Corks 20d. Nails 6d.				2s	2d
	To Mary Goodyear 1 Year's Wages			£3	3s	
	To John Harmston 1 Year's Wages			£1	15s	
	To -ditto- Earnest Money				2s	6d
	To my wife			£2		
15	Of Mr B. Bowers, White House	£3	3s			
16	Of John Wells, Labourer		10s 6d			
	One Sack of Oats of Mr Wilkinson				7s	
17	By Retail and Small Bills	£1	1s 6d			
	Housebill this week			£1	1s	6¾d
23	Carriage of Druggs from F. & W.				2s	4d
	To Messrs Barrit and Robinson			£4	6s	
25	By Retail and Small Bills	£1	1s 6d			
	Housebill this week			£1	1s	5¾d
26	Of Mr Chambers, Wigtoft, by bill	£1	1s 0d			
	Of James Clark, by bill		8s			
	Of the Parish of Swineshead, by bill	£5	5s			
	Of R. Patison, Gosberton, in part		8s 6d			
	To Mr Samuel Ward for Stuff				11s	
	Of -ditto- for Interest of £10, 6 Months		5s			
	Of James Hides, Swineshead North End, by bill		5s 6d			
	One Stew Pan of Mr Bedezly				9s	6d
	One Tin Funnell of -ditto-					4d
	Of William King, Bicker	£1	1s			
	Remainder of Mr Bowers's bill		11s 6d			
27	One Pair of Beaver Gloves of Mr Weeks				2s	
	Cost me at the Charitable Card Assembly				5s	4d
28	Church Assessment £4 at 8d				2s	8d
	Twenty Bottles of Mrs Burr					10d
29	Of Captain Roberts at the Cow		5s			
31	Retail and small Bills		17s 6d			
	Housebill this week				17s	5¾d
	Turnpikes No 8 this Month				1s	
	Trifles during the Month					6d
[Carried over]		**£110 11s**	**6d**	**£88 19s**	**8¾d**	

[f.23v]
June 1777

		Received		Paid		
Brought over		**£110 11s**	**6d**	**£88 19s**	**8¾d**	
2	Two Dozen Bottles of Mrs Burr				1s	
5	Of Henry Everitt Junior by bill		15s 6d			
7	Of the Parish of Quadring by bill	£4	8s 0d			
	Of Mr Baldwick by bill (Quadring)		15s			
	By Retail and small bills	£1	14s			
	Housebill this week			£1	14s	2d
	Four Lancets grinding and carriage				1s	6d
8	Medical Magazine No 42				1s	

June 1777 (cont.)		Received			Paid		
10	Of Mr William Golding		11s	6d			
11	Auxung. Porcina,[136] 6lb at 5d					2s	6d
	To Mr William Ward a bill in full				£2	6s	
12	Of John Garner by bill		17s				
14	By Retail and Small Bills	£1	3s	6d			
	Housebill this week				£1	3s	7¾d
15	Of William Gould by bill		10s	6d			
16	Of my Brother for Phials & Carriage	£1	17s	9d			
	Paid to -ditto- for Druggs				£1	2s	11d
	Annual Register 1775 of Mr Albin					6s	
	Cost me going to Spalding					1s	
	Insurance Money to Mr Waite, Boston					9s	6d
19	Of J. Thompson (Hostler) by bill		18s				
21	Of Mr Thacker, Wigtoft Marsh		7s	6d			
	By Retail and small bills		19s				
	Housebill this week					18s	11¼d
23	Ten Gallons of Ale of J. Lee at 1s 2d					11s	8d
	Twenty five -ditto- Small Beer at 2d					4s	2d
	Of Mrs Clifton Senior by bill		10s				
	Betsey's Entrance at Mrs Moor's School					1s	6d
25	Gave Mr Green's Servant the 23d & 24th					1s	6d
	Breeches mending (to Mr Clark)						6d
26	To Mrs Flinders, Donington, one Brass Pot					7s	9d
	One Horse Lock of Mr Wicks						8d
27	Exchange of a Hat of Mr Ward					1s	6d
	Two Pounds of Fine Flax Spining					2s	
28	Of Mrs Orme, Quadring, by bill		10s	6d			
	To Mary Pigot for Bleaching					6s	4½d
	Retail &c. 16s 6d. Housebill 16s 4¼d.		16s	6d		16s	4¼d
29	Of Benjamin Blackwell by bill		8s				
30	Of P. Moor's wife by bill		5s	3d			
	To -ditto- for 22 Weeks' Schooling					3s	10d
	Nine Toll Barrs in June					1s	1½d
[Carried over]		**£127**	**19s**	**0d**	**£100**	**6s**	**10d**

[f.24]
July 1777

Brought over		Received			Paid		
		£127	**19s**	**0d**	**£100**	**6s**	**10d**
4	Of a Weaver, Donington, by bill		14s	6d			
	Of Mr Parker, Bicker Frist		5s	6d			
5	Of H. Holland, Swineshead Fen Houses		6s				
	By Retail and small bills	£1	5s	6d			
	Housebill this week				£1	5s	5¼d
8	Of Mr Thomas Pike by bill	£2	7s				
12	Carriage of Druggs from Swineshead						9d
	Of James Bucknell by bill		11s				
13	By Retail and small bills		14s	6d			
	Housebill this week					14s	8d

[136] See n.130 above.

July 1777 (cont.)	Received		Paid	
Medical Magazine No 43			1s	
17 7lb Rosin[137] 1s 2d. Arsen. alb.[138] 7lb: 2s 4d of				
Mr Ward			3s	6d
Of Mr Gleed's Servant Man by bill	7s			
18 18 Yards of Harden[139] weaving &c.			5s	2d
19 Of Mr Hand, Wigtoft, by bill	9s	6d		
Of Mr Garner by bill	8s	6d		
20 By Retail and small bills	£1 0s	6d		
Housebill this week			£1 0s	4d
21 Of John Smith, Bicker, by bill	11s	6d		
26 By Retail and small bills	£1 10s			
The weekly bill			£1 10s	2¾d
27 The Remainder of Luke Tebbs' bill, Northorp	4s	6d		
28 One Quarter's Land Tax			3s	
30 Of John Collingworth, Bicker, by bill	16s			
31 One Pair of Gloves of Mr Kew			1s	6d
Five Turnpikes to Swineshead in July				7½d
[Carried over]	**£139 10s**	**6d**	**£105 13s**	**1d**

Friday July 25. Dislocated Radius.

One Ketton a boy from Quadring Eaudike came to me with a dislocated Radius (a case I had never seen before). It happened by being pushed down from a ladder. It was clearly dislodged from its situation on the end of the humerus, to the back and upper part of that bone; the boy could by no means extend his arm. After examining the skeleton, and the other arm, I reduced it much indeed to my satisfaction. Standing sideways against him, with my left hand I took hold near the wrist to extend, and with my right thumb pushed strongly against the end of the Radius, and at the same time brought the arm gradually to a right line; the bone went in, and the boy had all the motions of his arm perfect again. August 12, 77.

Visiters

Aug. 7. My Uncle and Aunt H[ursthouse] with their Daughter[140] (now Mrs Decamps of Fleet) paid us a Visit. They staid the following day to dine & then left us. It is many Years since I saw my aunt & she is very hearty and well, and fatter than ever I saw her.

Aug. 17. My Brother, his son and Daughter paid us a Visit, & returned in the Evening. Jackey is to return to school again very shortly. It was not convenient for my Sisters to come.

[f.24v]
August 1777

Brought over	Received		Paid	
	£139 10s	**6d**	**£105 13s**	**1d**
2 Lancets grinding No 3 & Carriage			1s	
Of Mr J. Stimson, Bicker, in part	£2 2s			

[137] A variety of rosins was available. See *Supplement*, 203–209.

[138] *Arsenicum album*, or white arsenic (*Supplement*, 286–287).

[139] See n.80 above.

[140] Sarah, daughter of Matthew Hursthouse, married David DeCamps of Fleet (*Lincolnshire Pedigrees*, 1265; PRO, PROB 11/1446).

August 1777 (cont.)		Received			Paid		
	Of Mr Willoughby for the late Mr Gibbs		8s				
	Of Mr Wm Wells by bill	£2	5s	6d			
	Paid to him a bill in full				£2	4s	6d
3	The weekly bill				£1	3s	1½d
	By Retail and small bills	£1	3s				
	Of Mr Trimnel's Man, Bicker		6s	6d			
	Medical Magazine No 44					1s	
4	Of John Lammin by bill		14s				
5	To Richard Jackson a bill in full					18s	3d
	Of R. Coles wife by bill		10s	6d			
6	Of the Revd Mr Powell by bill	£3					
8	Of Symon the Irishman		10s	6d			
	Of J. Uffindale (by virtue of the Acts)		11s				
9	Four Grose of Phial Corks & Carriage					1s	2d
	By Retail and small bills	£1	6s	6d			
	The weekly bill				£1	6s	9d
	Of Mr Warrington by bill		8s	6d			
10	Of Mr Golding for the late Mr Pierrepont		17s	9d			
	To Mary Tunnard for Nursing					15s	
	Of Wm Edinborough by bill		12s	6d			
11	Of Mrs Orry by bill		6s	6d			
	Of Dimock Goodyear by bill		8s	6d			
12	Of Mr T. Root, Swineshead, by bill	£1	1s	0d			
	Of Mr Cortin, Gosberton, by bill		12s				
16	To Mr Tory for mending a Lancet Case						6d
	By Retail and small bills	£1	2s				
	The weekly bill				£1	2s	1d
18	Gave my Nephew & Neice the 17th					4s	
	Remainder of Samuel Ashton's bill		9s	6d			
	To the Revd Mr Powell for Churching					1s	
20	Tripoli polishing powder, 4oz.						6d
21	One Stand of Mr Parker, Joiner					3s	6d
	To my Wife, August the 6th				£2		
	To Mrs Wm Ward for a Gown					18s	
23	In part of Widow Reynolds's bill, Bicker		4s				
	Of Mrs Edwards, Donington, by bill		15s				
	To J. Wells for a pair of Shoes					6s	
	Retail &c. £1 1s 6d. Weekly bill £1 1s 7¾d.	£1	1s	6d	£1	1s	7¾d
26	Of Mr Barnet Mason by bill		5s				
30	Retail and small bills		16s				
	The weekly bill					15s	9d
31	Sacrament Money on the 24th						6d
	Eleven Turnpikes in August					1s	4½d
[Carried over]		**£161**	**7s**	**9d**	**£118**	**18s**	**8¾d**

Sacrament, August 24.

My self and wife attended the Holy Communion on Sunday August 24, we hope to our great advantage.

Brother's Visit, September 8.
My Brother having occasion to visit a patient at Quadring[141] came on & drank tea with us, and returned in the evening.

[f.25]
September 1777

		Received			Paid		
	Brought over	£161	7s	9d	£118	18s	8¾d
4	Of Mr Duckett, Quadring Eaudike		12s				
6	By Retail and small bills	£1	1s				
	The weekly bill				£1	1s	11¾d
7	Of Thos Alsop by bill		10s	6d			
	The Medical Magazine No 45					1s	
8	Of Mr Barber, Gosberton Risgate		7s				
10	Of J. Thompson, Labourer, in part		10s	6d			
13	Of Wm Story, Bicker Gauntlet, by bill	£1	1s				
	Retail and small bills	£1	1s				
	The weekly bill				£1	0s	11½d
16	Of Matthew Jackson, Shoemaker		5s				
19	Thos Melliday's bill (by Virtue of the Act)		11s	3d			
	Mr Brewster's Man's bill (by -ditto-)		8s	6d			
	Of John Damms, Swineshead Fenn, by bill	£1	1s				
20	By Retail and small bills	£1					
	The weekly bill					19s	11¾d
22	To Wm Morris, Blacksmith, a bill					6s	5d
25	To Messeurs Fernyhough & Wilson for three Parcels in full				£12	9s	
27	Of ~~ Elsom, Donington Northorp		15s				
	Of Widow Ketton, Quadring Eadike		5s				
	Of John Barret, Bicker, by bill		11s	6d			
	The weekly bill				£1	2s	2¼d
	By Retail and small bills	£1	2s				
30	Twenty three Toll Barrs this Month					2s	10½d
	[Carried over]	**£172**	**10s**	**0d**	**£136**	**3s**	**1½d**

Money to Mr Samuel Ward, September 4 1777.
I let Mr S. Ward have £20 on Note which with the £25[142] I let him have some time before makes £45. I am to make it up £50 at the October Fair, when he will take in the Notes, and give me a bond or other approved security. I thank God that hath enabled me to do this.

Illness, September 12 1777.
About this time I begun to be very much out of order with the common prevailing Autumnal Fever, and was for near a fortnight very poorley, and with great difficulty pursued my Business. I found considerable benefit from two Emetics of Tart. Emet.[143] and afterwards the Bark with Wine and Conf. Cardiaca[144] – for

141 Approximately 2 miles south-east of Donington.
142 MS '25th'.
143 See n.70 above.
144 *Confectio Cardiaca*, also known as Sir Walter Raleigh's Cordial (*Supplement*, 381–382).

after an Emetic I find Cordials suit best in this Low Autumnal Fever and that V.S. and Evacuations protract the disorder.

Court of Requests, September 19.
I had 3 Causes in our Court this day, viz. Melliday, Kirton Holme, 11s. 3d.; Brewster's Man, Swineshead, 8s. 6d., and William Smith, Donington, 15s. 6d. The 2 first paid without appearing in Court. I paid 3s 6d Costs for the latter, which together with the Bill the court ordered to be paid in 5 weeks, but at Smith's request I agreed to take at 1s per Week. October 15.

Mr W. W... d's Failure
I am very sorry to remark the failure of Mr Wm Ward contrary to every body's sentiments of him.[145]

[f.25v]
October 1777

		Received			Paid		
Brought over		£172	10s	0d	£136	3s	1½d
2	Of Joseph Wilkinson, Boston, by bill		15s				
	One Stone of Honey of J. Crompton					7s	
	Gave to Mr Gee's Servants					1s	6d
3	Of John Chapman, Hoflit, by bill		19s	6d			
4	To Mr Tory for cleaning the clock					2s	
	By Retail and small bills		17s				
	The weekly bill					17s	1½d
5	Medical Magazine No 46					1s	
7	Of Mr Bartol, Gosberton, by bill		14s	6d			
	Of Stiles Mapletoft by bill	£1	1s				
	Paid to -ditto- for two years Shaving and Hairdressing due the 5th Inst.				£1	4s	
8	To Mr Lynet, Druggist, in full				£1	19s	
	One & half Chaldron of Coales at 24s.				£1	16s	
	Expences relating to -ditto-					4s	1d
	To John Wells for Shoes Soling					2s	
9	Of John Clark Junior by bill		12s	6d			
11	Paid Out Rent at the Wikes Court					8s	5d
	By Retail and small bills	£1	2s				
	The weekly bill				£1	2s	2¼d
15	Of Thos Cook, Quadring, by bill	£1	2s				
16	One Chaldron of Coals 24s. Expences 2s 11d.				£1	6s	11d
17	Of Wm Story, Bicker town, by bill		6s				
	Of Mr Holbourn, Wigtoft, by bill		14s	6d			
	Of Thos Foster, Gosberton, in part		4s				
	Of Mr Love, Swineshead Abbey, by bill	£3	17s				
	Of Mr Copeland, Swaton, by bill	£1	16s	6d			
	Of Mr Jefford, Wheelwright, by bill		4s	6d			
	Of Mr Dowse, Burtoft, by bill	£1	18s				
	Of Joseph Clark, Swineshead Fen Houses in part		10s	6d			

---

[145] It is clear (31 Jan. 1775) that there had been problems between the two men in the past. There are also several mentions of seemingly routine financial dealings between Flinders and both Samuel and William Ward – but there are no other clues as to what specific matter this intriguing entry relates to.

October 1777 (cont.)	Received			Paid		
	Half a dozen knives and forks				5s	
18	By Retail and small bills	£1	7s			
	House bill this week			£1	6s	11¾d
22	Paid to Mr Weeks a bill				14s	
	Received of -ditto- by bill		4s			
	To Messrs Barrit & Robinson in full			£5	9s	
24	Turnpikes to & from Deeping					10½d
	Paid at the Bull at Deeping				2s	5½d
	Paid at John Sharpe at Spalding				3s	2d
	Gave my Brother's Servant Maid				1s	
	Admission Money at the Court at Deeping			£1	16s	
	Of the Brother of the late Moler		5s	6d			
25	Of Mr Kirk, Bicker, by bill		15s	6d			
	Of Mrs Marshall at Mr Lamb's, Quadring		13s				
	Of Mr Howeson, Bicker, by bill		7s				
	Retail &c. £1 9s 6d. Weekly bill £1 9s 8¾d.	£1	9s	6d	£1	9s	8¾d
26	Of John Smart, Swineshead, by bill		12s				
27	½ Year's Window Money 10s 2d. Land Tax 3s.				13s	2d
28	To Wm Morris, Blacksmith, 2s				2s	
29	Received Balance of Mr Matthew Hursthouse		12s	2d			
[Carried over]		**£195**	**10s**	**2d**	**£158**	**0s**	**8¾d**

[f.26]
Journey to Deeping[146]
Wednesday October 22, I went to Spalding in the Evening, and according to expectation found my Uncle & Cousin H. at my Brother's. We that Evening went to Mr Sanderson, to take his opinion concerning the division of the Deeping, Maxey & Spalding Estates, to which opinion we have all agreed & which is, that the Spalding Lands go to the two heirs, Mr J. H[ursthouse] & my Brother, as the late Mr J.H. dying without Issue had no power to give it by will, according to the will of his Father Mr Matthew H., as these lands were a seperate bequest to him & heirs with the above Proviso. The Deeping Estate, viz. £10 10s 0d Copyhold in Tenure of Mr Marshall, as the late Mr J.H. bought & surrendered to the use of his will, undoubtedly goes according to that will, viz. my Father's moiety into six equal shares, four to Mr M.H.'s family and two to ours; and the £10 10s 0d Freehold in tenure of Mr Osborn, goes exactly in the same manner, according to the late Mr J.H.'s will, as his Father gave this to him & heirs without the Proviso of dying without Issue. Two of Mr Matthew H.'s Daughters being dead (but of age) their shares devolve to their heir, viz. their Brother Mr J.H. who consequently has 3 shares, or a Moiety of the Moiety. The day following, viz. Thursday the 23d we all went to Deeping to attend the Court in order to be admitted Tenants to the Lord of the Manor of East & West Deeping. The Admission cost us £1 16s 0d each which we thought high as the shares are so small, but I find the admission money is the same, of whatever value the estate. As we are all desirous of selling this so intermixed and divided estate, the proposal was make to Mr Marshall, and he has agreed to give £230 for what he rents at Michaelmas next (about 22 Years Purchase). An agreement was drawn, and we hope he will adhere to it. In regard

---

[146] Market Deeping and nearby Maxey are 23 miles south of Donington.

to my Uncle's moiety, I fancy we shall give up to him the whole of Osborn's freehold for his Life (from which about the same neat money is received) and so divide the Purchase money into Six shares as above, viz. three to Mr J.H. and the other shares to Mr J. Flinders, myself & Mrs De Camps. My Brother & self came to Spalding that night though dark; the two Mr H's staid at Deeping and bargained with Mr Marshall. I returned home on Friday Morn the 24th.

Money Matter, October 17. 1777.

I forgot to mention this in the order of time, but now with gratitude to Providence note that I made up the money Mr S.W.[147] had of me £50, for which he pays me 5 per Cent. The Security he has at present given me is his Note, and the writings of his dwelling house, but if he keeps it any long time, proposes giving me a bond.

Mr Hall, November 9th 1777

My old acquaintance Mr Hall paid me a visit. He dined and left us soon after; he has been in the country some time and has had a very ill bout, & continues remarkably deaf.

[f.26v]
November 1777

		Received			Paid		
Brought over		£195	10s	2d	£158	0s	8¾d
1	Retail &c. £1 2s 6d. Weekly bill £1 2s 8¾d.	£1	2s	6d	£1	2s	8¾d
3	Of Richard Smith, Swineshead, by bill	£2	1s	6d			
6	Of Mr Pullin, Northorp, by bill		9s				
7	Carriage of Druggs from Barrit & Co.					3s	9d
8	Of Mr Robert Jennings, Bicker Gauntlet		19s				
	By Retail and small bills this week	£1	1s	6d			
	The weekly bill				£1	1s	3¾d
9	Of Mr Hardy, Swineshead, by bill		10s	6d			
	Medical Coms. No 16, 1s 6d. Brit. Biog. No 68, 6d					2s	
13	Journey to Spalding cost me					1s	9d
	Of Mr Wm Gee, Hale, by bill	£7	17s	0d			
15	Remainder of Mr Stimson's bill, Bicker	£2	4s				
	By Retail and small bills	£1	3s	6d			
	The weekly bill				£1	3s	10¾d
16	Annual Register 1776 of Mr Albin					6s	
17	Writing Paper 8d. Walking Stick 6d.					1s	2d
	Paid for one Sack of Oats to Mr Boldron					6s	
18	Of Mr Fisher, Swineshead, by bill		16s				
	Of Mr Hull, Weaver, by bill (Swineshead)		6s				
	Paid to my Wife on the 6th Inst.				£2		
20	Of Mr Strapps by bill		11s				
	Paid to Hill a bill					7s	6d
	Of John Mitchell by bill		10s	6d			
22	Of Mr Marsh, Quadring, by bills	£3	13s				
	By Retail and small bills		19s				
	The weekly bill					18s	10¼d
23	Of Mr Bull, Swineshead, by bill		7s	6d			

---

[147] Samuel Ward.

November 1777 (cont.)		Received			Paid		
27	Of Mr Caswell, Quadring	£1	11s	6d			
28	Of Mrs Maples by bills	£1	4s				
29	Of Mr Torks, Bicker, by bill		18s				
	By Retail and small bills		15s	6d			
	The weekly bill					15s	4½d
	One Pair Pedestall Scales of a Stranger					6s	
[Carried over]		**£224**	**10s**	**8d**	**£166**	**17s**	**0¾d**

Journey to Spalding, November 13.

We made a Journey to my Brother's, my wife not having been there a consider-able time. We went double but the mare performed the Journey very badly. I staid agreably that night, and sent for my wife a few days after not being able to go on account of Business.

Books

I have to note that I have discontinued the Medical Magazine and take the Medical Commentaries in its stead, this being but half the expence and containing only new matter, whereas that consists principally of old & almost useless writings. I have to note that I have got another volume of that agreable and entertaining work the Annual Register[148] for 1776. Wishing is a bad employ-ment, otherwise I regret I did not take this work instead of Magazines some years ago. December 15, 77.

[f.27]
December 1777

		Received			Paid		
Brought over		**£224**	**10s**	**8d**	**£166**	**17s**	**0¾d**
3	To Mr Lowe for 2 Stone 9 Pound of Pork at 4s					10s	6d
5	To Mr Green for 3 Stone 2 Pound of Cheese						
	at 3s 9d					11s	9d
	Four Lancetts grinding & Carriage					1s	6d
7	By Retail and small bills	£1					
	The weekly bill				£1	0s	0¼d
13	Of Mr Holbourn, Hoflit, by bill		14s	6d			
	By Retail and small bills	£1	0s	6d			
	The weekly bill				£1	0s	7¾d
16	Expence of 26 Gallons of Ale and the small beer,						
	Malt 4 Strike, 16s. Hops 2½lb, 3s 4d. Brewing 2s.				£1	1s	4d
20	Of Mr Retchill, Gosberton Risgate, by bill		4s	6d			
	By Retail and small bills		16s				
	The weekly bill					15s	10d
22	To Mr Spendley for one Sack of Oats					7s	
26	Of Mary Twell in part		6s	6d			
27	By Retail and small bills	£1	5s				
	The weekly bill				£1	5s	1¾d
[Carried over]		**£229**	**17s**	**8d**	**£173**	**10s**	**9½d**

---

148 A general almanac of national and international events which had commenced in 1758.

Receipts and Payments in 6 Years	£1073 11s 7½d	£761 10s 5d
Total Receipts and Payments in 7 Years	£1303 9s 3½d	£933 1s 2½d
Total Gained in 7 Years	£368 8s 1d	

Inoculation

December 7. The small Pox having made their appearance in this Parish, the season being favourable and my Son & Daughter of a very convenient age, Inoculated them this day, and have this among the innumerable other mercies of God to remark, that they have passed through that calamitous disorder in the most favourable & easy manner. I have also to remark that I have also inoculated several others with the greatest success and expect more Business of this kind before we stop.[149] December 31, 1777.

Year Concluded

I have again to remark that through the divine mercy we are yet continued in Life, and that life made comfortable by God's good Providence. I thank God I have gained something above £50 this year, and in my 7 Years of Business £368 8s 1d as above appears, far beyond my expectations and deserts. I am convinced a sufficiency is a very desirable thing, but far from being the whole necessary to human happiness, we ought with all humility and resignation to demean ourselves to the divine will and to follow after that plan which Reason & the Scriptures point out as most excellent. January 1. 78.

[f.27v]
January 1778

		Received			Paid	
1	Took from the Retail Money	£5	5s			
2	Of Mr Corby, Wigtoft, by bill		16s			
	A Map of America 1s 3d. Gave the Newsman 6d.				1s	9d
3	By Retail and small bills		15s			
	The weekly bill				15s	1d
4	Medical Commentaries No 17				1s	6d
10	By Retail and small bills	£1	3s	6d		
	The weekly bill				£1 3s	6½d
13	Of J. Mapletoft, Parish Bills	£1	16s	4d		
	To -ditto- Poor Assessment to Easter 1777				5s	4d
17	Of Mr Godley, Bicker Gantlet, by bill	£1	13s			
	By Retail and small bills		19s	6d		
	The weekly bill				19s	8½d
20	The late T. Hillyard's Account of Mr Golding	£1	15s			
22	To Mr Spendley for one Sack of Oats				6s	6d
23	Carriage of Druggs from London				6s	

[149] This is some 20 years before Edward Jenner's introduction of vaccination. The concept of introducing a mild form of the disease in order to provide future immunity is said to have been brought to Britain from Turkey in 1721. It carried a small risk of the patient contracting full-blown smallpox and eventually death, but smallpox was a major cause of death at this time and it was often felt worth the risk. Using this method, Flinders probably infected his children by scratching or cutting them and exposing them to smallpox puss. Jenner's discovery was that exposure to the relatively harmless disease of cowpox provided a safer method of long-term protection against smallpox (*ODNB*).

January 1778 (cont.)	Received	Paid
Spent at the Court[150] Dinner 1s. Liquor 6d.		1s 6d
Of Mr Shilcock by bill	5s 4d	
Paid to -ditto- for Veal & Hog's Lard		3s 7d
24 Of Thos Blow, Swaton, by bill	5s	
Of Mr James Taylor, Donington Eaudike, by bill	8s 6d	
By Retail and small bills	£1 13s	
The weekly bill		£1 13s 1½d
29 Cost me at Mr Gee's Funeral 21d. Ferrit 3d.		2s
31 By Retail and small bills	17s 6d	
The weekly bill		17s 7½d
[Carried over]	**£17 12s 8d**	**£6 17s 3d**

Christmas Entertainments 1778

Thursday January 15. A considerable party of us, of both sexes, got tea, supped and passed the Evening untill Midnight at Mr Shilcock's. This was an agreable party.

Tuesday January 20. I was with a party at Mr Whitehead's.

Wednesday January 21. The following of our Friends honored us with a Visit and staid untill midnight.

Mr Mrs & Miss Shilcock, Mr & Mrs Pakey, Mr and Miss Golding, Mr & Mrs Birks, Miss Cole, Miss Shepherd, Mrs Maples, Mrs Ward, Mr Charles Trimnell, Mrs Jarvis, Mr & Mrs Whitehead, in all 17. The following though invited did not come: Mr Jarvis, Mr David Trimnell, Mr & Mrs Gleed, Mr S. Ward, Mr W. Ward, Mr Harvey, in all 7.

[f.28]
Court of Requests

Friday January 23. Being Court day, and for this time held at the Rose & Crown, I attended nearly the whole day, dined there with 9 or 10 other Commissioners, but did not stay in the Evening untill all the Business was finished; this is the first time I have dined at the Court.

Birth Day

Tuesday February 17, 78. I compleated my 28th Year and with humble gratitude again acknowledge the goodness of the Almighty Creator, in thus preserving and blessing me. The weather proved bad, notwithstanding which, my good Brother came to tea & spent the Evening with us, & left us the next Morning.

Money

Saturday April 4. J. Kendall, an honest and industrious Labouring Man of this Place, having requested of me the use [of] Six Guineas (to purchase a Cow) for a Year, I ventured to let him have it, for which he has given me a Note with Interest. I thought I might safely venture as both himself and wife are industrious People.

Marshall's Purchase

Wednesday April 8, 1778. Mr Marshall having before wrote us word, that it would be more agreable to him, to pay the purchase money & enter on the estate

---

150 MS 'Club', struck through.

the present Lady Day, than to stay untill Michalemas, as agreed on, and having fixed this day, I set off very early for Spalding, and went about 9, along with my Brother, our Uncle H., Mr J.H. & Mr and Mrs De Camps[151] from Spalding to Deeping which we reached before noon. This being the Court day, and our Uncle having agreed to give up his moiety, we were all obliged to be at the expence of a second admission to that moiety before we could properly surrender it to Mr Marshall and they also charged us very high for the fine, viz. £12 – £4 higher than before. Mr Marshall paid the purchase money, viz. £230, after which we all surrendered it to him & his Grandson. I received a 6th Part of this as my quota, viz. £38 6s 8d – but all expences being deducted, I brought home in neat Cash only £34 4s 8d. I have wrote the particulars of the expences in my Debt Book. I am gratefull to Providence for this further instance of favour to me; it will I hope considerably overpay the expence of the great repairs I am now about.

Repairs & Improvements
On account of receiving the above, which I thought I could conveniently spare, I determined on some considerable improvements and repairs at my [f.28v] house, such as building up the back wall Brick, also the two sides of the Brewhouse of the same materials (before Mud), together with the making a rain water Cistern (16 Hogsheads), making the door in the Brewhouse instead of the (before) Kitchen, ceiling the Kitchen, turning the open Chimney into a stove, whereby we have gained 3 Closets, and made it a snug and convenient keeping room. We have converted the (before) Brewhouse into a Kitchen, removing into it the Ironing & Furnace Stoves, and setting the Still on the other side. Mr Fielding of Boston, a distant relation of my wife, with his assistants, did the Brick work, the materials I had of Mr Wells, & R. Jackson did the carpenter's work. I believe I have been used tolerably well by the workmen. I expect the whole will cost me not less than £25, but I hope upon the whole it will in time be a saving, especially in regard to Coals, as one fire in the general will now serve us, also there will be a mate[152]rial advantage in having a constant supply of rain water for washing and other domestic Purposes, exclusive of the great advantage to our Health, as the water in this county is in general bad. I have also to remark that Mr Torry has glazed anew the Parlour Windows with Crown Glass, the old Glass doing for the House new Window & that for the (now) Kitchen. Edward Gibson is about putting up new spouts in the front of the house, by which means I hope we shall have a good supply for our Cistern. We have also a small new Pump to put down in the cistern; we do not intend to let the water into this Convenience untill the work is thoroughly dry. May 19. 78.

[f.28v]
February 1778

		Received			Paid		
Brought forwards		£17	12s	8d	£6	17s	3d
	One quarter's Land Tax					3s	
3	Of Mr Hunt, Draper, by bill		9s	6d			
	To -ditto- for 18 Pound of Candles					9s	9d

---

151 See n.140 above.
152 The section from here to the end of the paragraph is inserted at the foot of f.29.

February 1778 (cont.)

		Received			Paid		
	To Jonathan Warriner a bill in full					14s	8d
	Highway Assessment at 4d per Pound					1s	4d
4	Lump Sugar 1½lb for shop use at 10½d.					1s	3¾d
6	Of Benjamin Upton in part		5s				
	One Pound of fine flax Spining					1s	
7	Of Mrs Vicars Senior, Swineshead	£3	3s				
	Of Mr Gleed's Servant Maid (Jenny)		7s	6d			
	By Retail and small bills	£1					
	The weekly bill				£1	0s	3½d
10	Of Mrs Dodd for Inoculating &c. her Grandson		10s	6d			
13	Cloth 2 Yards & ¼ for shop use					2s	4d
14	Of Mr Green, Bicker, by bill		12s				
	By Retail and small bills		18s	6d			
	The weekly bill					18s	6¼d
	To my wife on the 6th Instant				£2		
20	One Sack of Oats of Mr Spendley					6s	6d
21	By Retail and small bills	£1	4s				
	The weekly bill				£1	3s	11¾d
22	Of Joseph Clark, Swineshead Fen Houses, by bill		10s	6d			
26	To Mr Wilkinson, Gardener, for a day's Work					1s	6d
27	Of Mr Pycroft, Donington Eadike, by bill	£1	7s				
28	By Retail and small bills		14s	6d			
	House Bill this week					14s	4½d
	[Carried over]	**£28**	**14s**	**8d**	**£14**	**15s**	**9¾d**

[f.29]
March 1778

		Received			Paid		
	Brought forwards	**£28**	**14s**	**8d**	**£14**	**15s**	**9¾d**
2	Phial Corks 4 Grose & Carriage					1s	3d
	One Chaldron of Coales				£1	4s	
	Port. 7d. Ale 4d. Man 6d. Barr 9d.					2s	2d
3	Of John Walker, Quadring, in part	£1	1s				
4	To Mr Ward in full					18s	
5	Of Mr Clay, Swineshead, by bill		14s				
	Cera flava[153] ½lb (of Mr Hunt)					1s	2d
6	Of Sam. Brand, Wigtoft, by bill		13s	6d			
	To Wm Boldram for a Sack of Oats					6s	
7	Of Mr Jarvis, Bicker, by bill	£2	12s	6d			
	By Retail and small bills		14s	6d			
	The weekly bill					14s	9¾d
9	Of Mr Baxter, Swineshead, by bill		6s				
11	Of Mr Rolls, Swineshead Clay Hills	£1	1s				
	Of Mr Watkin, Hoflit, by bill		16s	6d			
12	Of Wm West (Tawer) by bill		8s	6d			
14	By Retail and small bills		17s				
	The weekly bill					17s	2¾d
20	Writing Paper 1 Quire 10d. A Letter 2d.					1s	
21	Of Mr John Jackson, Bicker, by bill	£1	7s				
	By Retail and small bills	£1	11s	6d			

---

153 See n.63 above.

March 1778 (cont.)	**Received**		**Paid**	
The weekly bill			£1 11s	6¾d
22 Of J. Alvey, Donington, by bill	5s	6d		
To J. Barret's Son, Earnest Money			1s	
23 Of Mr Kenting, Swineshead, by bill	£1 3s	6d		
26 Of Mr Boyfield, Quadring Edike, by bill	£2 5s			
Of Mr Brown, Hoflit, by bill	£3 15s	6d		
27 Of Mr Gleed's Servant Maid by bill	7s	6d		
28 By Retail and small bills	18s			
The weekly bill			18s	3¾d
White Wine 1½lb 1 Pint & ½ (Shop use)			1s	6d
29 Of Mrs Trimnel's Man by bill	6s	6d		
31 One Hankerchief of Mrs Wicks			1s	3d
[Carried over]	**£49 19s**	**2d**	**£21 15s**	**0¾d**

[f.29v]
April 1778

	Received		**Paid**	
Brought forwards	**£49 19s**	**2d**	**£21 15s**	**0¾d**
3 Carriage of Druggs			5s	7d
5 Reckoned with Mrs Flinders and paid a balance in full to this day			£2 7s	
A Letter from Messrs Ferneyhough				7d
By Retail and small bills	14s			
The weekly bill			13s	10½d
6 A Pair of Gloves 1s 6d. Trifles 6d.			2s	
7 Of Mr Clifton, Donington, by bill	15s	6d		
Of Edward Laykins by bill	19s			
Paid to -ditto- a bill			£1 2s	8d
9 To Mr Jennings, Spalding, for a Grate			7s	6d
10 Of Mrs Barker, Swineshead Fenn, by bill	13s	6d		
11 To Mr Ashworth a bill for meat			£1 12s	9d
Of -ditto- a bill	£1 5s	3d		
Of Mr Torry by bill	£1 2s			
Paid to -ditto- a bill in full			9s	
Of Mr Caswell, Quadring, by bill	9s			
Of -ditto- Quadring Parish bill	£3 12s			
By Retail and small bills	16s	6d		
The weekly bill 16s 4d. Spent at the Cow 9d.			17s	1d
12 Gave at the Sacrament				6d
Of John Daff at J. Kendall's by bill	11s	6d		
15 Of Mr J. Birks by bill	13s	6d		
17 To Wilkinson for a day's Gardening			1s	6d
18 Of Mrs Barber, Gosberton Risgate, by bill	9s	6d		
Of Mr Sam. Ward. Bol: a balance	15s			
Paid to -ditto- for flax 12s & Tow 3s			15s	
Of Mr David Trimnel by bills	£4 2s			
By Retail and small bills	£1 1s			
The weekly bill			£1 0s	11¼d
22 To J. Lammin for work &c.			5s	
23 Of Richard Jackson a bill	6s	10d		
24 Half a Year's Window Money			10s	2d
A Quarter's Land Tax			3s	

April 1778 (cont.)

		Received			Paid		
25	By Retail and small bills	£1	7s	6d			
	The weekly bill				£1	7s	4½d
27	The Salary for Wigtoft Poor of Mr Jackson	£4	4s				
28	Of Mr Woods, Bicker, by bill		7s				
	Easter dues to the Revd Mr Powell						8d
29	To Edward Gibson by bill					13s	6d
	Of -ditto- by bill		4s	6d			
[Carried over]		**£74**	**8s**	**3d**	**£34**	**10s**	**9d**

Servants

In regard to our Servants this May Day: we continue on our Maid Mary Goodyer as usual at £3 3s 0d. I have parted with J. Harmston & have hired a Son of J Barret's, Bicker Fenn, at £2 2s 0d. The lad seems active & capable & I hope will do. I with pleasure note that Mr Shilcock the assessor tells me such servants as mine who are instrumental towards their Master's Business are exempt from the late new heavy Tax on Male Servants. May 19. 78.

[f.30]
May 1778

		Received			Paid		
Brought forwards		**£74**	**8s**	**3d**	**£34**	**10s**	**9d**
1	Of J. Berry, Donington, by bill		10s	6d			
2	To Mr Wm Wells a bill					9s	
	Of -ditto- by bill		7s	6d			
	By Retail and small bills		16s				
	The weekly bill					15s	10¾d
4	3 Chaldrons of Coals at 24s (2 Loads)				£3	12s	
	Porterage 2s. Ale for the Porters 1s.					3s	
9	The Salary for Bicker Poor of Mr Wilton	£4	4s				
	Of Mr Northern, Bicker, by bill		11s				
	By Retail and small bills	£1	5s				
	The weekly bill				£1	5s	2¼d
	To Mr Lynch, Druggist, in full				£3	14s	6d
12	To J. Harmston a Year's Wages				£2	10s	
	To -ditto- a Gratuity					2s	6d
	Of Samuel Brown, Swineshead Fen Houses	£1	11s	6d			
	Of Mr J. Hanley, Swineshead, by bill		8s	6d			
	A small Fish skin Lancet Case					1s	
14	To Messrs Barret & Robinson in full				£5	7s	6d
	A Paving Hammer & Trowel					1s	6d
16	Of Elizabeth Warsop by bill		12s				
	By Retail and small bills		19s				
	The weekly bill					19s	1d
17	Of Mr Lettin by bill		10s	6d			
	A Couple of tame Rabbits					1s	
19	Cost me at the Cow at Mr Powel's Exhibition					2s	9d
	Of Wm Moor, Taylor, Donington	£1	1s				
23	Of —— Chevens, Gosberton, by bill		12s				
	Of Mr Sandall, Wigtoft, by bill		10s				
	By Retail and small bills		16s	6d			
	The weekly bill					16s	6½d

May 1778 (cont.)	Received			Paid		
25 To Mary Goodyer One Year's Wages due the						
present Old May Day				£3	3s	
26 Of Jacob Tomlin, Quadring, by bill		8s				
Of Mr Bones, Bicker, by bill		13s				
Of Mr Palmer, Quadring, by bill		6s				
Of Mr Copeland, Swaton, by bill	£2	4s	6d			
Of Mr R. Caltrop by bill		5s				
Of R. Hudson, Swineshead, by bill		14s				
28 Church Assessment at 6d per Pound					2s	
Gave at the Charitable Assembly the 27th					2s	6d
29 Carriage of Druggs from Barrit & Co					8s	
One Strike of Oates of Mrs Flinders					1s	6d
Of Wm West by bill		12s	6d			
30 By Retail and small bills	£1	5s	6d			
The weekly bill				£1	5s	8½d
Of Mr John Birks by bill	£1	11s	6d			
[Carried over]	**£97**	**3s**	**3d**	**£59**	**14s**	**11d**

Windows

I have to remark that we have lathed and reeded up two Windows which reduces the Number I pay for to 12, which is an annual saving of 3s 4d. [I] pay now but 17s & before £1 0s 4d. Mr Shilcock told me it was in time.[154]

[f.30v]
Powell the Fire Eater

On Monday May 18th I attended the long famous Mr Powell's exhibition (at the Cow). I cannot say that it came up to his Bill or our expectations, yet what he really & fairly does, is amazing. He is now above 70, and has performed in this way above 50 years, hence some allowances is due to his Years, as I make no doubt his performances were more dextrous in his Younger Time. A set of us staid with him some hours after; he seems but a very moderate companion, for the variety of scenes and company he must have pass'd through, and moreover is a good deal of a Sloven. He showed us his large Silver Medal the Royal Society gave him in 1751. The Motto chosen by Sir Hans Sloane I much admire, viz. Mors aliis sed vita mihi.[155] I conceive he has by long Practice enured himself to extraordinary heat, but he does not absolutely lick the Iron Red Hot and his charcoal he mouths very tenderly. I ventured to ask him if he was sensible of heat, he acknowledged he was, and sometimes by chance burnt himself; he excused himself through his age & retired to rest. I believe he was afraid we should press him with too many questions – there have been doubts, whether he be the heretofore famous Fire Eater, but for my part I have not the least doubt about it. At present he is rather in a reduced situation, travelling without a Servant &c. whereas he formerly had a Carriage & was well attended. He told us he had been stripped of all his Property in France, on what account I know not. He appears to

---

154 Windows had been taxed since 1696, but by Flinders's era, and in the absence of an income tax, virtually everything else from wigs to dogs incurred a tax, particularly during time of war.
155 Loosely, *Death for others, but life for me.*

be much given to drink, not often sleeping Sober. He also performs dexterity of Hand, but I have seen these done equally well before.[156]

Court of Requests

I am sorry to note, that Lord Exeter, thinking that our act infringed on his Priviledges as Lord Paramount of the Soke of Kirton, has procured a Repeal of the same; indeed his Court is to be held every 3 Weeks at Kirton, but from what I have yet learnt its Powers are inadequate to any good purposes to the Community.[157]

Books

As I was not possessed of a single Law Book, I thought the most usefull ones I could purchase would be Burn's Justice, which I have just got, in 4 volumes octavo. These contain a summary of the whole English Law, & any particular is easily referable to; they are rather expensive, but quite necessary to every Man who would wish to know any thing of the Laws whereby he is governed.[158]

I also got at the same time Truslers Cronology, a very usefull and extremely compendious little Book.[159] Also the Pocket Farrier[160] – I can say but little to this, but think each[161] of these ought not to bear the price they are sold at. (June 2.)

[f.31]
June 1778

		Received			Paid		
Brought over		£97	3s	3d	£59	14s	11d
1	Of Mr Harness, Ball Hall, by bill	£2	1s	6d			
	Of Benjamin Fallowell, Gosberton Risgate, by bill	5s					

---

[156] Robert Powell. Harry Houdini mentions Powell and reproduces one of his advertisements: "SUM SOLUS: Please observe that there are two different performances the same evening, which will be performed by the famous MR POWELL, FIRE-EATER, FROM LONDON who has had the honor to exhibit, with universal applause, the most surprising performances that were ever attempted by mankind, before His Royal Highness William . . . at Windsor Lodge May 7th, 1752 . . . before Sir Hans Sloane and several of the Royal Society, March 4th, 1751, who made Mr Powell a compliment of a purse of gold, and a fine large silver medal, which the curious may view by applying to him . . . N.B. He displaces teeth or stumps so easily as to scarce be felt. He sells a chemical liquid which discharges inflammation, scalds, and burns, in a short time, and is necessary to be kept in all families . . ." Houdini says that Powell's career lasted over 60 years, and that his advertisements show that he was performing until shortly before his death, approximately two years after Flinders saw him. Houdini also gives details of some of the ways in which performers like Powell accomplished their feats. See Houdini, *Miracle Mongers and their Methods* (New York, 1920).

[157] The Lord Paramount was the senior civil official of the soke, which was an ancient administrative district similar to a manor. The soke of Kirton (about 7 miles east of Donington) was his area of private jurisdiction – hence his lordship's indignation on hearing of the cosy little arrangement which had sprung up at Donington.

[158] Richard Burn (1709–85), *The Justice of the Peace, and Parish Officer*, first published in 1755. The thirteenth edition in four volumes was published in 1776. It was the standard reference work for JPs of that time.

[159] John Trusler (1735–1820), *Chronology: or, a concise view of the annals of England*, first published in 1769.

[160] Probably Henry Bracken (1697–1764), *The Traveller's Pocket Farrier: or, a treatise upon the distempers and common incidents happening to horses upon a journey*, first published in 1743.

[161] MS 'think' ('each' struck through).

June 1778 (cont.)	Received			Paid		
2 Funeral Expences for the 2 Children (in part)					6s	6½d
4 Of Thos Harrison, Bicker, by bill	£1	3s				
6 Of Henry Robinson, Donington, by bill		5s				
Of Revd Mr Cotes by bill	£1	7s				
By Retail and small bills	£1	7s	6d			
The weekly bill				£1	7s	11¼d
8 Of Mr Hanley, Shoemaker, Donington, by bill		11s	6d			
9 Of Wm Swallow by bill		6s				
12 Of Thos Walker by bill		7s	6d			
13 By Retail &c.		14s				
The weekly bill					14s	1¾d
15 To Mr Morris, Blacksmith, a bill					3s	11d
Interest of Mr S. Ward for £50 from October last						
to June 11	£1	12s	6d			
16 Of Mr A. Burr by bill		7s	6d			
18 Of Mr Bell, Wigtoft, by bill		8s				
Of Wm King, Donington Eaudike, by bill	£1	1s				
Of Mr Christian, Bicker, by bill	£1	1s				
19 Of Mr Lowe by bill		18s	8d			
To -ditto- for 5½ Stone of Pork at 4s 6d				£1	4s	9d
20 By Retail &c.	£1	5s				
The weekly bill				£1	5s	1d
23 To Martin Cottam for Weaving 26 Yards of Cloth						
at 9d per Yard				£1	0s	6d
Received of -ditto- by bill		17s				
Gave Mrs Trimnell's Maid the 22d					1s	
24 One double Linnen Girt of J. Strapps					1s	4d
Gave Mr Green's Servant Maid the 23d						6d
Of John Newton by bill		12s	6d			
To -ditto- a bill					2s	3d
27 Of the Parish of Pinchbeck a bill	£1	7s				
Of Mr Parker, Bicker Frist, by bill	£2	5s				
Of James Bucknell in part	£1	1s				
Expences of a Journey to Guilsborough					19s	6d
A Present to my Neice Henny					5s	6d
A Year's Insurance Money to the Sun Fire Office					9s	
28 By Retail and small bills		13s	6d			
The weekly bill					13s	4¾d
30 Of Mrs Moor by bill		15s	6d			
To -ditto- for Teaching the Children to this day					13s	10d
Of Mr Disney, Quadring, in part	£1	1s				
[Carried over]	£129	17s	5d	£69	4s	1¼d

[f.31v]

Bird Cassowar[162]

May 26. Being the Fair an opportunity offered of seeing that large & Beautifull Bird, from Java. Tis reckoned the 2d in magnitude among Birds. I have a good description together with a Cut in the Christian's Magazine, 'tis a great Curiosity.

---

162 Cassowary: a large cursorial bird, related to the ostrich (*OED*).

Mare

The Mare which I have rode 3 years, but very ill suiting me, especially in the Winter, I sold this Fair. I expected to loose considerably by her; and indeed I have. I gave £14 14s and sold her but for £9 14s (loss £5 for 3 years use) – but indeed I believe it was her worth – since which my Brother S. Ward has let me[163] have a strong Galloway,[164] but upon about 10 days' trial, I have returned him as unsound and not able to do my Business, since which he has let me have a four year old Mare which I like much, and hope she will do, he asks £14 14s.

Family Increase

Early in the Morn of May 28 my wife was delivered of 2 Sons John & Samuel. I thank God she seems doing very well, but as she wanted about 6 weeks of full time the Children are both dead; one the same day, and the other the next, and they were intered in one Coffin on Sunday May 30. I must not omit my humble gratitude to Divine Mercy for sparing my Partner through these perilous times and also at the same time for not burthening me with the additional Care of more Children; she has now had 4 Children in about 11 Months.

Donington Assembly

May 27. Being the little Fair, was held a Charitable Assembly[165] at the School Chamber. A great deal of genteel company more so than I ever expected to see in Donington. The preceeding Year it was for the Benefit of Mrs Burgess, this year to be divided among several in Distress. I was called away early in the Evening on account of my wife's Illness.

Dislocated Radius, Thursday May 29

One R. Holmes, Bicker, dislocated the upper end of the Radius. I found it exactly in the same manner as Ketton's (see July 25, 1777) and reduced it much to my own and my Patient's satisfaction.

Money Matters, June 11

I made up the money Mr S. Ward has of me £100, for which he has given me a Bond at 5 per Cent per Annum bearing date as above. Also he had a further sum of me on a particular emergency on a Note only, as he proposes paying this in October. How ought my gratitude to be again warmly renewed for these gracious & unmerited Mercies. Securities in these precarious times ought to be scrupulously weighed – but from the testimonies he has shown I do not doubt his. June 15, 78.

[f.32]
July 1778

		Received			Paid		
Brought over		**£129**	**17s**	**5d**	**£69**	**4s**	**1¼d**
	To my Wife of the 6th of May				£2		
2	To Mary Tunnard for Nursing					16s	
4	The weekly bill				£1	2s	7d

---

163 MS 'my'.
164 A small but strong breed of horses, originally from Galloway (*OED*).
165 At this period "assembly" invariably meant a ball of the Jane Austen variety.

July 1778 (cont.)	Received			Paid		
By Retail and small bills	£1	2s	6d			
6	Of Mr Lammin, Donington, by bill		10s	6d			
9	Of Uriah Castor by bill		11s				
11	Of Mr Pillings, Bicker, by bill		15s				
Of Mr Jarvis, Bicker, by bill		14s	6d			
Remainder of Mary Twell's bill		4s				
By Retail and small bills		16s				
The weekly bill					15s	10d
12	Of Mr Elveson by bill		14s				
13	Of John Sivers by bill		12s				
Of Mrs Broughton (late Bennit), Bicker	£1	18s				
Paid to -ditto- a bill					10s	
Horse Hire to Bolingbroke twice &c.					6s	6d
16	Of Mr Elsey, Bicker, by bill		14s	6d			
17	Carriage of Druggs from London					3s	
18	By Retail and small bills		16s	6d			
The weekly bill					16s	8½d
19	Of Henry Everit Junior		10s	6d			
To John Wells, Shoemaker, a bill					6s	2d
20	To Ed. Gibson a bill (funeral expences)					9s	
21	Of Mrs Edwards a bill		6s	6d			
25	Land Tax one quarter to Mr Elveson					3s	
By Retail and small bills		17s	6d			
The weekly bill					17s	9d
A Pair of Linnen Hose of Mr Weeks					2s	4d
26	Of Samuel Ashton by bill		5s				
28	Remainder of James Bucknell's bill		3s				
29	Mr Dove's Man's bill of Mr Harvey		13s				
Subscription to Mr Wilton's Paraphrase on the						
Liturgy					3s	6d ·
Trifles in Charity &c. during the Month						10d
[Carried over]	£133	1s	5d	£77	17s	3¾d

[f.32v]

Bicker Feast, Monday June 22

I dined [and] spent the afternoon & Evening at Mr Trimnel's and the 23d went in the afternoon and spent the Evening at Mr Green's. As we had no invitation to Mr Jarvis's, I imagine he has now quite dropt it.

Guilsborough Journey, June 24

I had dropt all thoughts of accompanying my Brother to fetch his Son from School, but coming round this way with the Wiskey[166] to call on me upon hazard, · I ventured for once this considerable Journey.[167] We set off from Donington in afternoon of Wednesday June 24 and observed the Solar Eclipse during our going to Bourn which we reached about 6 o clock. It was above 20 miles about for his coming by Donington; it would have been even nearer if we had returned by Spalding again. We got tea, & staid scarce an hour, when we went through

---

166 An open, one-horse cart.
167 A village about 10 miles north-west of Northampton and just under 70 miles from Donington.

Deeping for Peterborough which we did not reach till near 11. Here we slept at the Talbot inn, not much liking our treatment. We did not get off before seven Thursday June 25 and we reached Oundle (12 Miles) very little before 10. Here we breakfasted comfortably at Mr Ellis's, the Talbot inn, and met with very civil treatment while our Mare rested. We walked about the town, which is nearly as large as Spalding, but has a very dull appearance and many of the Buildings mean. The country is delightfull travelling, the Prospects very extensive, and charmingly diversified, with beautifull Seats & Villages. Northamptonshire has been termed the Garden of England, and indeed it is a sweet country. We passed through Thrapston, a good market town 8 Miles from Oundle; we did not stop there but went forwards to Kettering, a town as large or rather larger than Oundle, and seventeen miles from it. It was 3 o'clock 'ere we reached it. We dined at Mr Roberts's, the White Hart, met with very good accommodations, refreshed ourselves, got barbered &c. Hitherto we had travelled on Turnpike road only, but now we had 15 miles of very cross country road to Guilsborough. We did not get off untill turned of 5, and after many twinings and going out of our Road several times, we reached Guilsborough somewhat after 10. In our return we got better informed of this road, which I will now note down for future caution. About 3 miles from Kettering we pass near the town of Broughton leaving it on the left, about 2 or 3 Miles further we pass thro the town of Ould;[168] further on through the Town of Scaldwell (which last we wrongly omitted, and went through Lamport, considerably too much to the right of us), we now pass on to Brixworth, a considerable village, passing very near to the town but leaving to the left (this Town we wrongly passed through, which led us to another puzzling village called Spratton which we passed through, though some Miles to the left of our right road). We now passed over a kind of common to a little Village called Creighton,[169] about 2 miles from Guilsborough. We made [f.33] (I dare say) 20 Miles, of what ought not to be above 15. As my Brother had been twice before, I wonder he should not find it better. It was so late, part of Mr Clark's family were gone to rest, but he was so complisant as to rise again.[170] I found them very agreable good sort of people as far as one can judge of a family in so short a stay. We had some agreable walks the next morning, Friday June 26. Sir Thomas Ward[171] has a seat in the Village, an exceeding pretty place; we saw his Gardens, and indeed were introduced to the Knight himself, who very affably & Politely asked up to dine with him, but this our time would by no means admit off. I heartily wished we could have stayed a day or 2 in a situation so exceeding fine (supposed to be one of the Highest parts in the kingdom)[172] and among Gentlemen so very obliging and Worthy, but above all I wished to stay that I

---

[168] The village of Old.
[169] Creaton.
[170] Revd John Clarke MA, Master of Guilsborough Grammar School from c.1769 until his death in 1811. "At Guilsborough, in the County of Northampton (a most healthy Air, and pleasant Situation) Young Gentlemen are Boarded, and Taught the Latin and Greek Languages, at Fourteen Pounds a Year, One Guinea Entrance, by the Rev. John Clarke . . ." (*Northampton Mercury*, quoted in Ethel L. Renton and Eleanor L. Renton (comp.), *Records of Guilsborough, Nortoft and Hollowell, Northamptonshire* (Kettering, 1929), 98).
[171] Sir Thomas Ward (1717–1778), High Sheriff of Northamptonshire 1761 in which year he was knighted by George III (*Records of Guilsborough*, 91).
[172] Although the locals might have liked to believe this, it appears to have no basis in fact!

might have traversed Naseby Field but 4 miles from Guilsborough where[173] Martial relicts are to this day frequently picked up; but as I was obliged to be at Donington on Saturday, we left Mr Clark's about 10½ & reached Kettering about 2, where[174] we dined. We now walked about this town, to the church &c. which is a fine Spire. I think I never saw a church yard so full of graves as this is. I think Kettering a better built town than Oundle. We left Kettering about 4 nor stopt untill we reached Oundle about 9, where[175] we supped & slept. We got off early in the Morn, viz. 5 o'clock, and reached Peterborough by 8 where[176] we comfortably refressed ourselves with Coffee at the Angel Inn, not chusing to Visit our old quarters. We got from Peterborough soon after nine, nor stopped till we reached Spalding about 2 o'clock; my Brother leaving Henny at our House, in the Evening came forwards with the Wiskey, and I reached home about 9 o'clock. They returned to Spalding that night, which I was sorry for, as it proved Stormy and they were obliged to take up at Gosberton. I thank God I found my family all well, but the usual allay (a labour had happened in the interval), Mrs Samuel Pike. I do not recollect that I ever before this Journey slept 3 succeeding nights from Donington (since I begun Business). I have two other circumstances to remark, viz. that the common People in Northamptonshire are much more civilized & courteous than in our vulgar part of the Kingdom and that in those inland towns there does not appear half the hurry and bustle, and that you meet by far fewer travellers than in our towns and roads.

My Wife's Journey to Bolingbrook, Sunday July 5
My Wife made a Visit along with her Brother Samuel to her friends at Bolingbrook and returned the Sunday following. Mr Ward returned on the Mare I have had upon trial, as I found she will not suit me, as she leaps, nor will stay long in any ground; so that from this time I have been without a horse and have made an agreement with Mr Harvey from this Date.

[f.33v]
Agreement with Mr Harvey
On Wednesday July 29, 78 I made an agreement with Mr Harvey to find me a Horse any time when I want. He asked me £5 5s 0d per Annum, which I think very reasonable and a considerable saving to me both of Money, Trouble, Hazard &c. As I begun to have horses of him from July 5 the agreement takes place from that date; I have found no inconvenience hitherto, but how we shall manage about night work I have not yet experienced.

Commentary on the Liturgy
Wednesday July 29, 78. A Revd Mr Wilton being at Donington on his Journey soliciting subscriptions to a Commentary on the Liturgy he has written, I amongst many others put down my Name with 3s 6d the money paid down. He

---

173 MS 'were'.
174 MS 'were'.
175 MS 'were'.
176 MS 'were'.

appears a very sensible clever man, but I think somewhat unsteady;[177] he has travelled almost the Island over, and has collected he tells us upwards of 16000 Subscribers, an amazing Number. If well executed the work may prove of general utility – it is in quarto. We are to pay 5s more on the delivery of the Book which he thought would be in October.

Theatrical Magazine
In the beginning of September 1778 we begun to take the above Monthly work. Each Number contains a Tragedy, Comedy & Farce, with 2 good engravings. It is certainly the cheapest way of collecting Plays yet published; the Print is small and rather too crouded, but this must be expected from its cheapness. There are 22 Numbers Published before I began; which I am afraid I must have, to be compleat.

Whale, Monday September 21, 78
That enormous and in these parts of the world uncommon Fish a Whale being chased on shore from Boston Deeps by the crew of the King's Smack or Cutter, & brought up the Witham[178] to very near the town of Boston a few days before this date, I made a Journey to Boston, in company with Mr Harvey, to see so uncommon a Creature. I wish we had gone 2 or 3 Days sooner, that is before they had begun to cut him up, as a sight of him entire must have been an amazing curious Spectacle. Even the mess we now saw was curious from its amazing Bulk – when entire he measured 52 feet in length, his tongue as large as a Calf and each finn joining at the Shoulder about two yards long; the Ball of the Bone going into the Pot at the Shoulder, as large or larger than the Human Head. I suppose it was not that species of Whale from whence long whale bone is procured. The older inhabitants report that a whale was thrown up about Butterwick 53 years ago & these are the only ones within memory cast upon these parts of the Lincolnshire coast.

[f.34]
August 1778

Brought over	Received £133 1s 5d			Paid £77 17s 3¾d		
1	By Retail and small bills	17s				
	The weekly bill				16s	9½d
	Of John Barrat, Bicker Fenn, in part	10s	6d			
	Of Luke Tebb, Northorp, by bill	15s				
3	Present to my Nephew John				2s	6d
	Horse Hire & Barrs to Spalding for -ditto-				1s	9d
5	Of Robert Catlin, Quadring Edike, by bill	16s	6d			
	Two Groose of Yellow Gallipots[179]				12s	
	Sugar for Wine 1 Stone & ¼ at 9s				11s	3d
	One Hankerchief of Mr Weeks				1s	2d
7	Of Mrs Shilcock by bills	£2 15s				
	To my wife on the 6th instant				£2	

177 This was to prove truer than Flinders realised at the time, as the entry on 15 March 1779 will show.
178 MS 'Withan'.

August 1778 (cont.)	**Received**			**Paid**		
	Of Richard Cotes Junior by bill	11s				
	To Mrs Worley, Boston, a bill				£1	16s	6d
8	By Retail and small bills	£1	5s			
	The weekly bill				£1	4s	11½d
	25 Yards of Cloth Bleaching					3s	11d
12	Of Rebecca Thomson Junior by bill	5s				
13	Of John Ablewight by bill	12s				
14	Of Mr Jennings, Bicker Gantlet, by bill	19s	6d			
	Of Mrs Thimbleby, Donington, by bill	8s				
	To Mr Hunt a bill in full					18s	11d
	Of -ditto- a bill	16s	6d			
	To Mr Lane, Druggist, a bill					10s	5d
15	Of Benjamin Brand, Wigtoft, by bill	£1	3s			
	Of Mr Stringer, Swineshead, by bill	12s				
	The weekly bill					17s	7d
	By Retail and small bills	17s	6d			
19	Of Thos Berry, Bicker, by bill	5s				
22	By Retail and small bills	£1	2s	6d		
	The weekly bill				£1	2s	8¼d
25	Of John Kenning, Donington, by bill	13s	6d			
27	Of Mr Lee, Donington, by bill	£2				
	Paid to -ditto- for Ale 14 Gallons					17s	
	To -ditto- for my Mare keeping from April 5 to July 5 1778				£1	6s	
29	Of Mr Thos Tenny by bill	£2	10s	6d		
	By Retail and small bills	£1	1s	6d		
	The weekly bill				£1	1s	8½d
30	Of John Bettison by bill	9s	6d			
	Of Mr Rickaby, Kirton Holm	15s				
31	Of Wm Williamson, Quadring Edike, by bill	6s	6d			
	Of John Wells, Cutler, Donington, by bill	6s	6d			
[Carried over]		**£155**	**15s**	**5d**	**£92**	**2s**	**5½d**

Universal Magazine, October 3 1778

I have begun to take in my old Magazine again – as much wanting the Maps of the Seats of War[180] in the Critical & important Crisis of England – & which one cannot obtain from any other channel so well as the Magazines & I believe this is the best published.

[f.34v]
September 1778

		Received			**Paid**		
Brought over		**£155**	**15s**	**5d**	**£92**	**2s**	**5½d**
1	A Man's bill at Mark Wassop's	9s					
2	Of Charles Fever, Hoflit, by bill	£1	4s				
3	Of Mr Crampton, Northorp, by bill	15s					
	To -ditto- for 2 Stone of Honey at 6d lb					14s	
	To -ditto- for Wax 3lb 14oz at 1s 6d. A Pipkin 5d.					6s	3d

---

179 Gallipot: a small earthen glazed pot, used for ointments and medicines (*OED*).
180 American War of Independence.

September 1778 (cont.)	Received			Paid		
4 Of Mr Garner, Donington, by bills	£1	12s	6d			
5 Of John Bartram by bill		12s	6d			
To -ditto- for an Oak Table Tray					3s	
By Retail and small bills	£1	4s	6d			
The weekly bill				£1	4s	7¼d
6 Of Wm Blancher, Hoflit, by bill		5s	6d			
Of Samuel Wise in part		10s	6d			
7 To Messrs Ferneyhough & Wilson in full				£14	4s	
12 Of Mr Harrison, Quadring Fen, by bill		12s				
By Retail and small bills	£1	3s	6d			
The weekly bill				£1	3s	3d
13 Of Mr Shilcock's Man by bill		8s	6d			
15 Of Wm King, Donington Eaudike, by bill		8s				
19 By Retail and small bills		18s	6d			
The weekly bill					18s	4½d
20 Of Mr Pinion, Swineshead, by bill		8s				
21 Journey to Boston cost me					3s	6½d
22 Of Mr Gleed's Servant Maid by bill		7s	6d			
Of Mr Richard Bowles by bill	£1	1s				
23 Of Mr Dunn, Quadring, by bill	£2	8s				
Of Mr Percival, Bicker, by bill		5s	6d			
To Mr Grimbald, Swineshead, a bill					2s	6d
25 Carriage of Druggs from London					3s	2d
Theatrical Magazine 3 Numbers					1s	6d
26 By Retail and small bills	£1	4s	6d			
The weekly bill				£1	4s	4¼d
27 Remainder of J. Barrat's bill		6s	6d			
28 Of a Man at Wm West's by bill		7s				
[Carried over]	**£172**	**6s**	**11d**	**£112**	**11s**	**0d**

Journey to Spalding, October 11

We made a Journey to Spalding, my Brother's Birth Day (the 10th) happening on the Saturday, which being inconvenient on account of the Markett, we excused ourselves untill the Sunday. We spent an agreable day & Evening, and returned home on Monday forenoon, being desirous of reaching home in time to dine at the Wikes Court.

Mr Hall

Friday October 30. My old friend Mr Hall was kind enough to take a ride from Boston to see us. He came unexpected, took a bit of Dinner with us, staid a few hours, and returned in the Evening. He tells me he has some thoughts of passing his Winter in Liverpool.

[f.35]
October 1778

	Received			Paid		
Brought over	**£172**	**6s**	**11d**	**£112**	**11s**	**0d**
1 Four Gallons of Vinegar for Distilling					5s	4d
3 Sold my Mare at our last May Fair to a Dealer for	£9	14s				
To Mr Sharp, Billingborough, for Eight Walnut						
chairs				£3	3s	

October 1778 (cont.)	Received	Paid
By Retail and small bills	£1 15s 6d	
The weekly bill		£1 15s 6½d
Universal Magazine for September		6d
6 One Hat of Mr Hunt		6s 6d
To -ditto- for 3½lb Bees Wax at 20d		5s 10d
10 By Retail and small bills	£1 1s	
The weekly bill ·		£1 0s 9½d
11 To Mr Wilcockson, Druggist, in full		£1 14s
Journey to Spalding cost me		2s 9d
12 To my Wife for a Gown		£1 1s
One Year's Out Rent at the Wikes Court		8s 5d
14 Of Mr Huddlestone, Swineshead, in part	10s 6d	
17 By Retail and small bills	£1 0s 6d	
The weekly bill		£1 0s 7d
Of R. Butcher, Hoflit, by bill	7s 6d	
Of J. Measures, Gosberton, by bill	4s	
Of Mr Jackson, Swineshead Fen Houses, by bill	13s 6d	
Of Mr Crow's Maid, Quadring, by bill	7s 6d	
Of Wm Story, Bicker, by bill	12s 6d	
Of Mr Overton, Quadring, by bill	6s	
Of Mr Jackson Junior, Donington Fenn, by bill	£1 0s 6d	
22 Theatrical Magazine Two Numbers		1s
24 Of Mr Holmes, Bicker, by bill	8s	
By Retail and small bills	18s	
The weekly bill		17s 4½d
26 Half of the Window Money 8s 6d. Land Tax 3s.		11s 6d
Of Mr French by bill	8s	
27 To Stiles Mapletoft for a Year's Shaving and Hair Dressing due the 5th Inst.		12s
Of -ditto- by bill	6s	
29 Of Thos Boots by bill	18s 6d	
To Messrs Barret and Robinson in full		£5 17s
30 To Mrs Maples a bill		£2 15s 3d
Received of -ditto- by bills	£1 6s	
31 Of Thos West, Wigtoft, by bill	13s 6d	
Of Mr Kircum's Housekeeper by bill	5s 6d	
By Retail and small bills	15s 6d	
The weekly bill		15s 7d
[Carried over]	**£195 18s 11d**	**£135 4s 11½d**

Money Matters

Nov 8th. Mr S. Ward on a particular emergency having occasion for 12 Guineas, I let him have that sum, which makes the Money he has had of me above £34 (exclusive of the bond). This he proposes paying in the Spring. He has given me two Notes, the first with Interest.

[f.35v]
November 1778

		Received			Paid		
Brought over		**£195**	**18s**	**11d**	**£135**	**4s**	**11½d**
2	Of Mr R. Bull, Swineshead, in part	£2	2s				
3	Of Tunnard Asplin, Swineshead Fen Houses,						
	in part	£1	1s				
	Of Wm Tinckley by bill		5s				
6	Of R. Hubbard, Donington, by bill in part		10s	6d			
	Theatrical Magazine, 2 Numbers					1s	
7	Universal Magazine for October						6d
	By Retail and small bills	£1	5s	6d			
	The weekly bill				£1	5s	4½d
8	Sacrament Money						6d
	To my Wife on the 6th Instant				£2		
9	Of Mr Grant, Baker, by bill	£1	3s				
	To -ditto- a bill in full				£1	3s	7d
10	To Edward Laykins a bill in full					3s	6d
13	Of Umph: Stimson, Bicker, by bill	£2	1s	6d			
	Of Mr Harmston, Bicker, by bill		9s				
14	Of Mr Abraham Jackson, Swineshead, by bill		14s				
	Of Mr Taylor, Donington Eaudike, by bill		6s	6d			
	By Retail and small bills		16s	6d			
	The weekly bill					16s	7d
16	Of Mr Torry by bill		16s	8d			
20	Of Mr Samuel Pike by bill		5s	6d			
21	Of Mr Burrus, Donington		10s	6d			
	By Retail and small bills		15s				
	The weekly bill					15s	0¾d
27	Carriage of Druggs from Barrit & Co					2s	7d
	The Ladies Diary for 1779						8d
28	By Retail and small bills	£1	5s				
	The weekly bill				£1	5s	0½d
29	Of J. Allvey, Donington, by bill		12s				
[Carried over]		**£210**	**18s**	**1d**	**£142**	**19s**	**4¼d**

Mr Daubney, Thursday December 24 1778.

Mr J. Daubney Junior, Butcher, fixed here (in the house lately occupied by Mr
Wm Ward) about 2 months, unhappily ended his mortal existence by Drowning
in one of the Engine drains in the Fenn,[181] on this day about 10 at night. He was
observed to be very unhappy & had given suspicious hints for some days
preceeding – which unfortunately were too little regarded. Various reasons are
suspected concurring to this unhappy affair, as a Marriage contrary to his inclina-
tion (for he had Married a lady of Sutton at the time of his fixing here), his Business not answering to his expectation as was supposed & several other reasons.
As he left his watch & Money in his desk, it shows his intention before he left
home: which was between 9 & 10 at night, telling the boy he should be home

---

181 Fenland drainage scoops and pumps were later driven by steam engines – but at the time Flinders
was writing, wind-powered machinery would have been the only technology available (T. W.
Beastall, *The Agricultural Revolution in Lincolnshire* (History of Lincolnshire VIII, 1978), 64).

presently. He was found the following Morn early drowned, the water scarce 2 feet deep. I attended the funeral Sunday December 27.

[f.36]
December 1778

		Received			Paid		
	[Brought over]	**£210 18s**	**1d**		**£142 19s**	**4¼d**	
4	Theatrical Magazine, 2 Numbers				1s		
5	Of Mr Wilkinson by bill	£1	4s				
	To -ditto- for Meat 6s 8d. -ditto- Hog's Lard 3s 4d.				10s		
	By Retail and small bills		12s	6d			
	The weekly bill				12s	7¼d	
	Nine Universal Magazines				4s	6d	
8	Of Mr Gleed by bills	£3	3s				
	To -ditto- a bill				5s		
9	Of Mr Sweeting, Quadring, in part		5s				
12	Of Elizabeth Wassop, Donington, by bill		10s	6d			
	By Retail and small bills		12s	6d			
	The weekly bill				12s	5½d	
13	Of Mr R. Smith, Asperton, by bill		9s	6d			
	Of James Clark, Donington, by bill		7s				
14	Of Mr Whitehead by bills	£3	12s				
18	A Tin Oven 7s. A Wheel mending 3s.				10s		
19	By Retail and small bills	£1					
	The weekly bill				£1	0s	0¾d
22	Of John Speed by bill		4s	8d			
	To - ditto's - wife for Milk				4s	8d	
26	Of Mr Love, Swineshead, by bill	£7	7s				
	By Retail and small bills	£1					
	The weekly bill				£1	0s	0¾d
30	Of Mrs Sudbury's Man, Hale Fen		7s				
	One Chaldron & ½ of Coals at 25s				£1	17s	6d
	Expences of -ditto-				3s	11d	
	Two Post Letters 14d. Writing Paper 10d.				2s		
31	Gave in Christmas Boxes				2s		
	My 6th Part of the Estate purchased by the Tenant Mr Marshall	£38	6s	8d			
	Paid Expences relating to -ditto-				£4	9s	4d
	My Part of the Rent due from -ditto-		7s	4d			
	Expences of the Repairs & Improvements of my House in 1778				£26	17s	4½d
	the particulars are noted at the end of my Debt Book						
		£270	**6s**	**9d**	**£181 12s**	**0½d**	

Receipts and Payments in 7 Years	£1303 9s 3½d	£933 1s 2½d	
Total Receipts and Payments in 8 Years	£1573 16s 0½d	£1116 13s 3d	
Total Gained in 7 Years	£457 2s 9½d		

Through the continuance of the Divine Mercy over us we are arrived to the end of another year & my 8th year of Business which I praise God has been exceedingly Prosperous. I have gained in the way of Business alone above £70 this year, and in the whole 8 Years £457 2s 9½d as by account appears. I praise my mercifull God & humbly hope the same mercy may continue with me & Mine. January 1, 1778.

[f.36v]
Company, Thursday January 14. 1779
I invited a few of my Friends & Neighbour[s] to spend this Evening with me – in the whole I invited 10 – but only the 7 following came, viz. Mr Jarvis, Mr Green, Mr Gleed, Mr Golding, Mr Hunt, Mr Birks and Mr Ashworth. Some staid untill about 2 in the Morn.

House Tax, Saturday Jan 23d 1779
I made my first payment of the new Tax on Houses.[182] The Assessors have charged my House at £5 which is the lowest rate that they could, as houses under that value are exempt: consequently I have 2s 6d more to pay annually. I lowered the window money some time ago more than sufficient to pay this new burden.

Christmas Visits
On Thursday Jan. 21. We spent the Evening with a Party at Mr Shilcock's.
On Wednesday Jan. 27. We had a party of female Visiters.
On Thursday Jan. 28. My Wife was with a party at Mr Pakey's.
On Friday Jan. 29. We were at Mr Gleed's.
On Saturday Jan. 30. – Ditto – at Mr Shepherd's. We were at home by 12 each of these Evenings.
On Monday Feb. 1. We were with a small Party at Mr Birks; we got home in good time.
On Tuesday Feb. 9. I was at Mr Golding's; home by 11.

February 17th 1779.
This day through a favouring Providence I compleated my 29th year, for which I offer my humble gratitude. We expected our friends from Spalding, but my Brother's Business has prevented us that pleasure.

My Brother's Visit
Sunday Feb. 21. My Brother being prevented from seeing us on the 17th by Business, did us the favour of a visit as above. He dined with us but was obliged to leave us in the Evening. My Sister would[183] have done us that favour also, but they could not at that time procure a Wiskey.

Lowe's Lectures
An ingenious man of the name of Lowe has paid this Parish a visit for about a week at Mr Harvey's. I saw his Exhibition on the Evening of March 3. We were highly entertained at his Satirical & Comic Lectures & at his wonderfull deceptions & machinery; he had a good company and the Evening was very agreable. I

---

182 The Inhabited House Tax (1778) was in addition to the Window Tax, being an assessment based on the rateable value of the property.
183 MS 'woud'.

went again on the Saturday Evening but the Repetition was flat in comparison of the other.

[f.37]
January 1779

		Received		Paid		
1	Overplus Retail money	£3	3s			
2	By Retail and small bills	£1				
	The weekly bill			£1	0s	2½d
4	Of Mr Trickett in part of the Parish account	£5	5s			
	Universal Magazine for December					6d
	Flannell for an under Waistcoat				1s	6d
	Spinning 1lb of fine flax				1s	
5	Of J. Kendall in part of his bill		10s			
	Of Jos. Wright Junior by bill		10s	6d		
6	Of John Chamberlain by bill		10s	6d		
7	Sugar 3lb at 6d for Shop use				1s	6d
	Of John Brown, Donington, by bill		15s			
9	Of Mr Spinks, Wigtoft, by bill	£1	15s			
	By Retail and small bills		17s	6d		
	The weekly bill				17s	5¾d
15	Theatrical Magazine, two numbers				1s	
16	A Magazine for November (omitted before)					6d
	By Retail &c	£1	3s			
	The weekly bill			£1	2s	11¾d
18	Of Mr Morris, Bicker Mill, by bill	£2	17s	6d		
	Common Writing Paper 1 Quire					7d
19	A large Map of Europe				1s	
23	Land Tax 1 quarter (£3 at 4s per Annum)				3s	
	The New House Tax 3 quarters (at 2s 6d per Annum)				1s	10½d
	Four Grose of Phial Corks & Carriage				1s	3d
	Of Mrs Burr by bill		5s			
	By Retail and small bills	£1	9s			
	The weekly bill			£1	9s	4d
	Of John Thomson, Hostler, by bill		5s	6d		
	To -ditto- for a Christmas Box				1s	
26	Of Mr Broughton, Bicker, by bill		11s	6d		
30	By Retail and small bills	£1	0s	6d		
	The weekly bill			£1	0s	9¾d
31	Of Francis Horn by bill		6s			
	Trifles during the Month				1s	8d
	Spining one Pound of fine flax				1s	
		£22	**4s**	**6d**	**£6**	**8s**	**2¼d**

Books
In the latter end of March I sent a Box of Books to Mr Hollingworth[184] of Lynn in order to have them bound, they were as follows: British Biography, 80 Nos to be bound in 8 Volumes; some few Nos of this work are wanting, which I have

---

[184] Probably T. Hollingworth, bookseller and publisher of Lynn, c.1748–c.1769. This entry confirms Plomer's suggestion that he was in business later than 1769 (Plomer).

ordered him to procure. Beauties of England, 2 vols (26 Nos compleat) in 2 Volumes, & 2 Years Universal Magazines.

Mr Matthew Hursthouse, April 3 1779[185]

Called of us having been to Spalding & Fleet. He paid me 14s being what was due to me of Mr Osborn's Rent up to Mr Marshall's purchase & which is the last I am to receive during Mr M. Hursthouse's Life.

[f.37v]
February 1779

		Received			Paid		
Brought over		£22	4s	6d	£6	8s	2¼d
1	Lost at Cards at Mr Birks's &c.					1s	6d
	Of John Pasmoor, Quadring, by bill		10s	6d			
4	Of Mr Sewerds, Quadring, by bill	£1	5s				
	Mrs Sharmon's bill of Northorp		7s	6d			
5	Theatrical Magazine, 2 Numbers					1s	
6	Of Mr Tenant, Bicker Gauntlet, in part	£1	1s				
	Of John Clark, Quadring, by bill		5s				
	By Retail and small bills		17s				
	The weekly bill					16s	11½d
	To my Wife				£2		
	Universal Magazine for January						6d
8	Chaldron of Coals 25s. Porterage & Ale 14d.				£1	6s	2d
9	Of Mr Barnet, Bricklayer, in part	£1	1s				
11	Of Mr Spendley by bill		5s	6d			
13	Carriage of Druggs 4 Stone					3s	
	Of Henry Torks, Bicker, by bill		11s				
	Of Mr Wm Gee, Hale, by bill		10s	6d			
	Of John Mayhorn in part		12s				
	By Retail and small bills	£1	2s				
	The weekly bill				£1	2s	2½d
17	Of Thos Stokes, Northorp, by bill		15s				
	Of Mr Birks, the late R. Bell's bill	£1	8s	6d			
18	Of Mr Parker (Joiner) by bill		8s	6d			
19	To Mr J. Weeks in full					6s	5d
	Of -ditto- by bills in full	£5	17s				
20	By Retail and small bills		19s	6d			
	The weekly bill					19s	6¼d
	A Pair of Shoes of John Wells					6s	
21	To my Brother an account					6s	
	Of Mr Caffen, Swaton, by bill		16s				
27	Of Mr Lamb, Quadring, by bill		6s				
	By Retail and small bills	£1	5s				
	The weekly bill				£1	5s	2½d
		£42	**8s**	**0d**	**£21**	**1s**	**3d**

My Aunt's Death

I am sorry to remark that my Aunt Shilcock going on Horseback to attend Mrs Stocks's (her late Husband's Sister) funeral at Burtoft: in the town of Wigtoft

---

185 His maternal grandfather was Matthew Hursthouse, but this is probably his son.

somebody fired a gun, by which her Mare took an affright & she was thrown backwards. I saw her a few hours afterwards, found no external hurt, but she raised much blood & seemed much hurt inwardly at the Stomach or Lungs. I bleed her & administered some medicines. The next day I found her very bad, a fever of the Putrid kind coming fast on, & I thought she would not live & so it happened, for she died in the next night. The accident happened Tuesday April 13th '79 & she died early on Thursday Morn, & I attended the funeral on Friday Evening. I doubt the younger part of her Family will much want her.

[f.38]
March 1779

		Received			Paid		
Brought over		£42	8s	0d	£21	1s	3d
1	Of Martin Wise, Donington, by bill	£1	10s				
	Paid to him a bill for Sundries					14s	6d
3	Cost me at Mr Lowe's Exhibition					3s	
	Theatrical Magazine, 2 Numbers					1s	
5	Of Mr Lee, Donington, by bill		17s	6d			
	Spent at the Cow						6d
6	Of Mr Palmer, Quadring, by bill		13s				
	By Retail and small bills		12s	6d			
	The weekly bill					12s	5¼d
7	Of Thomas Roberts, Gosberton Risgate, by bill		14s				
	Attending Mr Lowe's Exhibition					1s	
8	Two Handkerchiefs of Mr Hunt					3s	4d
	Two Rush floor matts					1s	3d
11	Of Wm Gaunt, Quadring Fen, in part		10s	6d			
12	Of Mr Carnal, Swineshead, by bill	£1	11s	6d			
13	Universal Magazine for February						6d
	By Retail and small bills		13s				
	The weekly bill					12s	10½d
15	Of Mr Root, Swineshead, by bill	£1	10s	6d			
17	Of Elizabeth Shepherd, Bicker, by bill	£1	1s				
18	Fine flax 1lb Spining					1s	
20	Six Stone Six Pound Pork of Mr Wilkinson at 4s 4d per Stone				£1	7s	10d
	Of John Barret, Bicker Fenn, by bill		8s	6d			
	By Retail and small bills		17s				
	The weekly bill					16s	10½d
22	Remainder of J. Kendall's bill		8s	6d			
24	Of H. Everitt Senior by bill		17s				
	Supplement to the Universal Magazine						6d
27	By Retail and small bills		17s				
	The weekly bill					17s	0¼d
		£55	**9s**	**6d**	**£26**	**14s**	**10½d**

Guardianship

I have to note that on Saturday May 8 '79, Mr Green, Mr Stocks and myself were sworn Guardians to the late Wm Shilcock's 2 Sons & Daughter. I have made a Book to keep our accounts in – there has been a Sale (May 14) and the Cash and Notes are deposited in my hands. I am to be as it were the Steward & they undertake the chief care & management of our Wards. The Eldest Son continues in the farm, the other Son as a Servant with Mr Stocks. The Girl is also at present with him. We hope there will be about £50 each when all debts &c. are paid.

Impostor

I am sorry to remark any additional instances of Deceit and Villainy among mankind, but truth obliges me to note, that we have heard nothing of Mr Wilton and his Commentary on the Liturgy – though the Book was to have been delivered in October.[186] May 15.

[f.38v]

April 1779

		Received			Paid		
Brought forward		**£55**	**9s**	**6d**	**£26**	**14s**	**10½d**
1	Of Mrs Pillings's Servant Man by bill		5s	6d			
2	Of Mr Johnson, Donington Wikes, by bill		19s	6d			
3	Of Mr Matthew Hursthouse, being the last Rent						
	due to me at Maxey		14s				
	Of Wm Moor, Northorp		5s				
	A Set of Fire Irons at Mr Daubney's Sale					17s	9d
	Of Thos Vellum, Gosberton, by bill		12s				
	By Retail and small bills		16s				
	The weekly bill					16s	3¼d
5	Of Mrs Clam by bill		8s				
	Bought of -ditto- an Ash-grate					5s	6d
7	Of Miss Golding by bill	£2	9s				
10	By Retail and small bills		19s				
	The weekly bill					18s	10¼d
11	To Messrs Ferneyhough & Wilson in full				£11		
	Of Mr J. Birks in part	£1	1s				
12	Of Mr Lowe's Servant Maid by bill		12s				
14	Of Mr Percival, Quadring, by bill		8s				
17	By Retail and small bills		17s				
	The weekly bill					17s	1½d
	Earnest Money to Mary Parker					2s	6d
20	To Wm Darcey Earnest Money					2s	6d
21	Of Richard Gray, Brick-Maker, Gosberton		16s				
22	Of Mr Edwards, Donington, by bill	£1	3s	6d			
23	Carriage of Druggs, 7 Stone at 9d					5s	3d
	Gave H. Baumford towards buying a Cow					1s	
	Of Wm Edinborough in part		11s				
24	By Retail and small bills		19s	6d			
	The weekly bill					19s	6d
28	Window Money 8s 6d. Land Tax 3s. House Tax 7½d.					12s	1½d
	Of Thos Speed by bill		5s				
		£69	**10s**	**6d**	**£43**	**13s**	**3d**

Servants

I have to note that we have this May changed both our Servants, chiefly from their wanting to raise Wages. We have hired Ann Parker, Daughter of John Parker

---

[186] See 29 July 1778.

farmer in this town, her Wages 55s & 2s 6d received, and Wm Darcey – his Wages 2 Guineas & 2s 6d received. I hope they will both suit us, if one can so soon judge.

Family Increase
With gratefull acknowledgement to Divine Mercy, I note that this day Saturday May 22 at 10½ in the Morning, my wife was safely delivered of a Daughter, a fine Girl,[187] and both are at present in a hopefull way.

Journey to Boston
Wed. June 9 '79. I took a ride to Boston, almost on purpose to dine with Dr Knolton[188] – which I did, and spent an agreable afternoon & returned in the Evening. Also paid my insurance Money – I did some other little Bussiness.

[f.39]
May 1779

		Received			Paid		
Brought forward		**£69**	**10s**	**6d**	**£43**	**13s**	**3d**
1	Of Mr Millington, Donington, by bill	£1	9s				
	To -ditto- for High-way Assessment due 1774					1s	3d
	Of Mr Weeks's Man Servant, Wigtoft, by bill		6s	6d			
	By Retail and small bills		18s				
	The weekly bill					18s	0¼d
3	Of Wm Swallow, Donington, by bill		13s				
5	Of John Bettison, Donington, by bill		12s	6d			
	Of Revd Mr Cotes by bill		10s				
7	Theatrical Magazines 4 Numbers					2s	
	By Retail and small bills	£1	5s				
	The weekly bill				£1	5s	0¼d
10	Of Mrs Godley, Bicker Gauntlet, by bill	£3	6s				
	Of Mrs Emmitt (late Maples) by bill		5s	3d			
	To -ditto- for 4 Strike of Malt at 33s per Quarter					16s	6d
	and 2½lb of Hops at 10d					2s	1d
11	Of Mr Sharp Junior, Hoflit, by bill		10s	6d			
12	To Mary Goodyear a year's Wages				£3	3s	
	To Thos Barrat a year's Wages				£2	2s	
13	Of Mr Caswell, Quadring, by bill	£1	6s				
	Of R. Gray, Gosberton, by bill		15s	6d			
	Of Mrs Burgess by bill		9s				
15	Of Mr J. Wires, Swineshead Fen Houses	£1	1s				
	Of James Taylor, Donington Eaudike, by bill		5s	6d			
	By Retail and small bills		15s	6d			
	The weekly bill					15s	4d
17	Of Mr Sharp, Hoflit, by bill		5s				
18	To Mr Wilcockson, Druggist, in full				£4	18s	
19	Of Henry Cook, Donington, by bill	£1	12s				
20	Of Mr Injelaw, Quadring Eaudike, by bill		14s				
22	To Messrs Barrit & Robinson in full				£4	0s	6d

---

187 Susanna.
188 Dr Knowlton of Boston. See n.113 above.

May 1779 (cont.)	Received		Paid	
Retail &c. 17s 6d. Weekly bill	17s	6d	17s	5¾d
23 Of Mr Bee, Bicker Gauntlet	£1 1s			
Of Mrs Dodd	5s			
24 Of Wm Cole, Wheelwright, by bill	£1 7s			
26 Half a dozen knives and forks			4s	9d
The Salary for Wigtoft Poor	£4 4s			
Of Mr Harrison, Alder church Fenn	£1 13s	6d		
Of Mr Marsh, Quadring, by bill	£1 9s			
Of Jos. Clark, Swineshead Fen Houses	12s	6d		
Of Mrs Gee, Swineshead, by bill	£1 1s			
Paid Mr S. Ward for the use of a Mare			14s	
To -ditto- for 12 Pound of 8d Flax			8s	
28 Of Mr Jackson, Bicker, by bill	10s	6d		
Of J. Kendall one year's Interest of £6 6s due				
April 5	6s			
Of Robert Smeeton at Mr Harvey's	6s			
29 Of Mr Nettleton, Swineshead, by bill	£1 9s			
Of Wm King, Donington Eaudike, by bill	£1 8s			
The Salary for Bicker Poor	£4 4s			
Of Mr Green, Bicker, by bill	£3 3s			
Retail &c. £1 3s 6d. The weekly bill £1 3s 8¼d.	£1 3s	6d	£1 3s	8¼d
Carried over	**£111 10s**	**3d**	**£65 4s**	**10½d**

[f.39v]

Journey to Sleaford[189]

Monday June 14. I was obliged to make a Journey to Sleaford, being one of the Witnesses to the Will of the late Mr Gee of Swineshead, which was proved this day. I was required to give evidence of the same. Had a disagreable rainy Journey home.

Bicker Feast

Tuesday June 22. We dined and spent the Evening with an agreeable Company at Mr Trimnell's & on Wednesday 23 we did the same at Mr Green's.

Money Matters, June 28

Mr Ward of Bolingbrook being over I have made[190] up the money he has of me £180 which at present is secured in the following manner, viz. £100 on Bond, on the back of which bond is a note of £51 10s purporting[191] to be secured in the same manner as the Bond, & the Remainder, viz. £28 10s he has given me another note for. I have also the possession of the writings of his Land, as a further security; it is to continue in this manner untill next June, when if he has occasion for it longer I am (if I can, which I hope I shall be able with God's Blessing) to make it up £200 when he will give me a Mortgage on his Land for that sum at £5 per Cent per Annum.

My Brother having requested the Loan of 10 Guineas for a few months, I have sent it him for which he has given me a Note dated June 29, so that I am at

---

189 About 16 miles north-west of Donington.
190 MS 'make'.
191 MS 'purpoting'.

present low in Cash, tho' I thank God, money has come in very well lately, notwithstanding it is allowed by most that times are very bad.

July 12. Mrs Flinders having also requested of me to assist her with 10 Pounds a few months, I am to have a joint note from her & Mr Thos Pike with Interest to be paid in[192] October or November.

Horse

It not being convenient to Mr Harvey to let me have a Horse as last Year, I have had one upon trial of Mr Clare's of Bicker, and finding him suit have purchased him (Horses being luckily[193] for me at this time very low), Mrs Flinders offering to keep me one again which I have accepted as being most convenient; begun with her on July 1st. The Horse that I have bought is a strong Chestnut one, 6 Years old, a range down the face, Tail nicked, rough hanging mane, his forelegs somewhat bandied. He walks a great pace, and at present carries me easier & better than I ever was carried before – is gentle & has several good properties suitable for me. All that can be said against him, he is not a very handsome one & is a Year or two too old.

[f.40]
June 1779

		Received			Paid		
Brought forward		**£111**	**10s**	**3d**	**£65**	**4s**	**10½d**
May							
30	Of Benjamin Blackwell by bill		13s				
June							
1	Of Miss Twell, by bill		4s	6d			
2	Of Mr Naylor, Gosberton Risgate, by bill		6s				
	Of Mrs Pike Senior by bill		7s				
4	Of Mr Turfit, Kirton Holm, by bill		6s				
	Theatrical Magazine 2 Nos					1s	
	Of Mr Torks, Bicker, some days ago		10s				
5	Of Mr Hooton, Donington Ing, by bill		7s	6d			
	Of Mr Christian, Bicker, by bill		6s	6d			
	By Retail and small bills		15s				
	The weekly bill					15s	1½d
9	Insurance Money to the Sun Fire Office					9s	
	Cost me at Boston					1s	6d
10	Of Mr Crain, Gosberton Belney, by bill		15s	6d			
12	Of J. Wells (Labourer) by bill		7s				
	By Retail and small bills	£1	9s				
	The weekly bill				£1	9s	2½d
13	Of John Smith, Kirk-hill, by bill		10s	6d			
	Remainder of Benjamin Upton's bill		6s				
14	Mare cost me at Sleaford						7d
15	Of Mr Blancher, Swineshead, on account of J. Day		5s				
	Interest Money of Mr S. Ward due the 11th Inst.						
	(£100 at 5 per Cent 1 Year) 4s 2d being deducted	£4	15s	10d			
	Of Mr Lowe, Donington		7s				

---

192 MS 'in in'.
193 MS 'lukily'.

June 1779 (cont.)	Received		Paid		
16 Remainder of Wm Gant's bill, Quadring Fen	13s	6d			
Three Spout Irons of Wm Morris				2s	3d
19 To my Wife on the 6th May			£2		
By Retail and small bills	13s				
The weekly bill				13s	0½d
Of Mr Elverson on the Parish account	£1	5s			
To -ditto- Poor Assessment from Easter 1778 to					
Easter 1779, £4 at 2s 3½d				9s	2d
20 To Mary Tunnard for Nursing &c.				18s	
Received of -ditto- a bill	5s				
21 Of Mr J. Ward by bill	£2	4s			
23 Cost me at Bicker Feast the 22d & 23d				3s	6d
24 Paid to Mr Lowe, Baker, a bill			£2	15s	
Received of him by bill	£2	12s 11d			
26 Retail &c. 17s 6d. Weekly bill 17s 6½d.	17s	6d		17s	6½d
30 Of Mr Kirk, Bicker, by bill	19s				
	£134	**11s 6d**	**£75**	**19s**	**9½d**

Journey to Tidd

On Wednesday July 28, we set off early to see our Freinds at Tidd; got to
Spalding by 7. Breakfasted. My Brother & Jackey went with us; we went on our
horse, they in a Wiskey. We got to Mr De Camps's (to dinner) at Fleet & staid tea
& went to Mr H.'s in the Evening, & staid there untill Friday Morning. We had an
agreable visit. We dined at Spalding and got home in the Evening. My Brother &
Jackey left Mr H. on Thursday afternoon. On Thursday in the forenoon we had
an agreable walk to see the shipping at Peter's Point.

[f.40v]
July 1779

	Received		Paid		
Brought forwards	**£134 11s**	**6d**	**£75 19s**	**9½d**	
June					
30 Of Mr John Birks by bill	£1 11s	6d			
July					
1 Of Mr Boyfield, Quadring Eaudike, by bill	£1 4s				
Remainder of the Parish account of Mr George					
Trickett to Easter 1779	£5 5s				
To my Wife for a Gown			£1 1s		
3 Remainder of the late R. Disney's bill	12s	6d			
Expences of 2 Chaldrons of Coals			4s	4d	
Of John Chevens, Gosberton, by bill	7s				
Retail &c. £1 3s 0d. Weekly account £1 2s 11½d.	£1 3s		£1	2s 11½d	
5 To Mr Parker, Joiner, a bill in full			£4 17s	9d	
Of -ditto- by bill	7s	9d			
To Mr Harvey for a Year's Horse Hire			£5 5s		
Of -ditto- a bill in full	£2 14s	6d			
Of Mary Tunnard for a Table	10s	6d			
Gave in Charity on the 3d Instant			6d		
6 Of Mr Lettin, Carpenter, a bill	£1 2s	6d			
Of Thos Mathers, Donington Eaudike, a bill	£1 1s				
9 Carriage of Druggs from Barrit & Co			3s	6d	

July 1779 (cont.)

		Received			Paid		
	Of Mrs Moor, Donington, by bill	17s	6d				
	To -ditto- for Schooling up to the 17th Inst.				17s	6d	
10	Of Mr Peach, Gosberton, a bill	£1	14s				
	By Retail &c. £1 4s. The weekly bill £1 4s.	£1	4s		£1	4s	
11	To Mr Clare, Bicker, for a Horse				£6	16s	6d
	Of him a bill	£1	1s				
12	Of Mr Thos Pike a bill	£4	1s				
	Of Mrs M. Flinders a Year's Rent due Old Lady Day last	£2	3s				
	Of -ditto- a Physic bill		11s	6d			
	To -ditto- for Leading 9½ Chaldron of Coals				£2	12s	
	Expences of 2 Chaldron of Coals					4s	6d
	Cost me at Gosberton Feast					1s	6d
15	Of Edward Laykins a bill		6s	10d			
	To -ditto- a bill					1s	8d
	Of Mr Fox a bill		12s				
17	A Silver Stock Buckle of Mr Tory					5s	3d
	Retail &c. 15s 6d. Weekly bill 15s 7¾d.		15s	6d		15s	7¾d
18	Wm Smith's Dr's account of Gosberton Overseers		8s				
	To Mr Bowles Church Assessment £4 at 8d					2s	8d
21	Floor Matting six yards & half					4s	11d
22	Of Mr Crosby, Gosberton Risgate, by bill		14s				
	Of Wm West, Donington, a bill		12s	6d			
23	Of Thos Olsop a bill		19s				
	Bees Wax 1lb 6oz, 2s. Matthew's Shoes, 2s.					4s	
24	To Jonathan Warriner, Taylor, a bill				£2	18s	
	Of him a bill	£1	11s	6d			
	Of Mr H. Woods, Bicker, a bill		18s				
	Retail &c. 18s 6d. The weekly account 18s 8d.		18s	6d		18s	8d
26	Land Tax 3s 1 Quarter. A pair of Shoes 6s.					9s	
27	To Mr Albin, Spalding, a bill in full					13s	
31	Expences going to Tidd St Mary's					4s	9d
	Two Glass Salts 3s. Gave my Nephew 2s.					5s	
		£169	**18s**	**7d**	**£107**	**13s**	**4¾d**

[f.41]

August 1779

		Received			Paid		
Brought forwards		**£169**	**18s**	**7d**	**£107**	**13s**	**4¾d**
(July)							
31	Retail &c. 13s. Weekly account 13s 2¾d.		13s			13s	2¾d
(August)							
3	Of the Revd Mr Coates a bill		6s				
7	By Retail and small bills		18s				
	The weekly bill					18s	2¼d
	Of Martin Cottam a bill		15s				
	To -ditto- for Weaving 21 Yards Table Linen				£1	1s	
	To -ditto- for Weaving 17 Yards of Flaxen					7s	
	Theatrical Magazine No 34						6d
9	Of James Hare, Quadring Eaudike, a bill	£1	4s				
10	Of Thos Speed a bill		10s	6d			
14	Of Mr Weeks a bill	£1	11s				

August 1779 (cont.)		Received			Paid		
	To him a bill in full				£1	16s	10d
	By Retail and small bills	£1	0s	6d			
	The weekly bill				£1	0s	9d
16	Of Charles Smith, Shoe maker, in part		10s	6d			
17	Of Thos Chapman, Bicker, a bill		6s	3d			
	To him a bill					5s	6d
18	Of Samuel Bacchus, Donington, a bill		10s	6d			
19	Of Thos Berry, Bicker Mill, a bill		6s				
21	Of John Tunnard, Donington, a bill		15s				
	By Retail and small bills	£1	7s	6d			
	The weekly bill				£1	7s	5¼d
22	Of Mrs Fox, Quadring, a bill		8s	6d			
23	Of Thos Moor, Northorp, a bill		15s				
	Of a Scotchman at Coggles's, Hoflit		5s	6d			
27	Of Rebecca Thompson a bill		10s	6d			
28	By Retail and small bills	£1	9s				
	The weekly bill				£1	9s	
29	To my Wife on the 6th Instant				£2		
	Of Mr Bingley, Hoflit, a bill	£3	3s				
	Of a Stranger at Wm West's		5s				
		£187	**8s**	**10d**	**£118**	**12s**	**10d**

Christening, Friday August 20th

We baptized our young child by the name Susanna, the Sponsors my Sister from Spalding & Mrs Shilcock, Mr J. Ward & Mr Gleed. We had an agreable party. My Sister & Jackey staid with us a few days; my Brother could not come thro' Business.

Visiter

Mrs Langley, my Wife's Mother from Bolingbrook, paid us a Visit this Summer. She came on Thursday July 29 & staid with [us] almost 3 Months.

Health

I have to remark that the Autumnal Sickness has been very severe this Season, not only in the great Number whom it has affected but also in the length of time it has continued. It begun with August & continued to the end of October. I myself have had a worse Autumn in regard to Health than for several [f.41v] years past, having been very poorly for 5 or 6 Weeks with a kind of Bilious Intermittent, sometimes better, at others the Disorder returning again, tho' I thank God never so bad as to keep me two days wholly from my Business. I have taken I think 3 Pukes, & also the Saline Mixture with T. Emet., I thought with considerable advantage, & have lately taken the Bark with Success.[194] At present I am tolerably well, & have a good appetite, but how long I shall continue so I can't tell. I have had so many returns I durst not presume much on a few days' health. November 9 1779.

---

[194] For *Tartarum emeticum*, see n.70 above. Several barks were used for medical purposes, including the grey and red cinchona barks from South America which were used in cases of fever (*Supplement*, 88–89).

September 1779

Brought over	Received £187 8s 10d		Paid £118 12s 10d		
3 Theatrical Magazine two Nos				1s	
Master Wing's bill of Mr Whitehead	18s	6d			
Of Stephen Dalton a bill	11s				
4 Of Mr Garner, Donington Fenn, a bill	18s				
By Retail and small bills	£1 3s	6d			
The weekly bill			£1	3s	5¾d
5 Of Robert Kirk, Bicker, a bill	8s	6d			
8 Remainder of John Thomson's (Labourer) bill	10s	6d			
Worstead 9oz at 3d for Matthew's Stockings				2s	3d
Cloth for Shop use 1s. L: Sugar 2lb -ditto- 18d.				2s	6d
10 Of Mrs Thornhill (late Story), Bicker Gauntlet	£1 1s				
11 By Retail and small bills	£1 0s	6d			
The weekly bill			£1	0s	3½d
13 To Messrs Ferneyhough & Wilson in full			£7	7s	
Various articles of Matthew's Clothing			£1	4s	3¾d
500 Nails in March last for the ceiling				2s	6d
3 Stone of Spanish white[195] for -ditto-				1s	6d
18 Of Mr Edwards, Donington, a bill	11s				
By Retail and small bills	18s	6d			
The weekly bill				18s	6½d
24 Five Nos of the Theatrical Magazine				2s	6d
Of Francis Horn by bills	18s				
25 The late Mr Cookson's account of his Brother	£3 3s				
By Retail and small bills	17s	6d			
The weekly bill				17s	7d
26 Of J. Day near Swineshead Abbey by bills	£1 3s				
27 Of a Man at R. Mead's, Wigtoft	6s				
Of John Wells, Cutler, a bill	7s	7d			
Paid to -ditto- for various Carriages				5s	7d
30 Of Mrs Gunthorp, Donington, a bill	8s	10d			
	£202 13s	9d	£132	1s	10½d

Dislocated Jaw, December 8. 79

I was sent for at night to Thos Cook's wife, Quadring, who had dislocated one side of the lower Jaw with yawning. She had frequently done the same before but always had been able to reduce it herself. It[196] had been out about 2 or 3 hours. I found her mouth gaping open & the jaw somewhat turned to one side. By yawning too wide the jaw gets past its center and slips forwards; by pressing downwards and backwards it was easily reduced. I never met with a similar case – therefore I note it.

[195] Finely powdered chalk used as a pigment (*OED*).
[196] The section from here to the end of the paragraph is inserted on f.42v.

[f.42]
October 1779

		Received			Paid		
Brought over		**£202**	**13s**	**9d**	**£132**	**1s**	**10½d**
2	Of Mr Harvey's Servant Maid		9s	6d			
	By Retail and small bills	£1	7s	6d			
	The weekly bill				£1	7s	8½d
5	To the Bicker Gardener for a day					1s	6d
	To Mr Harvey for a Hat					8s	
6	Of T. Mitchell, Donington, a bill		5s	6d			
	Of Joseph Kircum a bill		9s				
7	8 Yards Irish Cloth at 22d of Mr Harvey					14s	8d
	3 Yards & ¾ of -ditto- at 2s 6d of Mr H.					9s	4d
8	Carrige of Druggs from Wilson & Co					6s	1d
	Of Mr Witton, Gosberton, a bill		5s				
	Six Theatrical Magazines					3s	
9	Of Jos. Taylor, Donington North Ing		8s				
	By Retail and small bill	£1	2s				
	The weekly bill				£1	1s	11d
11	Of Mrs Lowe a bill		10s	6d			
	Copy Rent at the Wikes Court					8s	5d
15	Of Mrs Edwards at the Barr a bill		6s	6d			
	Of Mr Overton's Man, Quadring Eaudike, a bill		7s	6d			
16	By Retail and small bills	£1	5s	6d			
	The weekly bill				£1	5s	4d
18	Of Mr Ding, Gosberton Risgate, a bill	£2	2s				
	Of J. Philips, Gosberton Risgate, a bill		5s				
	Of Abraham Walker, Quadring Eaudike, a bill		12s	6d			
	Of Widow Hudson, Swineshead, a bill		8s				
	Of Mr Joshua Dowse, Swineshead Fen Houses, a bill		5s	6d			
	Of Thos Cook, Quadring, a bill	£1	11s	6d			
19	Of George Ingle, Donington Fenn, in part		10s	6d			
20	To S. Mapletoft of a Year's Barbering due the 5th					12s	
	Of -ditto- a bill		10s	6d			
22	Remainder of Wm Gould's bill		4s	6d			
	Paid for Bleaching Cloth at Sleaford & Carriage					4s	11½d
23	By Retail and small bills		14s	6d			
	The weekly bill					14s	3½d
24	Of Mr Morley's Man, Bicker, a bill		7s	6d			
	Of Mr Trickett, Donington, a bill	£1	6s	6d			
	A Grose of Gally-pots[197] of T. Knight					6s	
25	Of Anthony Robinson, Swineshead, in part	£1	12s				
27	Window Money ½ Yr 8s 6d. Land Tax 3s. House Tax 15d.					12s	9d
28	Bees Wax 3¾lb at 1s 6d					5s	7½d
29	Of John Hall a bill		8s	5d			
	Of -ditto- received by a Milk Score					8s	5d
	The Children's Firing at School					2s	
30	Of Mr Gibson, Carpenter, a bill	£2	4s	3d			
	To -ditto- a bill				£1	9s	6d

197 See n.179 above.

October 1779 (cont.)

		Received		Paid		
	By Retail and small bills	17s				
	The weekly bill				17s	5½d
31	To Mr R. Wilby for 4 Chaldron of Coals			£5		
	Of John Dickenson, Bicker, a bill	9s	6d			
		£223 19s 11d		**£149 0s 10d**		

[f.42v]

November 1779

		Received		Paid		
Brought over		**£223 19s 11d**		**£149 0s 10d**		
3	Of Mr Shepherd a bill	17s				
4	Of Mr Burrus, Cooper, Donington, a bill	£1 7s	6d			
	To -ditto- a bill				9s	
6	Of Mr Clarkson, Excise Officer, a bill	13s				
	Of Mr Jackson, Donington Ing, a bill	£1 1s				
	By Retail and small bills	£1 7s	6d			
	The weekly bill			£1	7s	8¼d
	To my Wife			£2		
11	To Mr Wilcockson, Druggist, in full			£4	2s	
13	By Retail and small bills	17s	6d			
	The weekly bill				17s	5¼d
15	Of Ann Kircum a bill	7s	10d			
18	To Messrs Barrit & Co in full			£4	19s	3d
	Four Brass Candlesticks cost				14s	
20	By Retail and small bills	18s				
	The weekly bill				18s	0½d
25	To Mr Harvey, Draper, a bill in full			£3	17s	6d
	Of -ditto- by bills	15s	6d			
26	Of Mr Spendley by bill	17s	6d			
27	Of Benjamin Wright by bill	14s				
	By Retail and small bills	£1 0s	6d			
	The weekly bill			£1	0s	3¾d
29	Of Mr John Harvey a bill	£1 17s				
	Paid to -ditto- for Cheese				15s	6d
		£236 13s 9d		**£170 1s 6¾d**		

Christmas Entertainments

On Tuesday Jan. 21. 1780. My Wife had her party of Female Visiters, viz. Mrs Shilcock, 2 daughters and a Miss Caltrop; Mrs Birks, Mrs Pakey & Miss Golding. Mrs Whitehead, Mrs Jarvis, Mrs Gleed & Miss Shepherd absent.

On Thursday Jan. 28. 80. I had my Company as follow – Mr Jarvis, Mr Green and son, Mr Trimnell (Mr C. Trimnell absent), Mr Gleed & Taylor, Mr Golding, Mr Whitehead, Mr Hunt, Mr Birks, Mr Ward, Mr Shilcock & Son, Mr Fletcher. We got to Bed between 2 and 3 o'clock. Before I asked my Friends I had been at 3 places, viz. Mr Gleed's, Mr Whitehead's and Mr Fletcher's.

Matthew's Schooling

Monday Jan. 24. 1780. We entered Matthew at Mr Whitehead's School for Reading only, for the first year. As I do intend to take the Benefit of the Charity I sent a handsome entrance, viz. 10s 6d.

[f.43]
December 1779

		Received			Paid		
	Brought over	**£236**	**13s**	**9d**	**£170**	**1s**	**6¾d**
3	Of Mr Stafford, Quadring, a bill		7s				
4	Of John Joys, Swineshead, a bill		9s				
	Of Mr Wilton, Bicker, a bill		17s	6d			
	By Retail and small bills	£1	2s	6d			
	The weekly bill				£1	2s	7½d
	High Way Assessment £4 at 2d						8d
6	Of Wm West, Donington, a bill		12s	10d			
7	To Mr Tricket Poor Assessment 1 Year						
	£4 at 1s 6d due Easter 1778					6s	
8	Of Master Molson at Mr W.		5s				
10	Carriage of Druggs from London					6s	6d
	Of Mrs Lowe, Donington, a bill		8s				
11	Of Mr Dixon, Donington, a bill		14s	6d			
	Of Mr Holbourn, Wigtoft, a bill		9s	6d			
	By Retail and small bills		13s				
	The weekly bill					12s	10½d
	Theatrical Magazine (No 38)						6d
13	To Mr Barnett, Mason, a bill				£3	7s	
	Received of -ditto- a bill	£2	14s	6d			
	Of Mr Morley, Bicker, a bill	£3	12s				
	To Sarah Rouse for Spining					2s	
18	Of Mr Jarvis, Bicker, a bill		17s				
	Retail &c. £1 2s 0d. Weekly bill £1 2s 1½d.	£1	2s		£1	2s	1½d
20	To Mr Goodwin for Malt 16s. Brewing 1s.					17s	
	To Mr Hunt a bill in full				£4	5s	6d
	Received of -ditto- by bills		18s	3d			
21	To Mr Harvey for 1½ Dozen Candles					9s	6d
23	Of Mr J. Birks a bill	£2	4s	6d			
	Paid to -ditto- a bill				£1	17s	
24	Of Mr Weeks, Wigtoft, by bill	£3					
26	By Retail and small bills	£1	2s	6d			
	The weekly bill				£1	2s	5½d
	Of Mr Nettleton, Swineshead, a bill the 20th		12s	6d			
31	Lost by Bad Silver this year					3s	
	To my Wife for a New Gown				£2	2s	
	[Carried over]	**£258**	**15s**	**10d**	**£187**	**18s**	**3¾d**

Gained in the Year 1779	£70 17s 6¼d
Gained in the 8 preceeding Years	£457 2s 9½d
Total Gained in 9 Years' Business	£528 0s 3¾d

I have to thank the Mercifull Author of all things that me and my Family are brought safely to the beginning of the Year 1780, & that his wonted Bounties are continued to us, who are so unworthy. Tho' my Expences have been uncommonly great this year my Receipts have proportionably encreased and enabled me to save something again above £70. January 1. 1780.

[f.43v]
January 1780

		Received			Paid		
	Of Mr Berry, Donington, a bill (December 26)	£3	1s				
1	Overplus Money from the Retail	£3	3s				
	Of Mr Holmes, Bicker, a bill	£1	3s				
	Of Mrs Taylor, Donington Eaudike		19s	6d			
	Of Mr Tasker, Quadring, a bill		6s	6d			
	By Retail and small bills	£1	5s	6d			
	The weekly bill				£1	5s	6¼d
2	Sacrament Money						6d
	Bottle of Red Port Wine of Mr Harvey					2s	2d
3	Of Mr Pepper in part of Quadring Parish bill	£2	2s				
	Of Mr Pillings, Bicker, a bill		6s	6d			
4	Of Mr Beets, Wigtoft, a bill		12s				
5	Phial Corks 4 Gr., 1s. Quarts -ditto- ½ Gr., 1s.					2s	
7	Theatrical Mag. No 39, 6d. Gave Stamford Newsman 6d.					1s	
8	By Retail and small bills		14s	6d			
	The weekly bill					14s	9¾d
11	Gave Mr Fletcher's Servant 6d. Lost at Cards 1s.					1s	6d
15	By Retail and small bills		17s	6d			
	The weekly bill					17s	7d
17	Of J. Haw, Northorp, a bill		12s	6d			
	To -ditto- for a roasting Pig at our Christening					7s	6d
20	Of Jos. Brown, Swineshead Fen Houses, a bill	£1	3s	6d			
	To Wm Morris, Blacksmith, a bill					2s	6d
	A Pack of Cards 2s. Red Wine 1lb 14d.					3s	2d
	Rum two Quarts at 10s 6d					5s	3d
	A Couple of Ducks 20d. A Cruet 1s.					2s	8d
22	By Retail and small bills	£1	6s	6d			
	The weekly bill				£1	6s	4¾d
23	Of Wm Wheatly, Donington, a bill		16s				
24	To Mr Whitehead for Matthew's Entrance					10s	6d
	Of Mrs Lowe for 1 Doz. Batemans-drops[198]		12s				
	Land Tax one Quarter					3s	
25	A Lock for the Coal House door					1s	2d
27	Of J. Allen, Swineshead, a bill	£1	2s				
	To J. Wells, Shoemaker, a bill					4s	6d
28	Of Martha Moor, Donington, a bill		8s	6d			
	Of Luke Tebb, Northorp, a bill		8s	6d			
29	To Edward Laykins, Bicker, a bill					11s	2d
	Retail &c. 17s 6d. Weekly bill 17s 4¼d.		17s	6d		17s	4¼d
31	A Windsor Elbow Chair at Quadring Sale					7s	
		£21	**18s**	**0d**	**£8**	**7s**	**3d**

Mr Stukeley's Sale at Quadring, Monday Jan. 31, Feb. 1 & 2
I attended at the Sale the 1st & last day, bought a Chair & 3 Prints, the Auctioneer
Mr Tatum I think clever. Am sorry Mr Stukeley has brought himself into such

198 Bateman's Drops: a patent medicine dating from the early eighteenth century. There were
several variant forms but the basic ingredients were castor oil, camphor, opium and aniseed. It was
used in chest complaints (*Supplement*).

disagreable circumstances, fear he will not reside at Quadring again. I have let Mr Marsh & Palmer have £30 on Note to assist in purchasing for Mr S. at the Sale; am promised it again in a few weeks. Feb. 7.

[f.44]
February 1780

		Received			Paid		
	Brought over	**£21**	**18s**	**0d**	**£8**	**7s**	**3d**
1	Making an Affidavit at Spalding					2s	6d
	Cost me at Spalding					1s	
2	3 Prints framed & glazed at Quadring Sale					7s	
4	Theatrical Magazine No 40						6d
5	Of Mr Ducket, Quadring Eaudike, by bill	£1	6s				
	Retail &c. 13s 6d. Weekly bill 13s 6¼d.		13s	6d		13s	6¼d
6	Of J. Thompson (Hostler) a bill	£1	6s				
9	To Mr Parker, Joiner, a bill					7s	6d
	A Currying Comb of Mr Hunt						10d
11	Carriage of Druggs from Mr Wilson					1s	6d
12	Of Wm Green, Bicker Fen, a Bill	£1	1s	6d			
	Of Mrs Lockton's Servant Maid, Swineshead		7s				
	Retail &c. 15s. Weekly bill 15s 2d.		15s			15s	2d
	Of Mr Trimnell, Bicker, a bill	£6	10s				
14	Of Mr Baldwick a bill (Quadring)		18s				
	One Table Cloth at Quadring Sale					12s	
	To Mr Harvey, Draper, a bill					14s	3d
15	Affidavit & Expences at Spalding					3s	3d
17	To Mrs Worley, Boston, a bill					8s	8d
	Of Mr Parker, Bicker Frist, a bill	£2	11s				
18	Of Thos Higgs, Northorp, in part		10s	6d			
19	Of Mr J. Smith at Mr Love's, Swineshead		13s				
	Retail &c. 17s. Weekly bill 16s 11½d.		17s			16s	11½d
	To my Wife on the 6th Inst.				£2		
22	The late Wm Shilcock's bill		13s	10d			
	Of J. Hanley, Shoemaker, in part		8s	10d			
	Of H. Lettin, Carpenter, in part		11s	10d			
24	Joints 4 Pair for the W. Shuters					4s	4d
	Sugar 1½lb for Shop use					1s	2¼d
26	Retail &c. 16s 6d. Weekly bill 16s 7½d.		16s	6d		16s	7½d
28	Of Evans, Donington, a bill		5s				
		£42	**2s**	**6d**	**£16**	**14s**	**0½d**

Family Concerns

I omitted noting that we put our youngest Child Susanna out to Mary Tunnard to Nurse at 3s per Week & 7d of Milk. I believe her Child has been very well used. We got her home again March 29. 1780, being just 26 Weeks. She has cost me £3 18s 0d in Cash besides the Milk which I [have] yet to pay for to John Kendall. She is a very fine Child & has done quite as well with her Nurse, as she could have done at home. It has saved us a great deal of troubles, but is expensive.

[f.44v]

Money Matters

I am like to have a good deal of trouble in procuring Mr Gee's (of Swineshead) Bill. He has been dead two years & his debts yet unpaid. I have been obliged to go to Spalding twice this Month, viz. Feb. 1st & 15th, to make affidavit to the truth of my debt before Mr Attkinson a Master Extraordinary in Chancery – the affairs being in Chancery – in order to sell some of the estate to satisfy the Creditors. When we shall be paid I cannot tell; these Journeys &c. have cost me about 7s – the account is £20 11s.

I have to note that in order to assist Mr Marsh & Mr Palmer to purchase furniture &c. at Quad.[199] Sale for poor Mr Stukeley, I assisted them with £30 on Note, to be repaid me in a few weeks.

I have also to note that the Money my Brother Mr S. Ward has of me, viz. £180 on a bond & Notes, he proposes when the Year expires (June 11) to reduce to the bond only of £100. He was here Feb 15th & 16th and has paid me £20 in part. I am to loose nothing in the Interest if I don't get that money out before that time. I have spoke to Mr Gleed to get me a good Mortgage[200] for £200 in June next, part of which money may be advanced any time to the half – as I believe I have £50 of my Ward's money for a year if necessary – as I think it is best to get good security for £200 if I borrow some part of the Money.

Books

I have procured from London Bell's Edition of Churchill's Poems,[201] 3 neat small Vols 4s 6d; the execution & plates are most elegant & the price moderate. I also got at the same time the Annual Register 1778.

Birth Day, Thursday Feb. 17. 1780

I have again to offer up my gratefull thanks to the Divine Mercy that I have safely & prosperously passed thro' another year of my Life, & have now compleated the 30th of my age.

N.B. Feb. 22. The Money mentioned above lent to Mr Palmer was repaid to me this day.

Servants

I have to note that we have agreed with our Maid Ann Parker to stay another Year, her Wages £3 & 2s 6d Earnest. I have also hired John Bettison, a lad of this Parish, his Wages 30s & 1s Earnest.

Visitors

Wed. March 29. Mr J. Hursthouse, Mrs H. & Daughter & Mrs De Camps came to see us about teatime. Mr H. left us the next morn. Mr De Camps came to us Friday afternoon & they all left us on Saturday Morn. Mr H's longer stay would have rendered this much more agreable.

---

199 Quadring.
200 MS 'Mortgate'.
201 Charles Churchill (1731–64), satirical poet: *The poetical works of Charles Churchill in 3 Volumes* (London: John Bell, 1779).

[f.45]
March 1780

		Received			Paid		
Brought over		**£42**	**2s**	**6d**	**£16**	**14s**	**0½d**
1	Of Michael Grant, Baker, in part		10s	6d			
	Three Yards of Muslin for 9 Stocks					13s	6d
4	Of Mr Ding, Gosberton Risgate, a bill		8s	6d			
	Retail &c. 15s 6d. Weekly bill 15s 9d.		15s	6d		15s	9d
6	Sugar 5lb at 7d for Shop use					2s	11d
8	Of Mr Vicars, Swineshead, a bill	£1	2s				
	Of Mr Chambers, Wigtoft, a bill		15s				
	Theatrical Magazine No 41						6d
11	Of Mr R. Gennings, Bicker, a bill		16s				
	Retail &c. 16s. Weekly bill 16s 2¾d.		16s			16s	2¾d
	Of Mr Tenny, Donington Wikes, a bill	£1	11s	6d			
13	To J. Cole, Shoemaker, for a pair of Boots				£1		
	Of -ditto- a bill		11s	6d			
	To Mr May of Catliff[202] for Phials				£3	10s	
	Of Mrs Knight, Quadring, a bill	£1					
	To Ann Parker earnest for next Year					2s	6d
	To John Bettison -ditto-					1s	
	Bettsy's Entrance at Mrs Codling's School					1s	
14	Of John Fairam in part		10s	6d			
15	Lemons ½ a Dozen					1s	
17	Lemons ½ a Dozen					1s	
18	Black Ribbon 7½d. Stockings & Ribbon 16d.					1s	11½d
	Retail &c. 19s 6d. Weekly bill 19s 10½d.		19s	6d		19s	10½d
25	Of Mr Wilton, Bicker, a bill		9s				
	Retail &c. £1 0s 0d. Weekly bill 19s 11½d.	£1				19s	11½d
	Of Mr Allcock, Gosberton poor bill		9s	6d			
	Of Mr Chamberlain, Gosberton Risgate, a bill		14s				
27	Of Mr Morris, Bicker Mill, a bill	£2	16s				
29	Of John Kenning in part		10s	6d			
30	To Wm Fairam towards a Horse					1s	
31	To Mary Tunnard for Nursing the Child from September 29. 79 to March 29. 80, being 26 Weeks at 3s per Week				£3	18s	0d
	Paid to -ditto- for 3 Days					1s	6d
	Received of -ditto- a bill		6s	6d			
	Retail &c. £1 4s 6d. Weekly bill £1 4s 5d.	£1	4s	6d	£1	4s	5d
	Remainder of Jos. Handley's bill		10s				
	To -ditto- for Matthew's Shoes					2s	
		£59	**19s**	**0d**	**£31**	**8s**	**1¾d**

April 15. I have to note that my Nephew John being wholly bent to try his fortune at Sea my Brother & Sister thro' the Interest of good friends have procured him a Midshipman's place on board the Apollo, Frigate of 32 Guns. My Brother sets off with him for Plymouth sometime the ensuing week. He this day came over to take

---

202 The May family took over William Fenny's glassworks at Catcliffe near Rotherham (Yorks.) in 1759. See G. D. Lewis, 'The Catcliffe glassworks', *Journal of Industrial Archaeology* 1 (1965), 206–211.

leave of us; may the Providence of God be over [him] & grant that this Adventure may be for his good.

[f.45v]
April 1780

		Received			Paid		
	Brought over	£59	19s	0d	£31	8s	1¾d
3	Of Mr Crane, Quadring, a bill		11s	6d			
6	Of Mr Nathan Foster, his Sister's bill	£1					
	Sacrament Money on Easter Day						6d
	Gave to Mary Castor						6d
8	Of Mr Garner, Gosberton Risgate, a bill	£2	2s				
	Retail &c. 18s 6d. Weekly bill 18s 6¼d.		18s	6d		18s	6¼d
	Theatrical Magazine No 42						6d
	A Pair of Buckles of Mr Hunt					1s	2d
10	Of Mr Sharp Junior, Horfleet, a bill		12s	6d			
12	Of Mrs Lowe, Donington, in part		8s				
13	A New Map of England					1s	2d
14	To Messrs Wilson & Co				£8	7s	
	Of J. Bartram, Carpenter, a bill		10s				
15	A Present to my Nephew Jackey					7s	6d
	Retail &c. 12s 6d. Weekly bill 12s 7d.		12s	6d		12s	7d
16	Of J. Alvey, Donington, a bill		12s	6d			
17	Of Mr Parr, Wigtoft, a bill		10s	6d			
19	Of R. Gray, Gosberton, in part	£2	2s				
	Of Mr Ashworth a bill	£1	5s	6d			
	Paid to -ditto- a bill in full				£2	10s	
	Of Miss Jaques, Donington, a bill		5s	6d			
20	Of Mr Bulley, Little Hale, a bill	£2	9s				
	Spent at the Cow with -ditto-					1s	6d
	Of Mr Thornton, Swineshead Green Lane		5s	6d			
22	Of Mr Birks's Servant Maid a bill		7s	6d			
	The Salary from Easter 1779 to Easter 1780 of						
	R. Holmes for Bicker	£4	4s				
	Retail &c. 15s 6d. Weekly bill 15s 6¾d.		15s	6d		15s	6¾d
24	½ Year's Window Money 8s 6d. Land Tax ¼ 3s.						
	House Tax ½ Year 15d.					12s	9d
	Of Thos Risebrook, Swineshead, a bill	£1	1s				
29	Of H. Everitt Junior, a bill	£1					
	Retail &c. 15s 6d. Weekly bill 15s 7½d.		15s	6d		15s	7½d
	Two Political Magazines					1s	
		£82	8s	0d	£46	14s	0¼d

Money Matters, May 4. 1780

I have (with gratitude to a mercifull Providence) to remark that I have advanced to J. Smith of Frampton West End £150 on seven computed acres (tho' I think 10 or 11 real) & two Messuages Copyhold, at £5 per Cent. The writings, Bond &c. were signed this day, and are now in my possession. Mr Gleed thinks it a good security for the Money. The Cash I raised as follows: £60 I had mustered up since Mr Ward had any of me last; £40 he has repaid, & the other £50 I have of the late Wm Shilcock's money, which I propose keeping 6 Months & pay interest for it.

Mr W. in Aug. or Sept. intends to pay the other £40 with £9 Interest, with which I propose to repay the above. N.B. the above Mr Smith lives on the premises.

[f.46]
May 1780

		Received			Paid		
Brought over		**£82**	**8s**	**0d**	**£46**	**14s**	**0¼d**
	Easter dues to Mr Powell						8d
3	Four Grose large Phial Corks & Carriage					1s	6d
5	Carriage of Druggs from London					7s	11d
	Two Chaldrons of Coals at 25s				£2	10s	
	Porterage 14d. Ale for the Porters 8d.					1s	10d
	Theatrical Magazine No 43						6d
	Of Mr James Shilcock a bill	£5	12s				
6	Of Mr Dennis, Donington Eaudike, a bill	£1	13s	6d			
	Retail &c. 17s 6d. Weekly bill 17s 8d.		17s	6d		17s	8d
9	Two Chaldrons of Coals at 25s				£2	10s	
	Porterage 14d. Ale for the Porters 8d.					1s	10d
	Turnpike 18d. Man's Expences 1s.					2s	6d
	Of Mrs Lowe, Donington		6s				
10	Of Mr Cew, Glover, a bill		13s	6d			
	Of Wm Moor, Taylor, a bill		5s				
	To Mr Cew for a Pair of B. Garts					2s	
	5½ Pounds of Hops at 9d of Mr Hunt					4s	1½d
11	A Day's Gardening					1s	6d
13	To Wm Darcey a Year's Wages				£2	2s	
	Paid Mr Walton for Brewing					1s	
	To Ann Parker a Year's Wages				£2	15s	
	Retail &c. 14s 6d. Weekly bill 14s 4¾d.		14s	6d		14s	4¾d
14	Of J. Day, Swineshead, a bill		9s	6d			
	Of Mrs Pakey's Servant Maid a bill		11s				
15	To Mr Wilcockson in full					18s	
16	Of Mrs Lowe, Donington, in part		12s				
	Of Mrs Moor a bill		5s	6d			
	Paid to -ditto- for Schooling					4s	6d
17	Remainder of Mr Pepper's Account, Quadring	£2	16s				
	Of Mary Speed a bill in full	£1	6s				
	Paid to -ditto- a Milk bill					15s	6d
18	Of Mr Lee 6s. To -ditto- for Small Beer 2s.		6s			2s	
	Cloth Shop use 13d. Bees Wax 1lb 6oz 2s 5d.					3s	6d
	To J. Strapps 14s 10d. Of -ditto- a bill 8s 3d.		8s	3d		14s	10d
19	To Messrs Barrit & Robinson in full				£8	12s	
20	Of Mr Bowers (White house) in part	£2	2s				
	Retail £1 3s 6d. Weekly bill £1 3s 6¾d.	£1	3s	6d	£1	3s	6¾d
26	Of Mr Fant, Swineshead, a bill	£1	0s	6d			
	Of Mr Anderson, Gosberton, a bill		11s				
	Of Mr Freestone, Swineshead, a bill	£4	3s				
	Of Mr Gee, Hale Fenn, a bill	£2	13s	6d			
	Remainder of R. Gray's bill, Gosberton	£1	1s				
	The Salary for Wigtoft Poor	£4	4s				
	Of Mr Bones, Bicker, a bill		7s				
	Of Mr Baxter, Swineshead, a bill		15s	6d			

May 1780 (cont.)	Received			Paid		
27 Of Mr R. Jackson, Bicker, a bill	6s					
Of Mr Crampton, Northorp, a bill	15s					
Of Mr Dring, Wigtoft Marsh	8s					
	£118	4s	3d	£72	2s	4¼d

[f.46v]
Mr Stukeley's Funeral, Sunday June 4. 1780

It is with some concern that I note the decease of my Friend Mr Stukeley in London on Monday May 22. He was taken ill the preceeding Wednesday of an Inflamatory Disorder, but the particulars I am unacquainted with. When I reflect on what has happened to him & the very embarrassed state of his affairs, we ought to consider his removal as a mercifull interference of Providence. The Funeral was a Military one, a Body of the Militia preceeding[203] the Hearse from Spalding with the Fife & Drum in Solemn March. A Mourning Coach also attended – the concourse of People amazingly great for such a village, estimated at 2000. I was invited & many others; we went in Procession before the Body & after the Military & their proper officers. The Procession stopped at his House about an hour where the Tenants & all those who had scarfs (white ones, Shoulder scarfs & Hat-bands) joined it; it was the compleatest thing of the kind I ever saw – many from Holbeach & Spalding attended.

Money Matters, Wed. June 28. 1780

I this day accounted with Mr S. Ward. He intends to keep of my money £150, viz. the bond £100 & £50 a note on the back of the Bond. Having before £40 above the £100, the £9 the Year's Interest & £1 I now advanced made the £150. Over & above I also lent him £20 on a Note, which I am to have again before October to go towards the £50 I have then to pay. If it please God I accomplish this matter in the manner I propose I shall have done very well for this year, as I shall then be clear & have £300 out on Interest.

Family Concerns

I have to note that my Brother has had a letter from his son informing that he has been in an action with a French Frigate in which the Apollo has lost her Captain & several men killed: they drove the Frigate on shore near Ostend but was obliged to leave her. The action happened the 15th June. I have seen John's Letter & have extracted the principal particulars from it.[204]

Mr Hall

I have to note that my old friend Mr Hall just called on me on Wed. Evening July 12 in his return from Folkinham to Boston. He has been at Boston sometime. I find he spent his last Winter at Liverpool again, & likes it so well that he intends to go there also the next season.

---

203 MS 'proceeding'.

204 The *Apollo* under Captain Philemon Pownoll, had come across the French frigate *Stanislaus* by chance. Despite the fact that victory was denied the *Apollo* (Ostend being a neutral port) the French ship was eventually bought from the authorities in Ostend by the Admiralty and became a British ship. Pownoll died in the arms of Lt. Edward Pellew (1757–1833), who went on to become one of the finest frigate captains of the day and was created first Viscount Exmouth in 1814 (*ODNB*).

My Wife's Visit

My Wife and Betsy[205] have made a visit to our friends at Spalding. They went Tues. July 11, being the Race Week. I intended to have gone to them but was by Business prevented. My Wife returned Mond. July 17, but at the desire [f.47] of my Brother & Sister, Betsey is to make some stay at Spalding, I imagine untill sometime in October when I intend to go over.

Tuesday September 19. Mr Hall & his Brother Mr Bailey were kind enough to take a ride over from Boston to dine with me – they also drank tea, and returned in the Evening.

June 1780

		Received			Paid		
Brought over		**£118**	**4s**	**3d**	**£72**	**2s**	**4¼d**
May							
27	Retail &c. £1 13s. Weekly bill	£1	13s		£1	12s	11¼d
	Trifles during the fair						9d
29	Tins, Earthen Ware &c. at the fair					4s	6d
	Chairwoman 1s. A Ribbon 7½d.					1s	7½d
	To my Wife on the 6th Inst.				£2		
31	Of Mr Parker's Daughter, Donington, a bill		12s				
June							
1	Remainder of Thos Higg's bill, Northorp		10s				
2	Of J. Barrat, Bicker Fen, a bill		6s	6d			
3	Of Mr Injelaw, Quadring Eaudike		7s	6d			
	Retail &c. 18s. Weekly bill 17s 10d.		18s			17s	10d
	Of Mr Grant, Baker, a bill	£1	3s	6d			
	Paid to -ditto- for Bread & flower &c.				£1	3s	6d
6	Of a Stranger (Gosberton)		5s	6d			
7	Of Mr Clark (Glover) in part	£1	1s	0d			
	Ol. Terebinth. 1lb, 1s 6d. Cappaper[206] 3d.					1s	7d
	Of Wm Morris, Blacksmith		5s				
9	Theatrical Magazine No 44						6d
10	Retail &c. 16s 6d. Weekly bill 16s 4¾d.		16s	6d		16s	4¾d
11	Of Mrs Lowe, Donington		5s				
12	Of Mr Sewerds, Quadring Eaudike		12s	6d			
13	Sugar 3lb Shop use, 2s 4½d. Thread -ditto- 6d.					2s	10½d
16	To J. Kendall for 8 Stone 10 Pound Pork				£1	11s	6d
	To -ditto- a Milk score 37 weeks at 7d				£1	1s	7d
	A Pair of Stockings of Mr Harvey					4s	
17	Quadring Parish of Mr Crow	£8	4s				
	Of Mr Torry, Glaizier, in part	£2	12s	3d			
	Paid to -ditto- a bill in full				£2	12s	3d
	Retail &c. 18s 6d. Weekly bill 18s 5¼d.		18s	6d		18s	5¼d
20	Of Mr Johnson, Donington Wikes, a bill	£1	4s				
	Sun Fire Insurance Money					9s	
24	Cost us at Bicker Feast 2 days					2s	6d
	Of Wm Fairbanks, Gosberton Wistrop		6s				
	Retail &c. 15s 6d. Weekly bill 15s 9d.		15s	6d		15s	9d
	Of Mr Mason, Swineshead, a bill		10s	6d			

[205] Their eldest daughter, then aged nearly 5.
[206] See n.93 above.

June 1780 (cont.)	Received		Paid	
25 Of Mr Whitehead by bill	£4 6s			
26 Of Mr Dixon a bill	18s			
Of John Wells, Shoemaker, a bill	6s			
Paid to -ditto- a bill			11s	6d
28 Of Mr S. Ward Interest of £180 for one Year due the 11th Inst.	£9			
30 Of Mrs Burgess, Donington, a bill	10s			
	£156 11s	**0d**	**£87 11s**	**4½d**

Health

About the end of September, finding myself somewhat disordered with head ach, lassitude and other feverish symptoms – and fearing [f.47v] the Autumnal Bilious remittent (which I suffered several weeks from last year) now generally prevalent – tho' by the bye not near so bad as last year: I took Tart. Emet.[207] 1 grain, which puked me finely 4 times, easing me of a considerable quantity of Bile, which gave me great relief – and I thank God I am now tolerably hearty. October 4. 1780.

July 1780

Brought over	Received		Paid	
	£156 11s	**0d**	**£87 11s**	**4½d**
Of John Thompson, Hostler, a bill	11s.	6d		
1 Retail &c. 14s 6d. Weekly bill 14s 4½d.	14s	6d	14s	4½d
2 Of Mr Dodds a bill	6s	6d		
3 Of J. Wells (Labourer) a bill	6s			
4 Of Mrs Barrett, Bicker, a bill	10s	6d		
Bees Wax one Pound			1s	8d
7 Of Mrs Pattison a bill	6s			
8 Sugar 2lb at 7d (Shop use)			1s	2d
Retail &c. 25s. Weekly bill 25s 3½d.	£1	5s	£1 5s	3½d
9 Of R. Crust, Bicker, a bill	6s			
11 Of Mrs Bradley, School Mistres	8s	6d		
13 Of Mr Shepherd a bill	£3	3s		
Of Mr Samuel Pike a bill	8s	6d		
To Elizabeth Hall for Quilting last week			2s	6d
15 To the Bicker Gardener for Work			1s	
Of Mr Marsh, Quadring, a bill	£3	6s		
Of R. Nicholls a bill	8s	6d		
Retail &c. £1 2s 0d. Weekly bill £1 2s 0d.	£1	2s	£1 2s	0d
18 To John Wells for Carriage			1s	6d
19 To Mr Hunt a bill in full			£1 2s	
21 Theatrical Magazine No 45 (last week)				6d
Hog's Lard 3 Pounds at 4d			1s	
Retail &c. £1 0s 0d. Weekly bill £1 0s 0d.	£1		£1	
25 Land Tax one quarter			3s	
Bees Wax 2lb 3oz at 18d			3s	3d
A Pair of Stockings for Matthew			1s	6d
27 Of Wm Ashton, Donington, a bill	17s			
29 Retail &c. 17s. Weekly bill 16s 10d.	17s		16s	10d

[207] See n.70 above.

July 1780 (cont.)

		Received			Paid		
30	Of Wm Fielding, Donington Eaudike	£1	1s				
	Of Samuel Ashton a bill		11s				
	Of Richard Hales, Mr Ward's Servant		6s				
	Paid to Mary Tunnard					4s	
31	To J. Warriner, Taylor, a bill				£1	14s	
	Received of him a bill		15s	6d			
		£175	**1s**	**0d**	**£96**	**6s**	**11½d**

Journey to Spalding &c., October 10. 1780 Tuesday

Being my Brother's Birth Day, I made a Journey to see them; staid all night and my Brother was kind enough to return with me on the 11th in a Wiskey, with his Daughter Henny & to bring home Betsy. Henny left us this day to go to Cressy-hall,[208] October 19 Thursday, [f.48] and returned to us again on Tuesday October 31. She staid with us again untill Sunday November 12, when I carried her to Miss Caltrop's, Gosberton, from whence she was to return in the Fly[209] to Spalding the next day.

August 1780

		Received			Paid		
Brought over		**£175**	**1s**	**0d**	**£96**	**6s**	**11½d**
3	Of Mrs Lowe, Donington		10s				
5	Of Mr Bonner, Bicker, a bill	£3	5s				
	One Dozen of Pigeons					2s	
	Retail &c. 18s. Weekly bill 17s 11¼d.		18s			17s	11¼d
7	Of Wm Hickabottom a bill		10s	6d			
	Paid for things bought at Spalding					17s	2d
	To my Wife on the 6th Inst.				£2	2s	
	Of Mrs Lowe, Donington		7s				
8	Of Mr Wright's Man, Gosberton		5s				
10	Lining &c. for Matthew's close					2s	7d
12	A Hat for Matthew 2s 6d. Gloves 1s 10d.					4s	4d
	Received by exchange of 3 Pair of Gloves		4s				
	Of Mr Sharp, Hoffleet, a bill		10s				
	Retail &c. 18s. Weekly bill 18s 2d.		18s			18s	2d
16	Of Mr Pigot, Butcher, Swineshead, a bill		9s				
17	To Mr Parker, Joiner, a bill					18s	5d
19	Retail &c. 18s 6d. Weekly bill 18s 9d.		18s	6d		18s	9d
22	Of Mr Gee, Hale Fen	£1	1s				
24	Of Mr Christian, Bicker, a bill	£1	9s	6d			
25	Of Ed. Sutton, Gosberton Risgate	£1	1s	0d			
	Carriage of Druggs from London					5s	
	A Bird Cage 4s. Carriage of -ditto- 4d.					4s	4d
26	Retail &c. 14s. Weekly bill 14s 3d.		14s			14s	3d
27	Of John Berry a bill		10s	6d			
31	Of Mr Crosby, Gosberton Risgate, a bill		15s	6d			
		£189	**7s**	**6d**	**£104**	**11s**	**10¾d**

---

[208] Cressy Hall, near Gosberton. Formerly the seat of the Heron family, the seventeenth-century house was purchased by Henry Smith esquire, who rebuilt it after its destruction by fire in August 1792. See below under November 1792. Henny's mother (Flinders's sister-in-law) lived there before her marriage.

[209] A one-horse carriage (*OED*).

1. Donington: the house and shop of Matthew Flinders. Copy of a drawing by Miss E. M. C. Morris. (From Boston Library, courtesy of Lincolnshire County Council)

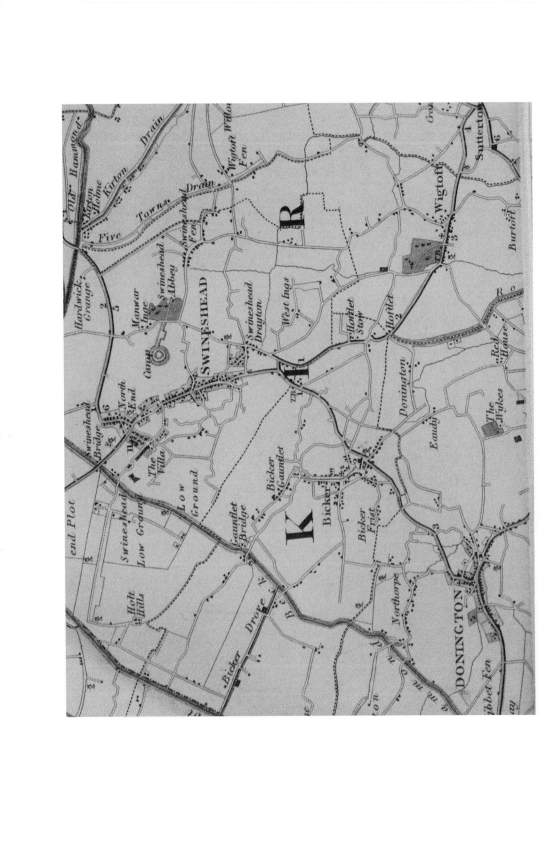

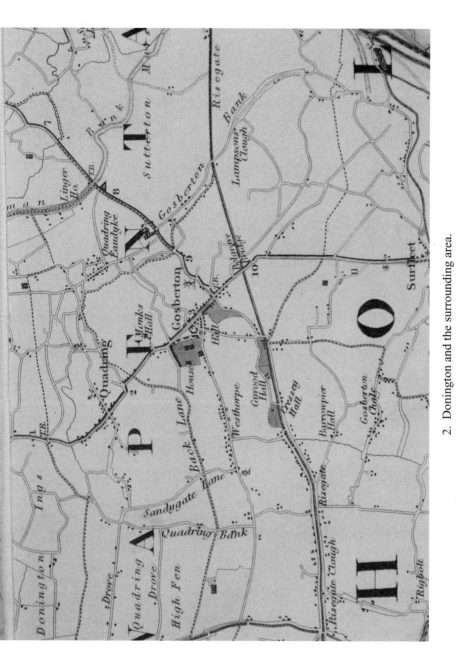

2. Donington and the surrounding area.
Detail from C. and J. Greenwood, *Map of the County of Lincoln* (London, 1830).
(Lincoln Cathedral Library)

Richard Grindall.

3. Richard Grindall, the apothecary with whom Flinders served his apprenticeship.
Soft ground etching. (Wellcome Library, London)

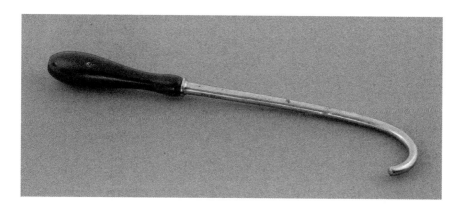

4. Above. Crochet:
a hooked medical
instrument.
(Wellcome Library,
London)

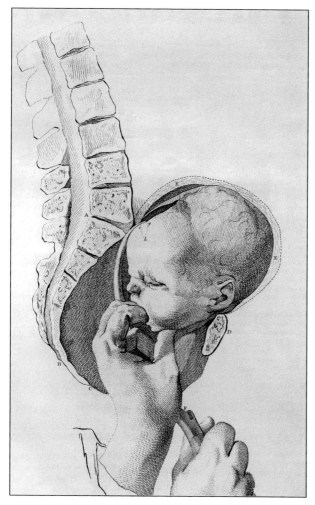

5. Left. Lateral view
of pelvis, showing
use of the crochet.
(Wellcome Library,
London)

Powell the Fire eater.

On Monday May 18th. I attended the long famous Mr Powells
exhibition / at the Cow / I cannot say that it came up to
his Bill or our expectation yet what he really if fairly
(Poles) is amazing he is now about 90, and has performed
in this way about 60 years since some allowance will be
to his Years, as I make no doubt, his performances were
more creatives in his younger years a set of us what it
him some hours after this performance, he seems but
a very moderate companion, for the variety of scenes,
and company he must have passd thro', and moreover
is good deal of a sloven, he shewd us his large silver
Medal the Royal Society gave him in 1751. the Motto
chosen by Sir Hans Sloane I much admire — viz

Mors aliis ved vita mihi.
However he has by long practice enurd himself to
extraordinary heat, but he does not absolutely lick

the Iron Red hot and his charcoal & mouths very
tenderly; ventured to ask him if he was sensible of
the heat; he acknowledged he was and sometimes by
chance burnt himself; he could himself; his
age pretend to not believe he was afraid we should
keep him with too many questions — there have
been doubts whether he be the heretofore famous
Tim Eaton; but for my part I have no the least doubt
about it; if prevent he is rather in a reduced situation, travelling without a servant & whereas he
formerly had a carriage and well attended, he billows
he had been stripped of all his property in France on
what account I know not. he appears to be much
given to drink not often sleeping sober; reals perform a dexterity of hand, but I have never there am
equally well before.

Court of Requests.

6. Matthew Flinders: diary for May 1778, recording the visit to Donington of Mr Powell the fire-eater.

7. Donington: Church of St Mary.
Lithograph from drawing by Stephen Lewin, from *An Account of the Churches in the Division of Holland* (Boston, 1843). (Lincoln Cathedral Library)

8. Bolingbroke: Church of St Peter and St Paul, where Susanna, Flinders's first
wife, was baptised, married and buried.
Drawing by J. C. Nattes from the Local Studies Collection, Lincoln Central
Library, by courtesy of Lincolnshire County Council.

April 1792.

		1st Month 30 Days			Received Paid		
		£	s	d	£	s	d
	Brought over	61	12	7	30	5	8½
Tu. 2	Of John Green Don: in part	1	1				
	Of Mr Pattison fixed a Bill		5				
Wed. 3	Of Mr Whitehead (by Bill)	6	3				
	Math: Schooling 2½ years by Carter						
	a present to Mr. Whitehead	1				3	3
	to him for Robinson Green 2 Vols		5				5
Sat. 6	Refait Weekly Bill		15			15	2½
Mon. 8	Capt Mr R. Ashworth a 2 Caud a Bill		19			19	
Th. 11	To C. Nicholas a Martha Nursing						
	Jonathan Ancell a Bill		12			10	
Wed.	Carriage of Drugs from Wilson						
	Probalife 1616 Weekly 1616	16	6		16	6	
						5	6
						16	6
Sun	Critical Review for Jan: Feby Mar:						
Mon 15	Lincoln Seal a Chaldon 10/ carriage 1/6					3	
						11	6

9. Matthew Flinders: accounts for April 1782, showing the purchase of *Robinson Crusoe* for his son Matthew.

Theatrical Magazine.

In the beginning of September 1790 We begun to take
the above monthly work, each Nº contains a Tragedy
Comedy & Farce with 2 good engravings, it is certainly
the cheapest way of collecting Plays yet published —
The Print is small and rather too coarse too, but there
must be expected from so Cheap a source, there are
22 Nºᵖʳ Publish'd before I began, which I am afraid
I never have, to be compleat.

Whale Monday Sept 21. 70.

That enormous and (in these parts of the world uncommon) Fish a Whale being chased on shore from Boston
Decʸ by the crew of the Rungo Smack or Cutter, & brought
as the Withan to very near the town of Boston, a few
Days before this date, made a Journey to Boston in

company with Mr Harvey how so uncommon a Creature
which we had gone 2 or 3 days extract that is Before
We had begun to cut him up, so a sight of him enter
we I have been an amazing curious Spectacle, even
the maß we now saw was curious from amazing
Bulk – when enters he measured 59 feet in length
his tongue as large as a Calf and each fin fore
of the Shoulder about 2 yards long; the Ball of the
Bone going into the Pot at the Shoulder so large on
larger than the Human Head. I suppose it was not
the species of Whale from whence long whale bone
extracted :- the elder inhabitants report that a
whale was thrown up, about Butterwick 53
years ago, & these are the only ones within memory
cast upon these parts of the Lincolnshire coast.

10. Matthew Flinders: diary for September 1781, recording the landing of a whale near Boston.

THE

New British Traveller;

Or, A Complete Modern Universal Display of

GREAT-BRITAIN AND IRELAND:

BEING A NEW, COMPLETE, ACCURATE, AND EXTENSIVE TOUR

Through England, Wales, Scotland, Ireland, the Isles of Man, Wight,
Scilly, Hebrides, Jersey, Sark, Guernsey, Alderney,
And other Islands adjoining to and dependent on the Crown of GREAT-BRITAIN.

Comprising all that is worthy of Observation in every County, Shire, &c.

And containing a full, ample, and circumstantial Account of every Thing remarkable in the several *Cities,
Market-Towns, Boroughs, Hundreds, Villages, Hamlets, Parishes, &c.* throughout these Kingdoms.

Being calculated equally to *please* the *Polite* — *entertain* the *Curious* — *instruct* the *Uninformed* —
and *direct* the *Traveller.*

THE WHOLE CLEARLY AND ACCURATELY DISPLAYED UNDER THE FOLLOWING GENERAL HEADS:

Situation, Etymology,	Agriculture,	Charitable Foundations,	Manufactures, Trades,
Extent, Roads, Capes,	Beasts, Birds, Fishes,	Institutions, &c.	Commerce,
Battles, Sieges,	Insects, Reptiles,	Customs, Manners, &c.	Revenues,
Skirmishes,	Amphibious Creatures,	Handicrafts,	Forces, Naval and Mili-
Civil Commotions,	Castles, Manors,	Commodities,	tary,
Trading and other	Military Ways, Camps,	Military and Naval Ex-	Polity, Power and Pre-
Companies.	Docks, Harbours,	ploits,	rogative of the King,

11. *The New British Traveller*, compiled by George Augustus Walpoole (London, 1784):
as acquired by Matthew Flinders by subscription. (Lincoln Cathedral Library)

12. The River Thames at Greenwich (from *The New British Traveller*). (Lincoln Cathedral Library)

13. Gosberton in 1797. Engraving, from a drawing by William Burgess of Fleet, published 1802. (Lincoln Cathedral Library).

Proposed Agreement with Mrs M. Flinders[210]

Mrs Flinders, from the badness of the farming Business intending to give it over, has made me an offer of what she holds of mine on Lease, 5 Years in which are to come at Lady Day 1781. She proposes giving them up at Lady Day 1781, on Condition of my paying £8 & letting her keep the smallest Ing Pasture the term of the Lease or till her Death if that happens before. These terms are quite in her favour, but to prevent broils & discontents, I imagine I shall close them at Old Lady Day 1781. As she has above £4 of mine in her hands, I shall not have much to pay her. The Ditches & Fences are much out of repair, and I doubt they will cost me a good deal to get them in proper order. I have already 2 men begun the ditching in the high Ing Pasture. Mrs F. tells me it cuts four Loads of Hay and consequently that I shall have hay to sell; but I don't imagine my horse will cost me less than he has done. December 1. 1780.

[f.48v]

September 1780: 9th Month, 30 Days

		Received			Paid		
Brought over		**£189**	**7s**	**6d**	**£104**	**11s**	**10¾d**
2	Retail &c. 14s 6d. Weekly bill 14s 3¾d.		14s	6d		14s	3¾d
3	Of Wm Stukeley, Donington (a Labour)		10s	6d			
	Of -ditto's- wife's Sister (a -ditto-)		10s	6d			
	Of Frances Ingerson a bill		5s				
	Of J. Chevens, Gosberton (a Labour)	£1	1s				
5	Of Mr Gadsby, Bicker Gauntlet, a bill		7s	6d			
6	To Messrs Ferneyhough & Wilson				£11	1s	9d
	Discount allowed by -ditto-		3s	9d			
7	Of Mr Dowse, Wigtoft Marsh, a bill	£2	14s				
9	Of Wm Thornhill, Bicker Gauntlet, a bill	£1	8s				
	Of Miss Boyfield, Quadring Eaudike, a bill		6s	6d			
	To -ditto- for 4lb 15oz Wax at 20d per Pound					8s	2d
	Retail &c. 17s 6d. Weekly bill 17s 4d.		17s	6d		17s	4d
10	Of Mr Reckaby, Kirton, the bill	£2	1s	6d			
11	Of Joseph Snell, Donington (a Labour)		10s	6d			
12	Of Wm Stukeley, Donington, a bill		8s				
13	Of R. Coats Junior, Donington, a bill		12s				
16	Retail &c. £1 1s 6d. Weekly bill £1 1s 7d.	£1	1s	6d	£1	1s	7d
17	Of Redhoof, Donington (a Labour)		10s	6d			
21	Of Mr Tenant, Bicker Gauntlet, in part	£2	2s				
22	Carriage 5 Stone 12 Pound of Druggs of Wilson					4s	4d
23	Statute Work on the Boston Road, 3 Days					1s	6d
	Retail &c. £1 6s. Weekly bill £1 6s 2½d.	£1	6s		£1	6s	2½d
26	Of J. Philipps, Gosberton Risgate, a bill		15s				
	Bees Wax 2¾lb at 1s 6d					4s	1½d
27	Honey 13½ Pounds of Mr Codling					6s	9d
	Of Mrs Orme for the 3 Prints		7s	6d			
	Worstead 10oz at 2½d					2s	1d
29	Of Mr Carby, Hale Fen (a Labour)	£1	1s				
	Of Miss Jarvis, Bicker (a Bill)	£1	1s				

[210] His father's second wife, Mary (see n.99 above).

September 1780 (cont.)	Received			Paid		
30 Of Mrs Orme, Quadring, a bill due to me from the late W. Stukeley Esq.[211]	£2	7s	6d			
Of Mrs Orme her own bill		5s				
To Mr Hunt for a Stone of Sugar					9s	4d
Retail &c. 18s 6d. Weekly bill 18s 3½d.		18s	6d		18s	3½d
	£213	**13s**	**9d**	**£122**	**7s**	**8d**

Silver Watch, December 23. 1780

Having been without a Watch several Years, but finding it very inconvenient especially when I am out at Labours where they have no clock, I spoke to Mr Tory of Hale to provide me with one, which he accordingly did on Sat. December 23. It is a very neat new Silver Watch, and he says a very good one. I am to have her 6 Weeks on trial, and if she suits the price is to be Five Guineas, the Marks (Henry Tory Great Hail No 2083).

[f.49]
October 1780: 10th Month, 31[212] Days

		Received			Paid		
Brought over		**£213**	**13s**	**9d**	**£122**	**7s**	**8d**
	One dozen of Lemons & Carriage					1s	10d
1	Of John Mayhorn (a bill)		11s	6d			
2	A Pair of small Blanketts					8s	3d
3	Paid to Mrs Gleed for a Tea Urn bought at Mr Moor's Sale, Frampton					16s	
4	Phial Corks 4 Groose 1s. Carriage 2d.					1s	2d
	1 Dozen of Lemons 20d. Carriage 2d.					1s	10d
5	Of Mr David Pike (a bill)		18s				
	To -ditto- for 3 Stone 8 Pound Cheese at 2s 6d					9s	
	Of H. Everitt Junior (a bill)		9s				
6	Of J. Newton (a Labour)		10s	6d			
7	Of Mr Broughton a bill (Bicker)		7s	6d			
	Of Mrs Pillings Senior, Bicker (a bill)	£1	3s				
	Of Mr Holmes, Bicker (a bill)		8s	6d			
	Cheese 2 Stone 7¾ Pound of Mr Hunt					7s	
	Sundries for Matthew at Mr Hunt's					2s	3d
	Retail &c. 28s. Weekly bill 28s 0½d.	£1	8s		£1	8s	0½d
11	Gave my Brother's Servant Maid					2s	6d
	Horse at Spalding 18d. -Ditto- at Donington 8d.					2s	2d
	1 Dozen of Lemons					2s	
	Half the Chaise Hire from Spalding					2s	6d
	To Mr Hollingworth a bill in full				£1	16s	
	Out-Rent at the Wikes Court					8s	5d
	Received of my Brother for Druggs &c.		10s				
	Paid to him for Sundries					9s	6d
14	Of Mr Broughton, Quadring (a bill)		7s				
	To J. Lee ½ the Poor Assessment					4s	8d
	Retail &c. £1 1s 6d. Weekly bill £1 1s 6d.	£1	1s	6d	£1	1s	6d

---

211 Sarah, widow of Walden Orme esquire, the sister and executrix of William Stukeley (PRO, PROB 11/1071).
212 MS '30'.

October 1780 (cont.)		Received			Paid		
17	Poppy Heads of a Woman at Bicker					1s	6d
	Of Mr Wiley, Wigtoft, a bill		14s				
	Of Mr Hodson, Gosberton Risgate, a bill		13s				
	Of Mr Crain, Gosberton Bolney, a bill	£3	17s				
	Of Mr E. Eastgate, Gosberton, a bill		8s				
18	Of Mr James Harrison, Bicker, a bill	£1	13s				
	Of J. Thompson, Hostler, a bill		10s				
	Interest of £50 ½ Year paid to Messrs Green and Stocks				£1	5s	
	A present to my Neice					10s	6d
21	Retail &c. £1 7s 6d. Weekly bill £1 7s 9½d.	£1	7s	6d	£1	7s	9½d
24	Of J. Northern, Bicker, a bill		10s				
28	Of Mr Garner, Donington Fenn, a bill	£1	13s				
	Retail &c. 19s 6d. Weekly bill 19s 8d.		19s	6d		19s	8d
	14lb of Lump Sugar at 9¾d of Mr Hunt					10s	9½d
	3½lb of Powder -ditto- at 7d of -ditto-					2s	0½d
	Of Mr Hunt for 1 Doz. of G's Cordial		4s				
	One Dozen of Lemons 2s. Carriage 2d.					2s	2d
30	Of Mr Smith at Mr Whitehead's a bill		11s	6d			
	Of Thos Cook, Quadring, a bill	£1	17s				
		£236	**5s**	**9d**	**£135**	**11s**	**8¾d**

[f.49v]

November 1780: 11th Month, 30 Days

		Received			Paid		
Brought over		**£236**	**5s**	**9d**	**£135**	**11s**	**8¾d**
1	½ Year's Window Money 8s 6d. Land Tax ½ 3s. House Tax ½ Year 15d.					12s	9d
	A Lock 9d. Matthew's Shoes mending 1s.					1s	9d
2	Powder Sugar 7lb at 7d, Shop use					4s	1d
4	Of Mrs Pattison a bill		13s				
	Of Mr Camm, Quadring, a bill	£1	5s	6d			
	Retail &c. £1 4s. Weekly bill £1 4s 0½d.	£1	4s		£1	4s	0½d
7	Of Mr Green's Man, Bicker, a bill		12s				
	Of the Revd Mr Powell a bill	£2	13s	6d			
9	Susan Bates's bill of Mr Gleed		9s	6d			
	To Mary Twell for Quilting					1s	6d
	1 Yard of Plad for Matthew's Bedgown					1s	6d
11	Retail &c. £1. Weekly bill £1 0s 3¼d.	£1			£1	0s	3¼d
	To my Wife on the 6th Instant				£2	10s	
	A present to my Sister at Spalding				£1	1s	
13	Matthew's School Feast Money					2s	6d
	To Mr Hunt a bill for Breeches					11s	6d
	Eleven Nos of the Field of Mars[213]					5s	6d
15	In Charity to Mary Moor						6d
16	Of Mrs Hanley Senior, Swineshead, a bill		14s				
	Spining 1lb of Flax to A. Smith						8d
18	Retail &c. 14s. Weekly bill 14s 7¼d.		14s			14s	7¼d

---

[213] Probably *The field of Mars: being an alphabetical digestion of the principal naval and military engagements, in Europe, Asia, Africa, and America, particularly of Great Britain and her allies, from the ninth century to the present period*, published in London in 1780 (ESTC).

November 1780 (cont.)	Received			Paid		
22 Of Mr West, Donington, a bill	18s					
Ladies Diary for 1781						9d
25 Of Mr Bingley, Horfleet, a bill	£3	2s				
Of Mr Harrison, Quadring Fen, a bill	18s					
Retail 9s 6d. Weekly bill £1 0s 3d.	9s	6d		£1	0s	3d
27 Of Mr Morris's Housekeeper a bill	9s					
28 Of Mr Woods, Bicker, a bill	16s					
29 Of Capt. Nettleton, Swineshead, a bill	£1	3s	6d			
	£253	**7s**	**3d**	**£145**	**4s**	**10½d**

Nephew, Sat. December 30

This day I got a Letter from my Brother, acquainting me that his Son John is come to Spalding (on a Visit for little untill the Ship is repaired) in good health and high Spirits, requesting me to come to see him if I can; he intends shortly to go fight the perfidious Dutch.[214] Accordingly on Monday Jan. 8. 1781 I made a Journey over (& returned in the Evening) on purpose to see him. I find he is not to wait for the repair of the Apollo, but goes in the Amphion a new Frigate of 32 Guns, just now launched. He sails with Capt. Bazeley and the Apollo's Crew; he seems to have taken such a real liking for the Sea, that I have now great hopes he may succeed in that way of Life. He expects to be called every day – indeed the sooner the better, as the present period seems a profitable harvest to the Seaman.

[f.50]
December 1780: 12th Month, 31 Days

	Received			Paid		
Brought over	**£253**	**7s**	**3d**	**£145**	**4s**	**10½d**
1 Of Mrs Thomson a bill	13s					
Paid to -ditto- a bill for Meat					7s	6d
Remainder of Mr Lettin's bill	13s	6d				
2 Retail &c. 13s 6d. Weekly bill 19s 2d.	13s	6d			19s	2d
3 Of Mr Johnson's Maid a bill	10s					
5 To Mr Harvey, Draper, a bill in full				£2	6s	10d
Remainder of Mr Clark's bill (Glover)	17s	3d				
Paid him a bill for Gloves in full					13s	9d
To Mrs Flinders for one Year's keeping of my Horse, due July 1.				£5		
To -ditto- for 2 Quarters & 1 Sack of Oats				£1	10s	
To -ditto- for Leading 4 Chalders of Coals				£1	2s	
To -ditto- for Steels Yards 5s 6d & Apples 4s					9s	6d
Of -ditto- for a Year's Rent due Apr. 5.	£2	3s				
Of -ditto- a Physic Bill	£1	4s				
Of -ditto- a Year's Interest of £10	10s					
8 Of J. Kendall a bill 10s 6d. Interest of -ditto- 7s.	17s	6d				
To -ditto- for Milk 7 Weeks at 7d					4s	1d
Child Bed Linnen & other necessaries				£1	0s	8d
To Mr Shaw for cleaning the Clock					2s	
9 To Mr Parker, Joiner, a bill in full				£1	5s	
Retail &c. 15s 6d. Weekly bill 16s 11¼d.	15s	6d			16s	11¼d

---

214 The Dutch had declared war on Britain in 1780 in support of the Americans in their fight for independence.

December 1780 (cont.)

		Received			Paid		
15	Of J. Mitchell, Donington, a bill		12s	6d			
16	Of Mr Brown, Horfleet, a bill	£2	1s	6d			
	Retail &c. 12s 6d. Weekly bill 14s 10d.		12s	6d		14s	10d
18	To Edward Laykins a bill in full					11s	
	Received of him by bill		6s	6d			
23	To Jonathan Warriner a bill in full				£1	1s	
	Retail &c. 8s 6d. Weekly bill £1 4s 3d.		8s	6d	£1	4s	3d
26	Of Ingle in part 6s. Carriage of Druggs 4s 6d.		6s			4s	6d
30	Retail &c. 12s 6d. Weekly bill 16s 2d.		12s	6d		16s	2d
	To Mr Hunt for 2 Dozen of Candles at 6s 4d					12s	8d
	Of Mr Root, Swineshead, a bill		12s	6d			
	To my Wife				£1	1s	
	Rum one Quart of Mr Harvey					3s	
Total Receipts & Payments in 1780		**£267**	**16s**	**6d**	**£167**	**10s**	**8¾d**
Payments in 1780 deducted		£167	10s	8¾d			
Total Gained in 1780		£100	5s	9¼d			
Total Gained in the 9 preceeding Years		£528	0s	3¾d			
Total Gained in 10 Years' Business		£628	6s	1d			

It is with the liveliest gratitude to Divine Providence I again note, the beginning of the new Year, my savings this year have been considerable indeed! This is the second time I have saved one hundred Pounds, notwithstanding times are confessed on all hands to be very bad. By Divine grace, I wish to be more deserving!

[f.50v]
January 1781: 1st Month, 31 Days

		Received			Paid		
	Of Mrs Jarvis, Bicker, by bill	£7	12s				
2	Mr Wells's Maid's bill, Northorp		7s				
4	Of Mr Bilsby Junior a bill (Bicker)	£1	2s				
6	Retail &c. 16s 6d. Weekly bill 19s 1¾d.		16s	6d		19s	1¾d
12	Of John Harrison, Bicker, a bill	£1	11s				
	To Mr Lowe for 8 Stone 13 Pound of Pork at 3s 6d				£1	11s	3d
13	Of Mr Jackson, Swineshead Fenn Houses		6s	6d			
	Retail &c. 10s 6d. Weekly bill 10s 11¼d.		10s	6d		10s	11¼d
15	Of Mr Walker, Hale Fenn (a bill)		10s	6d			
20	Of Mr Dennis, Donington Eaudike (a bill)	£1	4s				
	1 Stone of Lump Sugar of Mr Hunt at 10d					11s	6d
	Retail &c. 15s. Weekly bill 16s 0¾d.		15s			16s	0¾d
21	A Latin Grammar of Mrs Worley					1s	6d
23	Of Mr Shilcock's Maid a bill		7s				
27	Of Mr Cole, Burtoft, a bill		17s	6d			
	1 Quarter's Land Tax to Mr Bowers					3s	
	Retail 6s 6d. Weekly bill 16s 9½d.		6s	6d		16s	9¾d
29	Of Mrs Chester a bill (Bicker)		5s	6d			
30	To R. Codling for 40 Rods (each 20 Feet) and 1 Staff of Ditching at 8d a Rod				£1	7s	
	Received of -ditto- a bill		4s	6d			
30	The late Mr Spendly's Account of Mr Golding	£1	9s				
	To -ditto- for 3 Sacks of Oats					19s	

January 1781 (cont.)	Received	Paid
To Mrs Pakey for 20 Stone 2d Flower		£1 16s
To -ditto- for 5 Stone of Best Flower		10s
Of -ditto- a bill	£1 16s 9d	
Of Mr Golding a bill	£2 4s	
To -ditto- for 2 Quarters of Oats		£1
Carried over	**£22 9s 9d**	**£11 2s 2½d**

Mr Wm W—d
Sat. Feb. 10. Mr W. W—d came down from London, in order to settle such of his accounts as he is able. He has been with us a fortnight and at present is gone to Bolingbrook; he proposes to return to town next week. He has been out of the Public Business since September but proposes to get into some way of Business on his return if possible. Feb. 21. 1781.

Birth Day
Sat. Feb. 17. 1781. Thro' Divine Mercy I compleated my Thirty first Year. I expected my Brother from Spalding would have dined with me on the Sunday – but I imagine Business prevented.

Thursday March 1. 1781
Matthew begun to learn writing at Mr Whitehead's. I thank God he can now read tolerably well – have got a Latin Grammar, & he has begun these Winter Evenings to get lessons therein.

General Evening Post
Mr Shilcock, Mr Golding, Mr Hervey, Mercer, & myself have joined to take in the above London Paper. We got the 1st Paper on Saturday March 10. 1781.[215]

[f.51]
February 1781: 2nd Month, 28[216] Days

		Received	Paid
	Brought over	**£22 9s 9d**	**£11 2s 2½d**
1	Of Mr B. Crosby, Gosberton Risgate, a bill	19s	
	Of Wm Haw, Donington, a bill	6s	
2	Of Mrs Boots, Donington, a bill	15s 6d	
3	Retail &c. 8s. Weekly bill 8s 2¼d.	8s	8s 2¼d
5	Of Mr Burrus, Cooper, in part	£1 1s	
7	To Mr Main for 1 Year's Shaving &c.		17s
	Received of him a bill	12s 6d	
	Paid to R. Codling & B. Upton for 39 Rods of Ditching at 5d per Rod		16s 3d
	Of Mr Dodd a bill	13s 6d	
8	Of Mr Smith at Mr Whitehead's	15s	
	Of J. Hall a bill	11s	
	Paid to -ditto- a Milk bill		11s
9	Of Benjamin Wright, Donington Eaudike, a bill	15s	

---

[215] This was published three times a week and was circulated further afield than some other London papers.
[216] MS '29'.

February 1781 (cont.)	Received		Paid	
Of J. Winters, Donington Northorp, a bill	6s	6d		
10 Of Mrs Godley, Bicker Gauntlet, in part	£1	1s		
Retail &c. 13s 6d. Weekly bill 13s 7d.	13s	6d	13s	7d
12 Of Mr Samuel Pike a bill	£1	6s		
16 Pair of ground Lamb Gloves of Mr Cew			2s	
17 To Mr Tory, Hale, for a new Watch			£5	5s
Retail &c. 15s 6d. Weekly bill 15s 8¾d.	15s	6d	15s	8¾d
21 Of Mr Brooks, Gosberton Risgate, a bill	£1	2s		
To Wm Green towards the loss of his Cow			1s	
22 Of Miss Cole, Donington, a bill	6s	6d		
24 Remainder of Mrs Godley's bill	13s			
Retail &c. 16s. Weekly bill 17s 11½d.	16s		17s	11½d
To my Wife on the 6th Instant			£3	3s
25 Of Thos Stookes, Donington, a bill	10s	6d		
26 Of J. Parker, Donington, a bill	12s	6d		
To -ditto- for 4 Coup: Chickens 4s 4d. Bacon 2s.			6s	4d
28 Of Anthony Robinson, Swineshead, in part	10s	6d		
	£37	**19s 9d**	**£24 19s**	**3d**

Agreement with Mrs Flinders
April 3. 1781. Finished and signed the agreement with Mrs Flinders. Noted under August 1780.

Journey to Boston, April 4 1781. Wednesday
Attended the Justices' meeting at Boston, amongst other Creditors of the late Martin Wise on the Parish account in order to compell John Haw to settle the Parish Bills.

Birth of a Son
With gratitude to a mercifull Providence I note that my wife was delivered of a fine Boy very early this Morning (viz. half an hour after 12) Thursday April 5. – She had a severe but natural Labour, I thank God, both are hopefull.[217]

Child, Sat. Ap. 28. 1785
I thank God my wife is now recovered, & the child went this day to nurse at Bett: Wells's (the Labourer's wife) at 2s 6d per Week & 1d Milk per Day of John Kend-all's. It is at present a fine Child, & I hope this Woman will prove a good nurse.

[f.51v]
March 1781: 3rd Month, 31 Days

	Received		Paid	
Brought over	**£37 19s**	**9d**	**£24 19s**	**3d**
3 Of Mr Shepherd a bill	£3	1s		
Retail &c. 10s 6d. Weekly bill 15s 6½d.	10s	6d	15s	6½d
Dividend of the late Mr Cook's bill	5s	3d		
5 Pair of Leathern Baggs of Mr Ward			12s	
8 To Mrs Moor for 20 Weeks' Schooling at 4d			6s	8d

---

[217] This is the child who would come to be given the epithet "my unfortunate son John", as subsequent entries will show.

March 1781 (cont.)	**Received**		**Paid**	
Received of -ditto- a bill	5s	5d		
A Bread Tin 18d. A Tin Saucepan 9d.			2s	3d
Things mending at the Brazier's				9d
9 Of Mr Thompson, Donington, a bill	£1	16s		
To -ditto- for 1½ Chalders of Coals at 25s			£1 17s	6d
To -ditto- Carriage of the same			7s	6d
Porterage 14d. Ale for the Porters 4d.			1s	6d
Ten Oz Worstead for Boot Stockings			1s	8d
10 To Mrs Pakey for 10 Stone of best Flower			£1 0s	6d
Of Mr Vicars, Swineshead, a bill	10s	6d		
Of Mr Taylor, Donington North Ing, a bill	6s			
Of Mr Jackson, Bicker, in part	£1 11s	6d		
Retail &c. 12s. Weekly bill 13s 9½d.	12s		13s	9½d
Cambric a Yard, 22d			1s	10d
15 Of Mr J. Wires, Swineshead Fen Houses(a Labour)	£1	1s		
Writing Paper 9d. Cappaper[218] Paper 3d.			1s	
16 17 Nos of the Field of Mars (up to 28)			8s	6d
Of Benjamin Blackwell a bill	5s	6d		
17 Retail &c. 11s. Weekly bill 11s 2d.	11s		11s	2d
19 To Messrs Ferneyhough & Wilson in full			£10 1s	
To -ditto- towards the London Paper			10s	6d
20 Of H. Everitt Senior a bill	11s	6d		
To Ann Smith for 6 Pound of Honey			3s	
21 Of Mr Duckett, Quadring Eaudike, a bill	£2	14s		
22 Nutmegs 4oz of Mr Hunt			2s	4d
23 Of Mr Harvey, Draper, a bill	6s			
24 Retail &c. 15s 6d. Weekly bill 15s 7d.	15s	6d	15s	7d
26 Of Mr West, Donington, a bill	13s	6d		
To Wm Hall a Milk bill			16s	
Received of -ditto- a bill	16s			
30 To R. Codling for 3 Rods of Ditching			2s	
Retail &c. 11s 6d. Weekly bill 11s 6¾d.	11s	6d	11s	6¾d
	£55 3s	**5d**	**£45 3s**	**4¾d**

Improvements 1781

Since my agreement with Mrs Flinders, I have been obliged to do several things at the Yard and out Buildings. I have got a Cope Wall built in the front and have procured Raft for a pair of close Gates – have also had the Causway and Channell widened & repaired, & Ed. Gibson has repaired by splinting the Old Coal house and Barn, & also has made a partition in the Barn, the farther end for a stable, which I have had repaved. May 2.

May Feast Boston

Tues. 1. I made a Journey to Boston (by invitation from Mr Wayet Junior the Mayor) to dine at the May Feast; I returned in the Evening.

---

[218] See n.93 above.

[f.52]
April 1781: 4th Month, 30 Days

		Received			Paid		
Brought over		**£55**	**3s**	**5d**	**£45**	**3s**	**4¾d**
3	To Mrs Flinders the Consideration Money for quitting the Lease				£8		
	To -ditto- for keeping my Horse from July 1st 1780 to April 5th 1781 (3 Quarters of a Year)				£3	15s	
	To -ditto- for Ditching in the Green					6s	
	Of -ditto- for one Year's Rent due Apr. 5.	£2	3s				
6	Carriage of Druggs from London					6s	2d
7	Of Mr J. Haw, Northorp, a bill		19s				
	Retail &c. 14s 6d. Weekly bill 14s 5¼ d.		14s	6d		14s	5¼d
9	To Wm Morris a bill for Iron					4s	2d
10	Of Terebinth: 2lb of Mr Harvey					2s	6d
13	Of Mr Benington, Wigtoft, a bill		12s	6d			
14	Of James Hare's Daughter, Quadring Eaudike		5s				
	Retail &c. 15s 6d. Weekly bill 15s 9¼ d.		15s	6d		15s	9¼d
15	Of Joseph Haw, Donington, a bill		13s				
	Of J. Chamberlain, Surfleet, a bill	£1	0s	6d			
	Of Mr Injelaw, Quadring Eaudike, a bill	£1	10s				
16	To J. Wells, Shoemaker, a bill in full					10s	6d
	To Eliz. Bingham, Earnest Money					2s	6d
18	Sugar 4lb Shop use					2s	4d
19	Of Mr Mablestone, Bicker, a bill		16s	6d			
20	A Pair of Scissars of J. Bettison					1s	
21	Retail &c. 14s 6d. Weekly bill 14s 5½d.		14s	6d		14s	5½d
24	Window Money ½ Yr 8s 6d. Land Tax ¼ Yr 3s. House Tax ½ Yr 1s 3d.					12s	9d
25	Of Mr Brand, Hale Barr (a Labour)	£1	1s				
26	Of J. Beecroft Junior a bill	£1	2s				
28	Of Thos Risbrook, Swineshead, a bill	£1	3s				
	To J. Bettison Earnest Money					1s	
	Retail &c. 18s. Weekly bill 18s 3d.		18s			18s	3d
30	A Hat of Mr Harvey					10s	6d
Carried over		**£69**	**11s**	**5d**	**£63**	**0s**	**8¾d**

Child's Baptism
Th. May 31. We had our last Child John Baptized, the Sponsors Mr Golding and Mr D. Trimnell; Miss Eyre of Sleaford and Miss Shilcock. The rest of the Company Mrs Shilcock & Miss Martha, Mr & Mrs Gleed, Miss Cragg and Mr Taylor, Mr Pakey and Miss Golding, and my neice Henrietta. Mr Powell & Mr S. Ward were expected but did not come. It was an agreable party; we got to Bed about 2 in the Morning. If there is any benefit in this Ceremony, I pray God the Infant may have it.

Neice's Visit
Tues. June 5. My Neice from Spalding has been on a visit to us about a fortnight. She proposes leaving us tomorrow and intends to take Matthew with her to Spalding for a little time during his Witsuntide Holidays.

Health

Have been for several days troubled with a disagreable deafness in one Ear, I imagine from a cold. I took a little Blood from my left arm, and my wife Syringed that Ear with Sage Tea. It has gradually gone off, & have nothing of it at present.

[f.52v]
May 1781: 5th Month, 31 Days

		Received			Paid		
Brought over		**£69**	**11s**	**5d**	**£63**	**0s**	**8¾d**
1	Of Mr Crosby, Gosberton, the late Wm Garner's Account	£2	1s				
	Paid to Mr Garfit & Co a Raft bill				£1	10s	5d
2	Harden[219] 3 Yards at 10d for the Child's Bed					2s	6d
3	To Dorothy Beachill for Nursing					15s	
	To the Revd Mr Powell Church Money					1s	
5	Of a Woman at Th. Moor's, Northorp		15s				
	Of J. Tasker, Quadring, a bill		6s				
	To Wm Smith, Thatcher, for 4 Days and a half Daubing 13s 6d. Rushrope 3d.					13s	9d
	Retail &c. 18s 6d. Weekly bill 18s 8½d.		18s	6d		18s	8½d
	Carriage of Raff[220] from Boston					2s	
7	Of Wm Mapletoft a bill		19s				
	Bought things at his Sale					3s	10d
12	Of Mr Claxon, Quadring, a bill		7s	6d			
	Retail &c. 16s. Weekly bill 15s 10d.		16s			15s	10d
13	To Ann Parker a Year's Wages				£3		
	To J. Bettison a Year's Wages				£1	10s	
15	Of Mrs Robinson, Bicker Gauntlet, a bill		6s	6d			
16	To R. Jackson a bill in full					12s	6d
	Received of him a bill		7s				
17	To W. Fairam for Work 6s. 2 Coup: Rabbits 2s.					8s	
	Received of him in part		6s				
	Of Mr Samuel Pike a bill		7s				
18	To Messrs Barrit & Robinson in full				£6	12s	6d
19	Retail &c. 15s. Weekly bill 14s 10¼d.		15s			14s	10¼d
20	Of Mr Trimnell's Man a bill		12s				
	To J. Wells for Shoes Soling					2s	
26	Of A. Green, Wigtoft, a bill		17s	6d			
	Of Mr Wilcocks, Bicker, a bill		11s	6d			
	The Salary for Wigtoft Poor	£4	4s				
	Of Mr Stocks, Wigtoft, a bill		6s	6d			
	Quadring Parish Bill of Mr Ladd	£5	11s				
	Of J. Brumpton, Bicker, a bill		9s	6d			
	To Mr Holbourn, Horfleet, for 6 Trays					15s	
	Received of him a bill		5s				
	Of Mr Houseley, Bicker, a bill	£3	3s				
	Of Mr Harrison, Fosdike, a bill	£1	11s	6d			
	Weekly bill 18s 11¾d. Retail &c. 19s.		19s			18s	11¾d
28	Assembly Expences 5s.					5s	
29	Of Mr Clifton a bill	£1	5s				

---

219 See n.80 above.
220 Foreign timber, usually deals (*OED*).

May 1781 (cont.)	Received			Paid		
	Sugar 4lb Shop use 2s 4d				2s	4d
	To my Wife on the 6th			£3	3s	
30	Mett[221] of Coals of J. Wells				2s	
31	Of J. Brown, Donington, by bill	£1	5s			
		£98	**16s**	**5d**	**£86**	**11s**	**11¼d**

Journey to Boston

Wed. June 20. I took a ride to Boston, paid my Insurance Money, dined with Mr Hall at Mr Baily's & also got tea; and returned in the Evening. Mr Hall has been thro' Donington to Folkinham 2 or 3 times lately to see Mr Beatie & has called.

[f.53]
June 1781: 6th Month, 30 Days

		Received			Paid		
[Brought over]		**£98**	**16s**	**5d**	**£86**	**11s**	**11¼d**
1	To Mr Golding for two Oak Posts					6s	
2	To Mr Gunthorp a Meat bill					10s	9d
	Received of him a bill		5s	6d			
	Retail &c. £1 5s 6d. Weekly bill £1 5s 9½d.	£1	5s	6d	£1	5s	9½d
5	To Wm Kirk, Bicker, for 28½ Gallons of Ale				£1	8s	6d
	Received of him a bill	£1	4s	6d			
7	Of R. Kitchen, Northorp, in part		10s	6d			
9	Interest of £150 of Thos Smith of Frampton West End due May 4th	£7	10s				
	Of Jos. Wright Junior a bill		13s	6d			
	Retail &c. 16s. Weekly bill 16s 0½d.		16s			16s	0½d
12	Of Thos Bee, Bicker (a Labour)	£1	1s				
	Of Arthur Dickinson, Bicker Gauntlet (a Labour)	£1	1s				
13	To Mr Wilcockson, Druggist, in full				£3	10s	6d
14	Of Mrs Dixon Junior (a Labour)		10s	6d			
16	Of J. Ayre, Gosberton, a bill		5s				
	Retail &c. £1 2s. Weekly bill £1 2s 0½d.	£1	2s		£1	2s	0½d
18	Of Mr Torry's Maid Servant a bill		6s				
	Of J. Kenning a bill		14s	6d			
19	To J. Wells for Coals 2s. Carriage 6d.					2s	6d
	Two Chaldrons of Coals at 25s				£2	10s	
	Porterage 14d. Ale 6d.					1s	8d
20	The Salary for Bicker Poor	£4	4s				
	Sun Fire Office Insurance Money					9s	
	Pomfrett's Poems[222]					1s	
21	One Year's Servants Tax				£1	1s	
	Of Wm Edinborough, Caythorp (a Labour)		15s				
22	14 Nos of the Field of Mars (42)					7s	
	Of John Thompson (Hostler) a bill		7s				
23	Retail &c. 18s. Weekly bill 17s 11¼d.		18s			17s	11¼d

---

[221] A unit of measurement (*OED*).

[222] John Pomfret (1667–1702): his Poems were reprinted regularly throughout the eighteenth century. Flinders may have bought *The poetical works of John Pomfret. With the life of the author* (Edinburgh, 1779) (ESTC).

June 1781 (cont.)	Received	Paid
27 Of Mr Pepper, Quadring, a bill	18s	
28 A Scythe of Wm Morris		4s 6d
30 Retail &c. 14s. Weekly bill 14s.	14s	14s
Carried over	**£123 17s 11d**	**£102 0s 2d**

My Wife's Journey to Bolingbrook and Louth

Sat. June 30. My Wife went with her Brother to Bolingbrook, staid there untill Wed. July 4, then went with him to Louth & staid with her Sister & Friends untill Monday July 9 on which Evening she returned to Bolingbrook. On Tues. July 10 after Dinner I went to Bolingbrook and we returned on Wed. July 11. I thank God this Journey has been accomplished without any accident and during the little time I was out, was not very materially wanted.

Mr Wm W—d

I have to note that Mr & Mrs W. have been down from [damaged page] on what motive I can scarce say. They are returned, & have left their Son Wm at Mr Whitehead's School, & have desired me to take Thomas as a Servant, which I have consented to do, and expect him here ere long. September 18. 1781.

Health

Have been as usually I am at this Season troubled with a Bilious remitting Fever for about 10 days, insomuch [f.53v] as to render my Business excedingly fatiguing – being obliged several days to go to Bed at noon. I took an Emetic, which did me service, a Saline Mixture, and am now taking the Cortex,[223] & I thank God, am gaining my Appetite apace & am on the mending hand. September 18. 1781.

July 1781: 7th Month, 31 Days

	Received	Paid
Brought over	**£123 17s 11d**	**£102 0s 2d**
1 Of John Keel in part	10s 6d	
2 Bees Wax of Mr Codling 2 Pound ¾ at 18d		4s 1½d
Of Mrs Shepherd a bill	£4 2s	
To -ditto- for 3 Weeks Joice[224] of my Horse		6s
3 Of Mr Dunn, Quadring, a bill	10s 6d	
To Mr Barnett, Bricklayer, a bill		£2 4s 6d
Received of him a bill	£2	
4 Of Mr Smith at Mr Whitehead's a bill	11s 6d	
To Wm Smith, Thatcher, for a Job		1s
7 To B. Upton & Co for Mowing my 3 Acres		7s
Retail &c. 12s 6d. Weekly bill 12s 4¾d.	12s 6d	12s 4¾d
10 To John Strapps a bill in full		12s 2d
Of -ditto- a bill	7s 6d	
11 Expences to Bolingbrook and back		4s 2½d
14 Of Mr Trickett, Donington, a bill	15s	
Of J. Clark, Quadring, a bill	8s 6d	

---

[223] Bark. See n.194 above.
[224] Joice or joist: from gist or agistment, to pasture animals (*OED*).

July 1781 (cont.)		**Received**		**Paid**	
	Of Wm Moor (Labourer) a bill	10s	6d		
	To R. Codling for 4 Pound of Yellow Wax			6s	
	Retail &c. 15s 6d. Weekly bill 15s 4¼d.	15s	6d	15s	4¼d
16	Two Women 2 days at Hay at 8d			2s	8d
	A Lock for the Parlour door &c.			4s	
	A Lion's Head Knocker for the Outdoor			2s	9d
17	Brown Linnen 1 Yard for Shop use			1s	
18	To J. Wells for Carriage of Phials &c.			2s	8d
21	Retail &c. £1 4s 0d. Weekly bill £1 4s 3½d.	£1 4s		£1 4s	3½d
22	Of H. Everitt Junior (a Labour)	10s	6d		
25	Of Mr J. Ashworth a bill	14s	7d		
	Paid to him a bill for Meat			19s	7d
26	Of Mr Caswell, Quadring, by bills	£2 1s			
27	Of Mr Knight, Quadring, a bill	13s			
28	Retail &c. £1 1s 0d. Weekly bill £1 0s 10½d.	£1 1s		£1 0s	10½d
30	Paid to Mrs Pakey for Flower 5 Stone of the Best, 9s 6d; 5 -ditto- 3d Sort, 8s 3d.			17s	9d
	To Mr Hunt for 3 Hankerchiefs			4s	4d
	Of Mr Grant, Baker, a bill	15s			
31	Of J. Lammin a bill	7s			
	Currants for Wine			1s	
	20 Yards of Sheeting Cloth weaving at 5d			8s	4d
	Dressing and warping of -ditto- – 9d.				9d
	12½ Yards of Huckaback[225] weaving at 8d			8s	4d
	Dressing and warping of -ditto- – 8d				8d
	Of Martin Cottam a bill	6s	6d		
£29 2s 7d		**£142 14s**	**6d**	**£113 11s**	**11d**

[f.54]
August 1781: 8th Month, 31 Days

		Received		**Paid**	
Brought over		**£142 14s**	**6d**	**£113 11s**	**11d**
1	The late Ed. Harrison's bill, Bicker	£1 2s			
4	Powder Sugar 7lb of Mr Hunt			4s	
	Carriage of Druggs from Barrit & Co			3s	6d
5	Of J. Smith at the Barr (a Labour)	10s	6d		
	Retail &c. 15s 6d. Weekly bill 15s 6½d.	15s	6d	15s	6½d
	Of John Bettison a bill	12s			
6	To my Wife			£3 3s	
9	Of —- Hodge, Blacksmith, Swineshead, in part	15s			
11	Of J. Walker, Quadring, in part	£1 1s			
	Retail &c. 14s 6d. Weekly bill 14s 5¼d.	14s	6d	14s	5¼d
12	Of Mr Percival, Quadring, in part	10s	6d		
15	To Mr Harvey a bill for 3 Shirts			£1 4s	3d
18	Of Mr Tenny a bill	£1 12s	6d		
	Retail &c. 19s 0d. Weekly bill 19s 2½d.	19s		19s	2½d
20	Sugar Shop use 2s 10d. Rum a Quart 3s 4d.			6s	2d
22	Of Wm King, Bicker, a bill	6s			
23	Of Stephen Dalton a bill	£1 2s			

---

225 Huckaback: a stout linen fabric (*OED*).

August 1781 (cont.)		**Received**		**Paid**	
	Pair of Silk and Thread Stockings			5s	6d
25	Of R. Holmes, Bicker (a Labour)	£1 1s			
21	Retail &c. 17s. Weekly bill 17s 1½d.	17s		17s	1½d
27	Of Mr Duckett, Quadring Eaudike, a bill	7s			
28	Of Mr Gee, Hale Fenn (a Labour)	£1 1s	0d		
29	Of J. Kitchen, Quadring, a bill	5s	6d		
30	Of Mr French a bill	5s			
£34 6s 10¼d[226]		**£156 11s**	**6d**	**£122 6s 10¼d**	

November 23. 1781. Servants

I have to note that we have changed both our Servants this Martinmas. I had no intention of parting with the Lad, J. Bettison, but to oblige Mr Ward by taking his Son who came to me October 18, & I hope after the experience I have had of him, he will suit. In the place of Elizabeth Bingham, we have again hired our former servant Ann Parker, who left us last May, E. B. not being able to do our Business & too slow, otherwise the Girl had many good properties. The old Servants have left us this day.

Child at Nurse, Nov. 23

I have to note that we have put our young child[227] to Nurse at R. Nicholas's, at the usual price. He has been there a month & I believe it is a good place. The reason of taking him from Elizabeth Wells, was her[228] advanced pregnancy. We had him at home about a Month but found it so inconvenient that he was obliged to go out again; he was at J. Thompson's (Hostler) about a week, but his wife was soon tired. He is naturally a cross child.

[f.54v]
September 1781: 9th Month, 30 Days

		Received		**Paid**		
	Brought over	**£156 11s**	**6d**	**£122**	**6s**	**10¼d**
1	To Mr Parker, Joiner, a bill				10s	6d
	Received of him a bill	8s				
	Of Mrs Vessey, Gosberton, a bill	5s				
	Of Mr Samuel Ward £7 10s being a Year's Interest					
	of £150 due June 11th last	£7 10s				
	Paid to -ditto- a bill for Hemp and Flax			£1	7s	11d
	To Mrs Langley, Bolingbrooke, a present			£1	1s	
	Pair of Spatterdashes[229]				4s	6d
	To Messrs Ferneyhough & Wilson in full			£5	10s	
	Of -ditto- Discount of two bills	7s	9d			
	Retail &c. 12s 6d. Weekly bill 12s 3½d.	12s	6d		12s	3½d
2	Of Mr Cook, Donington, a bill	14s				
3	A Tin Salve Box sometime ago				1s	
	Of Charles Fever, Horfleet, in part	£1 1s				
	To Mr Ward for a large Tin Box				2s	

[226] Sum incorrectly calculated.
[227] John.
[228] MS 'here'.
[229] Long gaiters or leggings, the ancestor of spats (*OED*).

September 1781 (cont.)

		Received			Paid		
4	Of Mr Love, Swineshead, in part	£7	7s				
	Of Samuel Bacchus (a Labour)		10s	6d			
6	Of Thos Moor, Northorp (a Labour)		15s				
8	Of Abraham Jackson, Swineshead, a bill	£1	3s	6d			
	Retail &c. £1 1s. Weekly bill £1 1s 1½d.	£1	1s		£1	1s	1½d
10	A Pair of Spurrs of Mrs Porter, Boston					6s	6d
	Of Mr Sutton, Gosberton Risgate (a Labour)	£1	1s				
	Printed Linnen for the young Child's Frocks					6s	6d
	Of Wm Green, Bicker Fenn, in part		6s				
15	Of Francis Horn, Bicker, a bill		17s				
	Of Mr J. Godley, Bicker Gauntlet, a bill	£3	7s	6d			
	Retail &c. £1 5s 6d. Weekly bill £1 5s 7½d.	£1	5s	6d	£1	5s	7½d
19	To Elizabeth Wells for 20 Weeks & 2 days Nursing the Child at 2s 6d per Week				£2	11s	
	Received of -ditto- a bill		7s				
21	Carriage of Druggs from London					2s	8d
22	Retail &c. £1 1s 6d. Weekly bill £1 1s 10d.	£1	1s	6d	£1	1s	10d
27	One Week's Nursing the Child					2s	
28	Of Mr Gadsby, Bicker, a bill		9s				
29	Of Mr Nunnery, Gosberton, a bill	£1					
	Retail &c. 17s 6d. Weekly bill 17s 10¼d.		17s	6d		17s	10¼d
30	Bettsy's Schooling 29 Weeks at 4d					9s	8d
£48 9s 11d	**Carried over**	**£188**	**18s**	**9d**	**£140**	**8s**	**10d**

[f.55]

October 1781: 10th Month, 31 Days

		Received			Paid		
Brought over		£188	18s	9d	£140	8s	10d
6	Of Mr Jackson, Donington North Ing, a bill	£1	3s	4d			
	Weekly bill £1 1s 1½d. Retail &c. £1 1s.	£1	1s		£1	1s	1½d
7	Of Mrs Tenant, Bicker Gauntlet, in part		10s	6d			
8	Of Miss Jarvis, Bicker, a bill		9s				
9	Of a Stranger, Swineshead (for L.V. Cure)		15s				
10	Shirts making					2s	6d
	Journey to Spalding					1s	3d
11	Out Rent at the Wikes Court					8s	5d
13	Retail &c. £1 3s 0d. Weekly bill £1 2s 10½d.	£1	3s		£1	2s	10½d
15	Of John Kiel, Donington, in part		5s	6d			
17	Of Mr Trimnell's Servant Maid a bill		5s				
	Of Mr Brand, Hale Bar, a bill	£3	11s				
	Of the Revd Mr Fern's[230] Maid, Wigtoft, a bill		7s				
	Of Mr Jackson, Swineshead Fen Houses, a bill		8s				
	Of Mr Aspland, Holland Fen, a Labour	£1	1s				
	Of Mr Wilkinson, Gardener, Bicker, -ditto-	£1	1s				
18	Cortex Peruvian 3½lb at 5s					17s	6d
	Of Mrs Broughton, Bicker, a bill		4s				
	Of Mrs Peach, Gosberton, a bill	£1	11s				
19	A Peach Tree 1s 6d. A Pear -ditto- 16d.					2s	10d
	Work done in the Garden 2s 8d					2s	8d

230 Revd George Ferne MA, Vicar of Wigtoft with Quadring 1737–1790.

October 1781 (cont.)

		Received			Paid		
20	Retail &c. £1 5s. Weekly bill £1 5s 2½d.	£1	5s		£1	5s	2½d
26	Of J. Harness, Ball Hall, a Composition of 5s per £ for £3		15s				
	Of Mr Dixon, Donington, a bill		15s	6d			
	Two Chaldrons of Coals at 25s				£2	10s	
	Porterage 16d. Ale 8d.					2s	
27	A Pair of Stockings					2s	9d
	Of Mr Baldwick Junior, Quadring, a bill		13s				
	Retail &c. £1 5s 6d. Weekly bill £1 5s 6¼d.	£1	5s	6d	£1	5s	6¼d
28	Of Luke Tebb, Donington Northorp, a bill	£1	6s				
29	To Ed. Gibson a bill in full				£3	15s	6d
	Received of him a bill	£2	18s	6d			
30	Of Mr Samuel Pike a bill	£1	5s	6d			
31	Pair of Shoes of J. Wells						6s
£59 3s 1½d		**£212**	**18s**	**1d**	**£153**	**14s**	**11½d**

[f.55v]

November 1781: 11th Month, 30 Days

		Received			Paid		
Brought over		**£212**	**18s**	**1d**	**£153**	**14s**	**11½d**
3	Of Mr Green, Bicker, a bill	£3					
	Retail &c. £1 0s 6d. Weekly bill £1 0s 7½d.	£1	0s	6d	£1	0s	7½d
5	To Messrs Barrit & Robinson in full				£3	14s	
6	To my Wife				£3	3s	
9	Of Mrs Eyre (at Mr Shilcock's) a bill		16s	6d			
	Of Mr Cook, Northorp, a bill	£1	3s	6d			
	Of Mr Harvey, Publican, a bill	£2	9s				
	Of -ditto- his Servant's bill		6s				
	To -ditto- a bill for Liquors					16s	6d
	Of -ditto- the late Wm Cole's bill		15s	6d			
10	Retail &c. £1 1s 6d. Weekly bill £1 1s 9¾d.	£1	1s	6d	£1	1s	9¾d
11	Remainder of J. Keel's bill		5s				
12	To Mr Kirk, Bicker, for 18 Gallons Ale					18s	
	To -ditto- for 10 Gallons Small Beer					1s	8d
	Of Mr Harvey's Maid (Draper) a bill	£1					
13	To Edward Laykins a bill in full				£1	14s	6d
	Received of him a bill		10s	6d			
15	To Mr May, Glass Manufacturer,[231] in full				£3	1s	6d
17	To Mrs Pakey for 5 Stone of Flower					9s	
	Of Miss Golding a bill		15s				
	Of Mr Garner, Donington, for Arg. Viv.[232] 1lb		5s				
	Of — Bucknell, Donington Northorp, a bill		19s	6d			
	Retail &c. 14s. Weekly bill 14s 0¾d.		14s			14s	0¾d
18	Of Mr Wilson, Shoemaker, Great Hale		17s	6d			
20	Money for the Scholars' Feast					2s	6d
22	To Eliz. Nicholas for Nursing the Child 1 Month					10s	
23	To J. Bettison ½ Year's Wages				£1	1s	
	To Elizabeth Bingham ½ Year's Wages				£1	7s	6d
	A Copper Plate-warmer of Mr Brotherton					10s	6d

---

[231] See n.202 above.
[232] *Argentum vivum* (Quicksilver).

November 1781 (cont.)	Received			Paid		
Received of him a bill		6s				
24 Of Mr Wilton, Bicker, a bill		9s	6d			
Retail &c. 18s. Weekly bill 18s 3¼d.		18s			18s	3¼d
27 Of Miss Jaques a bill		10s				
£56 1s 2¼d **Carried over**	**£231**	**0s**	**7d**	**£174**	**19s**	**4¾d**

Mrs Carr's Visit

I have to note that my wife's Sister, Mrs Carr of Louth, has been over on a Visit to us. She came on New Year's Day, and left us this day, Jan. 12. 1782. The reason of her coming at this season of the Year was principally to consult me about a disorder on her Tongue, which by the Physician at Louth was feared to be Cancerous; but whatever its appearance may have been, she at present appears to me to be free from any thing of that kind, & what disorder she has to be a Nervous Affection.

[f.56]
December 1781: 12th Month, 31 Days

	Received			Paid		
Brought over	**£231**	**0s**	**7d**	**£174**	**19s**	**4¾d**
1 Of Thos Howett, Quadring, a bill		10s	6d			
Retail &c. 18s 6d. Weekly bill 18s 5d.		18s	6d		18s	5d
3 Of Benjamin Upton in part		6s				
4 Of Mrs Wolton Senior, Gosberton, a bill		17s	6d			
Of J. Allen, Swineshead, a Labour	£1	1s				
15 Pound of Flax at 10d. 3 Pound at 6d of Mr Toons.						
Spining 9d.					14s	9d
6 Of Mr Pearson, Excise Officer, a bill	£1	9s	6d			
7 A Glass for the keeping room					10s	6d
8 To Mr Wilcockson, Druggist, in full				£3	17s	
Retail &c. 17s 6d. Weekly bill 17s 9d.		17s	6d		17s	9d
11 To Mr Hunt, Draper, a bill in full				£3	15s	3d
To -ditto- ½ Year's Poor Assessment					5s	6d
Received of him on the Parish Account	£4	17s	3d			
Of -ditto- his own bill	£1	10s				
13 A day's Gardening 1s 6d. A B. Gilead Fir[233] 1s 6d.					3s	
15 Of Mr Jenings, Bicker Gauntlet, a bill		5s	6d			
Of Mr Marsh, Quadring, a bill		6s				
Retail &c. £1 0s 0d. Weekly bill 19s 10½d.	£1				19s	10½d
18 Of Captain Nettleton, Swineshead Abbey, a bill	£6	16s	6d			
Of Anthony Robinson, Swineshead, in part		10s	6d			
20 To E. Nicholas for Nursing the Child 1 Month					10s	
To Mrs Pakey for 6½ Stone of flower					11s	8d
22 Of Mr Carby, Hale Fen (a Labour)	£1	1s				
Retail &c. 16s 6d. Weekly bill 16s 5½d.		16s	6d		16s	5½d
23 The late Wm Morris's bill		17s				
27 To Mr Harvey, Draper, a bill				£1	19s	6d
Received of him by bills		15s	6d			
28 To Mr Gunthorp a bill for Meat					11s	

---

233 Balm of Gilead Fir (*Abies balsamea*).

December 1781 (cont.)	Received			Paid		
Received of him a bill		7s				
29 Retail &c £1 1s 6d. Weekly bill £1 1s 7d.	£1	1s	6d	£1	1s	7d
31 Betsy's Schooling 8 Weeks 2s 8d. Communion 6d.					3s	2d
Of Mr Jarvis, Bicker, a bill	£3	17s				
Total Receipts & Payments in 1781	**£261**	**2s**	**4d**	**£192**	**14s**	**9¾d**

Total gained in 1781	£68 7s 6¼d
Total gained in 10 Years' Business	£628 6s 1d
Total gained in Eleven Years	£696 13s 7¼d

Conclusion of the Year 1781

I have again to offer up to the Divine Creator of all things my most gratefull acknowledgements, for constant and manifold mercies – but it is a more especial manner for continuing myself, wife and 4 Children in Being[234] – and as good a state of health as these frail bodies can well expect. This has been a year of uncommon expence to me – and the times are universally complained off as bad from the consequences of the War, yet thro' mercy I have been enabled to save near Seventy Pounds, which added to my former savings is a considerable help. Jan. 12. 1782.

[f.56v]
January 1782: 1st Month, 31 Days

		Received			Paid		
	Overplus Money from the Retail	£5	5s				
4	17 Nos of the Field of Mars					8s	6d
5	Of Mr Turnhill at the Cow a bill		13s				
	Retail &c. £1 3s 6d. Weekly bill £1 3s 5¾d.	£1	3s	6d	£1	3s	5¾d
	Of Mr Thos Green, Donington		6s				
8	The late Mrs Robinson's bill of Mr Morris		14s	6d			
	Of Mr Morris, Horfleet (2 Labours)	£2	2s				
10	Of Wm Bell, Wigtoft Marsh, a bill		7s	6d			
	Of Thos Speed a bill		18s				
12	Of Mr Ward a bill	£1	4s				
	Retail &c. 16s 6d. Weekly bill 16s 5½d.		16s	6d		16s	5½d
15	Of Mr Ward's Man Servant a bill		8s				
16	Of Wm Fairam a bill		12s				
	Paid to him a bill for sundries					12s	2d
17	Of Mr Cheeswright, Gosberton Risgate, a bill		12s	6d			
	To E. Nichollas for Nursing the Child 1 Month					10s	
19	Of J. Sharrard (a Labour)		10s	6d			
	Retail &c. 19s 6d. Weekly bill 19s 8¼d.		19s	6d		19s	8¼d
21	To D. Shays, Taylor, a bill in full				£1	2s	6d
	Received of him a bill		18s	6d			
26	Carriage of Druggs from Barrit					3s	9d
	Retail &c. 18s 6d. Weekly bill 18s 9d.		18s	6d		18s	9d
27	Of Wm Moor, Taylor, a bill		14s				
	Of Charles Fever, Horfleet, in part		8s				
£12 16s 2½d	**Carried over**	**£19**	**11s**	**6d**	**£6**	**15s**	**3½d**

[234] At this point there were: Matthew (7), Betsey (6), Susanna (2) and John (9 months).

Agreement with John Tunnard

Feb. 1. 1782. I have this day let my 3 acre Ing Pasture to John Tunnard for £2 2s 0d per Annum, and I am to pay Parish and other expences. This is a very low Rent indeed, but this land has been abused many years, and is in very bad order; & John has engaged, instead of Carting the hay off, to Summer eating to cart 2 or 3 Load of hay into it and eat it off with Sheep; to level where it wants it and to keep the ditches in repair. Feb. 4. 1782.

Sunday Feb. 17, Birth Day

Thro' Divine Mercy I this day compleated my 32 Year. My Brother was kind enough to take a dinner with us & returned in the Evening. It is with concern that I was informed of the Death of Mrs Hursthouse Junior of Tidd by a Letter from my Brother on the 16th.

Health; Sore Throat

For about 3 days preceeding my Birth Day, I was troubled with a disagreable Sore Throat, first relaxation of the Uvula[235] then swelling of the left tonsil – much worse each night, but on the night of my Birth-day, very bad indeed. I took a Purge that day, which operated well. By my Brother's advice [I] had a Blister applied to left side of my Throat; it drew well, relieved that side, but the Uvula & Velum Pend. Palatinum[236] were much tumefied. Gargles I found of little or no use – but the Vapour of Acet. Bull. & Camp.[237] frequently applied I found very serviceable. Have been obliged to keep my Chamber on the 18th, & shall today Tues. the 19th, but I most humbly thank God I am greatly better.

[f.57]
February 1782: 2nd Month, – Days

		Received			Paid		
Brought over		£19	11s	6d	£6	15s	3½d
2	High Way Assessment £5 10s at 3d £					1s	4½d
	Retail &c. 19s 6d. Weekly bill 19s 5d.	19s	6d			19s	5d
4	To J. Kendall for 40 Weeks Milk at 1s 2d				£2	6s	8d
	To -ditto- for Cloth Bleaching					4s	
	Received of him a bill & Interest Money	19s	5d				
6	Paid Mary Holland for bottles					3s	4d
	Of Thos West, Carpenter, Wigtoft, a bill	12s	6d				
	Of Mr Holbourn, Horfleet, a bill	10s	6d				
7	Of R. Jackson, Carpenter, a bill	8s	3d				
	To -ditto- for a Wheel-barrow 5s 6d & a Ladder 6s.					11s	6d
9	Of Mrs Chrunkhorn, Swineshead, a bill	10s	6d				
	Retail &c. 12s 6d. Weekly bill 12s 8¼d.	12s	6d			12s	8¼d
	Paid to my wife on the 6th Instant				£3	10s	
13	To Mr Main a Year's Shaving &c. due the 5th					17s	
14	Of Mr Audis (late of Swineshead) in part	10s					
	Of Mr Brown, Swineshead, a bill	5s	6d				
	To E. Nicholas for one Month's Nursing					10s	

---

[235] The fleshy tissue hanging at the back of the throat.
[236] Soft palate.
[237] Perhaps the vapour of camphorated acetic acid (*Acidum aceticum camphoratum*).

February 1782 (cont.)	Received			Paid		
15 Of Benjamin Blackwell in part	£1	1s				
16 Of Mr Philips, Gosberton Risgate, a bill		11s				
Of Mr J. Jackson, Bicker, remainder of a bill	£1	3s				
Retail &c. £1 4s 0d. Weekly bill £1 4s 3½d.	£1	4s		£1	4s	3½d
17 Of Mr Elverson in part	£4	12s	8d			
Paid to him for a Quarter of Malt				£1	8s	
To him for half a Year's Tithe he paid Mr Powell					1s	8d
18 Of Widow Baxter, Swineshead, a bill		10s	6d			
Paid to my Brother for Trifles on the 17th					2s	6d
23 The weekly bill				£1	6s	0½d
28 Of Mr Lee a bill in full	£1	8s	0d			
To him for 5 Barrells of Small Beer					11s	1d
To him for 3 Quarters Land Tax, due in January					9s	
To him for ½ a Year's Window Money due in October					8s	6d
To him for ½ Year's House Tax due in October					1s	3d
To him for half a Year's Poor Assessment					3s	8d
£13 3s 0¾d Carried over	£35	10s	4d	£22	7s	3¼d

Money Matters, Friday April 5 1782

Thro' a kind Providence having (since I advanced J. Smith of Frampton £150
May 4 1780 – that is almost 2 years) again collected together £100 which I
thought I could spare, I applied to Mr Gleed, to procure me a good chapman[238]
for it; accordingly he informed me Mr Trimnell of Bicker would take it for one
Year. Accordingly Mr T. gave me a Bond for it this day with 5 per Cent Interest; I
have now £400 bringing me in £20 per Annum.

My Wife's Journey

On Sunday May 4 my wife went to Spalding, staid there that night, and the next
Morning went forwards to Tidd in the Fly. She staid at Mr J. Hursthouse's untill
Friday the 10th, in the forenoon of which day she returned to Spalding with Mr
H's young Child in a Post-chaise,[239] and I sent for her home that afternoon. I
should have gone also but could not.

[f.57v]
March 1782: 3rd Month, 31 Days

	Received			Paid		
Brought over	£35	10s	4d	£22	7s	3¼d
1 Of Mr Pycroft, Donington, a bill	£5	17s	3d			
Paid to him a bill for Sundries				£5	1s	3d
2 Retail &c. £1 2s 6d. Weekly bill £1 2s 5½d.	£1	2s	6d	£1	2s	5½d
3 Of Mrs Philips's Son, Gosberton, a bill		14s	6d			
4 Of Mr Sharp, Horfleet, a bill	£1	4s				
5 Sugar 4 Pound at 7d (Shop use)					2s	4d
Lump Sugar 1½ Pound at 1s (Shop use)					1s	6d
6 Of John Stalworth, Donington, a bill		15s				
To him for a day's work (Stacking)					1s	6d
To Wm Tooley for Carriage of the News Paper					3s	

---

238 The word is used here in its sense of 'customer' (*OED*).
239 A carriage hired from stage to stage (*OED*).

March 1782 (cont.)	Received		Paid		
8 To Wm Leedall for bottoming an Arm Chair				2s	6d
9 To Mr Goodwin for 16 Stone of flower at 16d			£1	1s	4d
Cambrick for Shirt Tuckers				2s	6d
Retail &c. 17s. Weekly bill 17s 0½d.	17s			17s	0½d
14 Of Mr Carby, Hale Fenn, a bill	10s	6d			
To E. Nicholas for a Month's Nursing				10s	
16 Retail &c. 16s. Weekly bill 16s 3½d.	16s			16s	3½d
19 Of Mr R. Mason a bill	12s				
20 Of Mr Lamb, Quadring, a bill	13s	6d			
To John Cook, Taylor, a bill				17s	11d
Received of him a bill	15s				
23 Retail &c. 19s. Weekly bill 18s 10½d.	19s			18s	10½d
25 Of J. Wells, Labourer (a Labour)	10s	6d			
27 Of Mr Morley, Bicker, a bill	£4	6s			
28 Of J. Battey at J. Beecroft's, Quadring		9s			
30 Of Robert Reding, Quadring Eaudike, a bill	£1	1s			
The Salary for Bicker Poor of Mr Torks	£4	4s			
To Mrs Pakey for 6 Stone of Flower at 1s 9d				10s	6d
Retail &c. 15s 6d. Weekly bill 15s 5½d.	15s	6d		15s	5½d
To Messrs Ferneyhough & Co in part the 22d			£2	14s	
£23 6s 10¼d **Carried over**	**£61**	**12s**	**7d**	**£38**	**5s**	**8¼d**

Weather

I may remark that the Spring Season has been remarkably Windy, rainy and Cold, & so continues. We have been a good deal flooded, and much damage done in the Fens, and low grounds; we have not had so much water in the Country for many years, I believe not since the great Flood in the winter of 1764. We had a great push of rain in 1773 in May, but not so much as at present. April & hitherto in May has been thought colder than in Winter, some few days excepted. For 3 years past we have had uncommonly dry Seasons, but now we are in the extreme of Wett, but I hope to God it may shortly cease. May 17.

Books

I have begun to take since the Commencement of the Year the Critical Review which I hope to find Instructive & Entertaining.[240] I have also finished the Field of Mars in quarto, in 60 Nos, 2 Vols. It is in Alphabetical order – I should have liked it much better in the Chronological or Historical method. Mr Hunt procured me this work; I was rather too hasty in taking this, as I think it scarce worth the cost. May 17.

[f.58]
April 1782: 4th Month, 30 Days

	Received		Paid		
Brought over	£61	12s	7d	£38	5s	8¼d
2 Of John Green, Donington, in part	£1	1s			
Of Mrs Pattison's Maid a bill	5s				
3 Of Mr Whitehead (by bills)	£6	3s			

[240] A monthly publication originally edited by the novelist Tobias Smollett, it "fearlessly defended public taste and morality, challenged abuses in writing and pretentiousness in publishing".

April 1782 (cont.)		Received			Paid		
	Matthew's Schooling 2¼ Years to this Easter						
	a present to Mr Whitehead				£3	3s	
	To him for Robinson Crusoe, 2 Vols					5s	
6	Retail &c. 15s. Weekly bill 15s 2¼d.		15s			15s	2¼d
8	Of Mr F. Ashworth, Quadring Eaudike, a bill		19s				
11	To E. Nicholas a Month's Nursing					10s	
	Of Jonathan Ancell a bill		12s				
13	Carriage of Druggs from Wilson					5s	6d
	Retail &c. 16s 6d. Weekly bill 16s 6d.		16s	6d		16s	6d
14	Critical Review for January, February & March					3s	
15	Lincoln Coal ½ Chalder 10s. Carriage 1s 6d.					11s	6d
16	Of Mr Petchill, Gosberton Risgate (a Labour)	£1	1s				
18	Of Thos Risebrook, Swineshead (a bill)	£1	3s	6d			
	Of Wm Kirk, Bicker (a bill)		12s				
	To him for Ale 18 Gallons 18s. Beer 10 Galls 1s 8d.					19s	8d
20	Of Wm Boldram, Donington, a bill	£1	10s				
	Paid to him for Leading 2 Chaldrons of Coals					10s	
	Retail &c. 12s 8½d. Weekly bill 12s 8½d.		12s	8½d		12s	8½d
22	Susan's Entrance & Battledore[241] at School					1s	2d
27	Of Mr Ephraim Eastgate's Man Cressy a bill		6s	3d			
	Retail &c. 13s 1d. Weekly bill 13s 1d.		13s	1d		13s	1d
	Paid half a Year's Tithe					2s	6d
29	Of Mr James Shilcock a bill	£6	14s	3½d			
	Paid to him a bill for Sundries				£2	5s	3½d
30	Of Mr Batty's Man Miller, Bicker, a bill		7s	6d			
	Window Money ½ Year 8s 6d. Land Tax ¼ 3s.						
	House Tax ½ Year 1s 3d.					12s	9d
£34 11s 10d	**Carried over**	**£85**	**4s**	**5d**	**£50**	**12s**	**7d**

Servants

I have to remark that our Servant Ann Parker has left us, and in her place we have hired a young woman from Bolingbrook, Ann Barton, sister to the lad I had of that name some years ago; I believe she will suit us. Tommy Ward is still with us as a lad and is like to continue so, untill his Father can do better for him. As we have now got the Child at home, my wife thought in her condition[242] she could not do well without a girl to nurse him, so she hired Mildred Thornton untill Martinmas at 14s.

Purchase of a Cow

As our Family is now increased to the number of 9,[243] we have thought it will be the most saving plan to have a Cow. Accordingly I got J. Tunnard to buy a heifer just at Calving, at Spalding on Tuesday the 18th Inst. She cost me £7, is 2 Years & a half old, and is judged by all who have seen her a fine Creature. We expect her to calve every day, till which time she is at J. Tunnard's & I must joist[244] her during the summer. June 25. 1782.

---

[241] Battledore: a horn-book, or simply a piece of cardboard, with the ABC, Lord's Prayer, etc. for teaching children to read (*OED*).

[242] He could be referring to the fact that Susanna would then have been around 4 months pregnant.

[243] This figure clearly includes servants: there were four Flinders children alive at this time.

[244] See n.224 above.

[f.58v]
May 1782: 5th Month, 31 Days

		Received			Paid		
Brought over		**£85**	**4s**	**5d**	**£50**	**12s**	**7d**
4	Retail &c. 13s 6d. Weekly bill 13s 5¼d.		13s	6d		13s	5¼d
6	To J. Strapps for Saddle mending					1s	
7	The Salary for Wigtoft Poor due at Easter	£4	4s				
8	To Mr Pycroft for 10 Hundred Weight of Pit-Coals					15s	
9	To E. Nicholas a Month's Nursing					10s	
11	My wife's Journey to Tidd					8s	5d
	To my wife on the 6th Instant				£3	10s	
	To Messrs Barrit and Robinson in full				£5	7s	
	The late Mr Jackson's bill, Swineshead Fen Houses		14s	6d			
	Critical Review for April					1s	
	Retail 13s. Weekly bill 13s 2¾d.		13s			13s	2¾d
13	To Ann Parker ½ Year's Wages due the 12th				£1	10s	
16	Of Mr Nunnery, Blacksmith, a bill	£1	3s	6d			
	Paid to him for a New Grate					16s	6d
17	To Mr Parker, Joiner, a bill in full				£1	1s	6d
	Received of him a bill		3s	6d			
18	Chairwoman 5 days 2s 6d					2s	6d
	Earnest to Ann Barton 3s. Carriage 1s.					4s	
	Retail 18s 6d. Weekly bill 18s 4d.		18s	6d		18s	4d
19	Communion Money						6d
21	An Horse-hair Tether of Wm Toons					2s	
22	Of Mr Baldwick, Quadring, a bill	£1	4s				
23	To Wm Kirk for Ale 18s. Beer 1s 8d.					19s	8d
25	To Mr Torry, Glazier, a bill in full				£5	4s	10d
	Received of him a bill	£3	18s	9d			
	One Grose of small Gally Pots[245]					4s	
	Two Metts of Coals of J. Wells					4s	
	Best Phial Corks 4 Grose 1s 4d. Carriage 2d.					1s	6d
	Retail £1 0s 0d. Weekly bill £1 0s 0¾d.	£1			£1	0s	0¾d
26	To Daniel Shays a bill in full					12s	
27	Of John Pepper, Gosberton Risgate, a bill		8s	6d			
	Of John Chamberlain, Surfleet		16s	6d			
	Of Th. Smith, Frampton, Interest Money due May 4	£7	10s				
28	Of Thos Cook's Maid, Quadring, a bill		9s	6d			
30	Remainder of the late B. Upton's bill		8s				
31	Of J. Harrison, Bicker, a bill		10s				
£34 7s 1¼d	**Carried over**	**£110**	**0s**	**2d**	**£75**	**13s**	**0¾d**

[f.59]
June 1782: 6th Month, 30 Days

		Received			Paid		
Brought over		**£110**	**0s**	**2d**	**£75**	**13s**	**0¾d**
	Of Mr Gleed's Servant Boy a bill		8s				
1	Ol. Lini[246] 3lb at 7d of Mr Torry					1s	7d
	Carriage of Druggs from Leicester					2s	2d
	One Chaldron and half of Coals at 25s				£1	17s	6d

---

245 See n.179 above.
246 *Oleum lini*, or linseed oil.

June 1782 (cont.)		Received			Paid		
	Porterage 1s. Ale 6d. Turnpike 1s 6d.					3s	
	Of Mr Trimnell a bill in full	£4	2s	4d			
	Of Mr Charles Trimnell, Bicker, a bill	£2	15s	8d			
	Retail &c. 16s 6d. Weekly bill 16s 5d.		16s	6d		16s	5d
2	Of Mr Brotherton, Brazier (a Labour)		15s				
	Of John Thompson, Hostler (a bill)		15s	6d			
3	To John Kendall for Milk 16 Weeks at 14d					18s	8d
	To Mrs Moor for Schooling Betsey 21 Weeks at 4d.						
	Susan 5 Weeks at 2d.					7s	10d
	Of John Philips, Gosberton Risgate, a bill	£1	3s				
7	Of Thos Cook, Quadring, in part	£1	1s				
	Of Thos Emmerson, Butcher (a Labour)		15s				
	Paid to him for Beef					6s	4d
	A Circular Board for a Map						8d
8	Of J. Hales, Gosberton Risgate, a bill		13s				
	To E. Nicholas a Month's Nursing due 6th					10s	
	Of Jos. Taylor, North Ing, a bill		5s	6d			
	Retail &c. £1 2s 0d. Weekly bill £1 2s 1d.	£1	2s		£1	2s	1d
11	Of Mr Wm Hunt the Parish Bill	£7	10s				
	Of -ditto- for 1 Doz. Godfrey's Cordial[247]		4s				
	Paid to him a bill in full				£8	7s	
14	To E. Nicholas a Week's Nursing					2s	6d
	A new Wheel and Axel for the Barrow					3s	6d
15	To Wm Harrison a bill for Meat					7s	8d
	Of Mr Birks (Boston) a bill	£2	18s				
	Retail &c. 12s. Weekly bill 12s 0¼d.		12s			12s	0¼d
	Entrance to Mildred Thornton					1s	
16	Critical Review for May					1s	
17	Of Mr Garner, Donington Fen, a bill		17s	6d			
	Of Mr Golding the late Mrs Boots's bill		17s	6d			
	To Mrs Pakey a bill for Flower				£2	0s	6d
19	Of Captain Nettleton, Swineshead, a bill	£1	0s	6d			
22	Retail &c. 14s 6d. Weekly bill 14s 5½d.		14s	6d		14s	5½d
	Paid for Spining at several times					11s	8d
24	Remainder of J. Green's bill, Donington		12s	6d			
25	Of Mr Crain, Gosberton Belney, a bill		8s				
	Journey to Spalding on Sunday the 23d					1s	8d
	A Cow bought at Spalding by J. Tunnard the 18th				£6	19s	6d
	Of Mr Thos Snell in part	£5	5s				
	To my wife					5s	
26	Insurance Money 7s. Treacle 1 Stone & Carriage						
	4s 6d.					11s	6d
	Of Mary Redhoof, Donington, a bill		11s	6d			
	Paid to her for Quilting					11s	6d
28	Of Daniel Walden, Swineshead, a bill	£1	6s				
	Half a Year's Poor Assessment due at Easter					5s	6d
£43 14s 2½d		**£147**	**9s**	**8d**	**£103**	**15s**	**5½d**

---

[247] A patent medicine, named after Thomas Godfrey of Hunsdon, Herts. (d.1721) and typically given to children with colic. There were several different preparations, usually including opium and treacle.

[f.59v]
July 1782: 7th Month, 31 Days

		Received			Paid		
Brought over		**£147**	**9s**	**8d**	**£103**	**15s**	**5½d**
June							
29	Of Mrs Walker, Quadring Eaudike, a bill		5s	6d			
	Of Mr Palmer, Quadring Parish bill	£4	10s	6d			
	Of -ditto- his own bill	£1	16s				
	Retail £1 6s 0d. Weekly bill £1 6s 3½d.	£1	6s		£1	6s	3½d
30	Of J. Bartram, Carpenter, a bill		11s	6d			
July							
5	To J. Tunnard for joist[248] 3 Weeks of the Cow, trouble of buying & attending her					10s	6d
6	Retail £1 0s 0d. Weekly bill 19s 10¼d.	£1	0s	0d		19s	10¼d
7	To Martin Cottam a bill for weaving				£1	1s	6d
9	Of Mr Gleed (Susan Bates's bill)	£1	2s	6d			
10	Of Mrs Pell, Bicker, a bill		7s	6d			
13	Of Mrs Lacey's Man, Wigtoft, a bill		6s				
	Retail 14s. Weekly bill 14s 1½d.		14s			14s	1½d
	Critical Review for June					1s	
17	Two Holdfasts for the fire irons						9d
18	To Mr Wilcockson, Druggist, in full				£2	7s	
	Journey to Spalding Races, the Play &c. &c.					6s	
20	Retail &c. £1 0s 6d. Weekly bill £1 0s 7¾d.	£1	0s	6d	£1	0s	7¾d
24	Of John Chevens, Gosberton (a Labour)	£1	1s				
25	Of Mr Brown, Horfleet, a bill	£1	17s	6d			
	Of Mr Dowse, Wigtoft Marsh, a bill	£1	11s	6d			
27	Retail &c. 19s 6d. Weekly bill 19s 4¾d.		19s	6d		19s	4¾d
29	A Quarter's Land Tax					3s	
30	Of Mr Harvey's Maid Servant a bill		5s	6d			
31	Cow Bulling at Mr Boldram's the 29th					1s	6d
	£52 17s 7¾d	**£166**	**4s**	**8d**	**£113**	**7s**	**0¼d**

Agreement with Mrs M. Flinders

Mrs Bradley the Schoolmistres dying the 7th of August, Mrs Flinders has obtained the School, which will be a happy circumstance for her & Children. Her place consequently being to let, I have taken it from Michaelmas next at £10 10s 0d per Annum, but she has annexed some disagreables to it such as buying her Cow, Heifer, Stack of Hay – and what is worse than those, about £8 worth of Furniture, fencing &c. We had the things appraised, and the whole together (with the Eddish[249] in the Ing, Orchard, and Homestead untill Michaelmas) came to £25 12s which I have paid her. We have an agreement drawn by Mr Gleed, she not to raise the Rent, or let it to any other person, or any ways disturb me except she wants it herself – also to do the outside repairs of the house myself, the inside & Fences. One great inducement to these conditions was my obtaining possession of my 2 acre pasture in the South Ing, which is 4 years before the expiration of the time Mrs F. was to have in possession rent free, & consequently as good as £8 or £10 to me, which is a material consideration, having two Cows, we have plenty of

---

248 See n.224 above.
249 Eddish: grass growing again; aftermath (*OED*).

Milk, make Cheese & get Butter. I have not yet got a tenant for the house, & fear I shall not untill Lady Day. October 2. 82.

[f.60]
August 1782: 8th Month, 31 Days

		Received			Paid		
Brought over		**£166**	**4s**	**8d**	**£113**	**7s**	**0¼d**
2	Of Mr Christian, Bicker, a bill	£1	19s				
	Sold the Calf to Mr Gunthorp for	£1	7s				
3	Of Mr Petchill, Gosberton Risgate, a bill		8s	6d			
	To John Hall for 3 Loads of Hay				£3	3s	
	Paid to him a Milk score					6s	1d
	Received of him a bill		16s	5d			
4	Of John Northern, Bicker, a bill		9s	6d			
	Retail &c. £1 2s. Weekly bill £1 1s 10¾d.	£1	2s		£1	1s	10¾d
6	To my Wife				£3	10s	
7	The late J. Houlton's bill of Mr Ward	£1	9s				
	Of J. Tunnard a bill		5s				
	Paid to Molly Tunnard for Bleaching					5s	6d
9	To John Tunnard for 2 days Stacking &c.					3s	
	Of J. Lammin a bill		6s	6d			
	Toll of a Load of Hay from Swineshead					1s	6d
10	A Pig Trough 2s. Critical Review July 1s.					3s	
	Retail &c. 17s 6d. Weekly bill 17s 5¾d.		17s	6d		17s	5¾d
12	Of Mr Samuel Sewerds, Quadring Bar, a bill				£1	8s	6d
	To Edward Laykins, Blacksmith, a bill					10s	6d
	Of Richard Leak a bill		11s				
14	Remainder of Mr Snell's bill		17s				
15	To H. Dennis for a ½ Hogshead Copper,						
	39½ Pounds at 8d per Pound				£1	6s	4d
	The Grate belonging to -ditto- (3 Stone)					7s	
	Copper Cover and Tun dish					2s	2d
	To Mrs Pakey a bill for Flower				£1	6s	
16	A Tarhib of Wm Toons					2s	
17	Retail &c. £1 0s 6d. Weekly bill £1 0s 5¼d.	£1	0s	6d	£1	0s	5¼d
19	To Mr Goodwin for 21 Stone of Flower				£1	17s	6d
	Of Jos. Wright Junior a bill		11s	6d			
	Of John Broughton, Horfleet, a bill		19s				
20	Honey 14 Pounds at 8d of Mr Broughton, Bicker					9s	4d
	Wax 3½ Pounds at 1s 6d of -ditto-					5s	3d
21	Of John Myland, Swineshead Woad Houses						
	(a Labour)	£1	1s				
23	Of Mr Tenny, Donington Wikes, in part	£3	3s				
24	Of Mr Harrison, Quadring Fen, by bills		17s				
	Retail &c. 13s 6d. Weekly bill 13s 4d.		13s	6d		13s	4d
27	Of Wm West a bill		12s	6d			
29	Of Mr Gee, Hale Fen, a bill		16s				
	To Thos Percival a bill (Blacksmith)					11s	11d
	Received of him in part		11s	11d			
30	Of Eliz. Hubbard in part		5s	6d			
31	Of Widow Holbourn, Wigtoft, a bill		9s				
	Of Uriah Castor a bill		13s				

August 1782 (cont.)

	Received		Paid	
Retail &c. 19s 6d. Weekly bill 19s 4½d.	19s	6d	19s	4½d
To John Hall for leading Bricks & Lime			2s	6d
£58 2s 4½d	**£190 14s 6d**		**£132 12s 1½d**	

Improvements

I have now fitted up the Old Barn into a Brewhouse. Have got a ½ Hogshead Copper fixed, & furnished myself with [f.60v] proper Tubbs &c. and we have Brewed once. I have hitherto found buying Beer inconvenient, generally bad and expensive; hope this will prove a saving & a convenience. Have also removed my Still from the Kitchen into the present Brewhouse. My Copper I chanced on second hand & tolerably reasonable of H. Dennis; my Mash Tub, I had also second hand of Mr Ward at ½ price. I imagine the whole expence, with the Chimney, Brick work &c., will cost me between £7 and £8, having already paid about £5 & the Bricklayer's Bill yet to discharge.

September 1782: 9th Month, 30 Days

		Received			Paid		
Brought over		**£190 14s**	**6d**		**£132 12s**	**1½d**	
3	Two Chaldrons of Coals				£2 10s		
	Porterage 1s 4d. Ale 8d. Turnpike 1s 6d.				3s	6d	
4	Of Mr Sewerds, Quadring, a bill	£2					
6	Carriage of Druggs from Lincoln 8 Stone at 5d				3s	4d	
7	Of — Stalworth, Northorp, a bill	5s					
	Retail &c. 19s 0d. Weekly bill 19s 0¼d.	19s			19s	0¼d	
8	To Messrs Ferneyhough & Wilson in full				£14 14s		
	Discount allowed on £12	6s					
9	Of George Bateman, Labourer, a bill	12s					
	Critical Review for August				1s		
15	Of Mr Goodwin's Man a bill	16s	6d				
	Of John Berry in part	10s	6d				
	Retail &c. £1 1s 0d. Weekly bill £1 1s 2½d.	£1 1s			£1 1s	2½d	
	Of Wm Fielding, Donington Eaudike, a bill	8s	6d				
	To Mr Hunt a bill (things for the Child)	4s	6d				
	Chaise Hire from Spalding				5s		
20	To Mrs Flinders a Month's Joist[250] of the Cow				6s		
	Of her by bills	11s					
21	To J. Strapps a bill: Saddle cloth 4s 6d.						
	Saddle mending 1s 6d				6s		
	Carriage of Druggs from London				3s	9d	
	Retail &c. 18s 6d. Weekly bill 18s 5¾d.	18s	6d		18s	5¾d	
22	Of Wm Story, Bicker, a bill	9s	6d				
	Of Mr Crow's Man, Quadring Eaudike, a bill	5s	10d				
25	Journey to Spalding				1s	2d	
26	A New Temms for Brewing				1s	6d	
28	Of Mr Pillings, Bicker, a bill	£1 16s					
	A cutting knife 1s. A yoke 1s 6d of Mrs F's				2s	6d	
	Retail &c. 13s 6d. Weekly bill 13s 7¾d.	13s	6d		13s	7¾d	

---

[250] See n.224 above.

September 1782 (cont.)	Received			Paid		
30 Of the Revd Mr Powell a bill	£1	12s				
Of Mr Thos Green (Arg. Viv.[251] 1lb extinct.)		6s				
£48 18s 7¼d Carried over	£204	5s	4d	£155	6s	8¾d

My Brother[252]

It is with much concern that I remark my Brother's leaving Spalding. He intends to remove on Monday Nov. 4 to Odiham in Hampshire – a great way indeed. He has been over too precipitately, and agreed with a Mr Eastland. It seems a remove from Spalding was become necessary, which I with sorrow & surprize remark – but with a little more patience I think he might have got a situation nearer than 150 miles, a distance which most likely will for ever preclude us seeing each other. My Sister was over for a Week some little time since & my Brother took his leave of us on Sunday last. October 30.

[f.61]
October 1782: 10th Month, 31 Days

	Received			Paid		
Brought over	£204	5s	4d	£155	6s	8¾d
2 Of Mr Nunnery, Gosberton, £1 0s 6d. Spent 6d.	£1	0s	6d			6d
To Ann Barton 19 Weeks' Wages				£1	0s	6d
5 Retail &c. 13s 6d. Weekly bill 13s 3¾d.		13s	6d		13s	3¾d
6 Critical Review for September					1s	
7 To Mr Hunt for 17 Pound of Cheese at 4s 6d					5s	6d
To M. Grant for Brewing 2s 6d. Overpaid Yeast 9d.			9d		2s	6d
10 Journey to Spalding					1s	6d
11 To J. Bettison for 5 Days' Gardening					1s	8d
Carriage of a Crate of Phials from Lincoln					4s	2d
12 Of Mrs Fox, Gosberton, a bill		5s				
Of Mr Allcock, Gosberton, a bill	£1					
Retail &c. £1 3s 0d. Weekly bill £1 3s 2½d.	£1	3s		£1	3s	2½d
13 Of — Johnson, Donington (a Labour)		10s	6d			
Of Zebidee Elsom a bill	£1	0s	6d			
14 24 Pound of Beef of Wm Harrison at 3s 6d					6s	
16 Of Mr Marsh, Quadring, a bill		17s	6d			
17 Of Wm Reckaby, Kirton Holm, a bill	£1	10s				
Of Mr Gadsby, Bicker, a bill		13s				
Of J. Witton, Gosberton, a bill	£1	1s				
Of Joseph Brown, Swineshead Fen Houses, a bill	£1	5s				
Paid to him for a load of Hay				£1	3s	
Two Pockett Knives					1s	
18 To Mary Taylor for 2 Weeks' service					2s	6d
19 Of H. Stanley, Gosberton Risgate, a bill		5s				
Of T. Lighten, Swineshead, a bill		6s				
20 Retail 18s 6d. Weekly bill 18s 4d.		18s	6d		18s	4d
22 Of Mrs Matthews, Donington Northorp, a bill	£1	2s	6d			
23 Of Thos Olsop in part		10s				
To Wm Burrus, Cooper, a bill in full				£6	6s	6d
Received of him a bill	£5	3s				

---

[251] See n.232 above.
[252] John Flinders.

October 1782 (cont.)	Received		Paid	
Of J. Clark, Quadring, in part	15s	6d		
26 Of Wm Green, Bicker Fen (a Labour)	£1	1s		
Half a Year's Tithe of the Ing Land			4s	1½d
Retail 16s 6d. Weekly bill 16s 3½d.	16s	6d	16s	3½d
28 Of Thos Higgs, Northorp, a bill	19s			
29 Of J. Cole, Shoemaker, 13s 6d. To -ditto- for				
Boots Soling 2s.	13s	6d	2s	
Window Money ½ Year 8s 6d. Land Tax ¼ Year 3s.				
House Tax 1s 3d.			12s	9d
30 To J. Wells for Shoes 6s. Splatts[253] Mending 4d.			6s	4d
To Mr Wilcockson, Druggist, in full			10s	6d
One Stone of Treacle (broke by J. Hall)			4s	
£57 2s 2d	**£227 16s**	**1d**	**£170 13s**	**11d**

Servants

In regard to Servants we have had a very quick succession indeed! Ann Barton did not prove so good as expected, got a hold of bad company. We therefore parted with her the 2d of October, having been 19 Weeks. We then got one that happened to be in town, but proving Lame she could not do her work & staid but 2 Weeks. We then got Elizabeth Abbot untill Martinmas; Mildred Thornton left us at Old Martinmas and we have now hired Mary Leak, untill May Day, intending to do with one if possible. T. Ward is gone & I have got J. Bettison again. Nov. 25. 82.

[f.61v]

November 1782: 11th[254] Month, 30 Days

Brought over	Received		Paid	
	£227 16s	**1d**	**£170 13s**	**11d**
2 Of Mr Duckett, Quadring Eaudike, a bill	£1	1s		
Retail £1 0s 0d. Weekly bill 19s 10¾d.	£1		19s	10¾d
3 Of the Parish of Swineshead a bill	7s	6d		
To Thos Speed towards the loss of Cow			1s	
7 Six Pound of Lump Sugar at 9½d (Shop use)			4s	9d
Lemons 1s. Chissels 1 Sack 2s 8d. Carriage 6d.			4s	2d
Ol. Lini 3lb of Mr Torry			1s	9d
9 Of Mrs Samuel Pike a bill	£1	13s		
Retail &c. 16s 6d. Weekly bill 16s 9d.	16s	6d	16s	9d
10 Critical Review for October			1s	
11 Matthew's Scholar feast money			2s	6d
Of Mrs Thos Wright (a Labour)	15s			
12 To Wm Kirk for Ale 10 Gallons 10s. Small beer 3s.			13s	
16 Of Wm Stukeley in part	10s 6d			
Of Mr Jackson, Donington Ing, a bill	£1	1s		
Retail &c. 17s. Weekly bill 17s 3d.	17s		17s	3d
17 Of Benjamin Wright a bill	£1	2s		
Flannel 2 Yards for the Child			1s	8d
To J. Tunnard for 4 Strike of Barley			11s	6d

[253] See n.229 above.
[254] MS '10th'.

November 1782 (cont.)	Received			Paid		
18 Drainage Tax for the South Ing Land due at Lady						
Day last 5a.3r.8p. at 1s 3d per Acre to Mr Shilcock					7s	3½d
23 Of Thos Fant, Swineshead, Baker (a Labour)	£1	1s				
Of Mrs Vicars, Swineshead, a bill	£2					
To Mildred Thornton Wages due this day					15s	
The late Robert Aubins's bill, Wigtoft Bank	£1	4s				
Of Mr Love, Swineshead, in part	£7	7s				
Of John Tasker, Quadring, a bill		12s				
Retail &c. £1 1s 0d. Weekly bill £1 1s 0¾d.	£1	1s		£1	1s	0¾d
24 Ladies Diary 9d. Rum 1 Quart 3s 6d.					4s	3d
Paid for Thos Ward various bills since he has been						
here £3 3s 9½d. To him in Cash 11s 6d.				£3	15s	3½d
26 Of R. Meads, Wigtoft, a bill		5s	6d			
29 Of Mr Harvey (Draper) the Parish bill	£6	18s	6d			
Of -ditto- his share of the News Paper		10s	6d			
Paid to him a bill in full				£5	9s	5d
To -ditto- ½ a Year's Poor Assessment due at						
Michaelmas					5s	6d
To my Wife on the 6th Instant				£3	10s	
30 Of Mr Sewerds, Quadring Eaudike, a bill	£1					
Retail &c. 15s. Weekly bill 15s 2¼d.		15s			15s	2¼d
£68 1s 11¼d	**£259**	**14s**	**1d**	**£191**	**12s**	**1¾d**

Birth of a Son

Sunday Nov. 3, about 8 in the Evening my wife was safely [delivered] of a very fine Boy, whom we have called Samuel. I thank God she had a good Labour, but had been very poorley a long time; had an Ague great part of her Pregnancy, and lost flesh a good deal. This has been a fatal lying and was 6 weeks before she got down stairs, at which time the Nurse left us. After being down until Xmas day she was forced to[255] her room again, and I am at this time in the utmost distress for her safety. I have noted the particulars in my Midwifery cases. The Child went to Mary Redhoof's to Nurse on the 17th for suckle. December 31. 82.

[f.62]
December 1782: 12th Month, 31 Days

	Received			Paid		
Brought over	**£259**	**14s**	**1d**	**£191**	**12s**	**1¾d**
2 Of Wm Thornhill, Bicker Gauntlet, a bill	£1	8s				
5 Flannell 3½ Yards at 14d, 4s 1d. -Ditto- ¼ Yard at						
1s 6d, 4½d.					4s	5½d
6 Interest of Mr S. Ward, due June 11th last	£7	10s				
To Mrs Langley a present for Coals					19s	
7 Carriage of Druggs from Robinson 5 Stone					3s	9d
Of Robert Jackson, Bicker, a bill	£1	5s				
Retail &c. £1 0s 0d. Weekly bill £1 0s 1d.	£1			£1	0s	1d
8 Critical Review for November					1s	
14 Retail &c. 19s 0d. Weekly bill 19s 1½d.		19s			19s	1½d
15 Of Mr Bones, Bicker, a bill		14s	6d			
To Dorothy Beechill for 6 Weeks' Nursing				£1	3s	

---

255 MS 'to to'.

December 1782 (cont.)		Received			Paid		
	To M. Redhoof for Nursing the Child a Month					12s	
17	Betsey's and Susan's Entrance at Mrs B's School					3s	6d
19	Of J. Sutton a bill		5s				
20	The late Mrs Bradley's bill of Mr Golding		11s	6d			
21	Of Robert Nailor, Gosberton Risgate, a bill		9s				
	Retail &c. £1 1s 6d. Weekly bill £1 1s 9d.	£1	1s	6d	£1	1s	9d
25	Of John Ward, Gosberton Risgate	£1	1s				
27	Of Mr Tooms, Roper, a bill		5s	6d			
28	Retail &c. 19s. Weekly bill 19s 2½d.		19s			19s	2½d
30	To Mrs Brotherton for teaching the Children					3s	2d
	Received of her for Rent of a Room	£1	1s				
31	Some of the Fruit from Mrs F's orchard sold for		6s	4d			
	Paid to Mrs F. September 20 for her Cow				£7	10s	
	To -ditto- for the Heifer £3 10s 0d. Hay £4 4s 0d.				£7	14s	
	For the Edish,[256] Green & Orchard untill						
	Michaelmas				£2	6s	
	Household Furniture, Wood &c. Appraised at				£8	2s	
	Received by the Sale of some of the things	£3	14s	4d			
	Paid to Mr Parker for selling 2s 6d. Crying 6d.					3s	
Total Receipts & Payments in 1782		**£282**	**4s**	**9d**	**£224**	**17s**	**2¼d**

Total gained in 1782	£57 7s 6¾d
Total gained in 11 Years' Business	£696 13s 7¼d
Total gained in Twelve Years	£754 1s 2d

Conclusion of the Year 1782

By the Providence of Almighty God we are now arrived to the conclusion of another Year, to me the most distressfull of any I have ever yet experienced: my poor wife, from her very ill recovery from her late lying inn, being at times most unhappily deprived in a great measure of her reason. Some days she is very well and capable of doing her Business, but on others in a most unhappy way indeed. I have taken notes of the case, and upon the whole it is the most extraordinary I ever met with. At sometimes I have the greatest hopes of her recovery, at others I am depressed to the lowest despair. At this time I am in the greatest uncertainty about it. I beseech the Lord day & night for her recovery. In regard to money matters I do not complain this year. Jan. 27. 83.

[f.62v]
January 1783: 1st Month, 31 Days

		Received			Paid		
Dec.							
28	Of Mr Jarvis, Bicker, a bill	£4	16s				
Jan.							
1	Of Mr Trickett a bill	£1	2s				
4	Retail &c. £1 2s 6d. Weekly bill £1 2s 6½d.	£1	2s	6d	£1	2s	6½d
5	Critical Review for December					1s	
6	Of Mr Hunt's Servant Maid a bill		6s				
9	To Messrs Swinfen & Co, Druggists, in full				£1	13s	6d

---

256 See n.249 above.

January 1783 (cont.)	Received			Paid		
To Mr Brotherton, Brazier, a bill					10s	8d
Received of him a bill		5s	3d			
11 Retail &c. 17s. Weekly bill 17s.		17s			17s	
12 Watch Repairing by Mr Shaw					4s	
To Mary Redhoof a Month's Nursing					12s	
16 Of Stephen Dalton a bill	£2	2s				
Paid to him a bill for flower &c.				£2	2s	5d
18 To Elizabeth Smith for Washing, Ironing &c.					3s	
Retail &c. 19s. Weekly bill 19s 1d.		19s			19s	1d
To Mrs Tunnard for attending on my wife				£1	1s	
20 To Mr Gunthorp a bill for Mutton					4s	6d
21 To E. Abbot for 14 Weeks' Service (5 at 1s, 9 at 8d)					11s	
22 Gave to A.C. in Charity					5s	
23 Of Mr Wilton, Bicker, a bill	£1	0s	6d			
Sugar 4 Pound for Shop use at 7d					2s	4d
25 18 Pound of Beef at 3s 6d Stone of W.H.					4s	6d
Retail &c. 18s. Weekly bill 18s 1d.		18s			18s	1d
27 One ¼ Year's Land Tax					3s	
29 Of Mary Winters, Northorp, a bill		6s	6d			
£2 2s 1½d	**£13**	**14s**	**9d**	**£11**	**12s**	**7½d**

Widow Flinders's Death[257]

Monday 6th. Mrs M. Flinders died which I may remark as a great additional Misfortune to me, as the Care of her Children will in some measure rest on me. My hands being full, I requested the Guardians (Messrs Ward & Pike) to undertake the funeral, & management of the affairs. She was interred on Wed. 8th. We had a Sale of her Goods on Monday 13th, which were mostly sold to the amount of £30. The funeral expences were paid (but no other), the money put into Mr Ward's hands & the children put to R. Jackson at 8s 6d per Week for the present. The Cloaths and things unsold are lodged with me.

Mrs Flinders's House Lett

On Sunday Feb. 2, I let the House and about 1 third of the Green to a Mr Isaac Lumby, Butcher, for £6 16s 6d per Annum. He is to divide it[258] at his charge. He is to pay £4 town's rates and myself 2. Some little repairs are to be done at the house; I am to keep the Cow hovel. I hope he will prove a good tenant, & I intend now to keep the place on.

Birth Day

Monday Feb. 17. Compleated my 33d Year, but on account of my present distressfull state I noted it not. On Wed. the 19th I removed my poor wife in Mr H's Chaise to Bolingbrooke in hopes that changing the Air & Scene may have its use. I have had information of about ½ a dozen similar instances which all recovered at different periods from 3 to 12 Months. Feb. 22d.

---

257   Mary Flinders, his father's second wife (see n.99 above).
258   'with a hedge' crossed through.

[f.63]
February 1783: 2nd Month, 28 Days

		Received			Paid		
Brought over		**£13**	**14s**	**9d**	**£11**	**12s**	**7½d**
1	Of the Revd Mr Cotes a bill	£1	11s	6d			
	Retail &c. 17s. Weekly bill 17s 3¼d.		17s			17s	3¼d
3	To Mr Barnet, Bricklayer, in full				£3	2s	2d
	Received of him a bill	£2	14s	5d			
6	Of Mrs Marshall, Quadring, a bill		11s				
	Of Mr Allcock, Gosberton (a Labour)	£1	1s				
7	Of Mr J. Ward a bill	£3	2s				
	To Edward Gibson a bill in full				£1	7s	3d
	Received of him a bill		15s	3d			
8	Retail &c. 16s. Weekly bill 16s 1½d.		16s			16s	1½d
9	Critical Review for January					1s	
10	Of Charles Smith, Shoemaker, a bill		11s	6d			
	Of Mrs Emminson a bill	£1	4s				
	To -ditto- for the Children's Entrance					2s	
	To -ditto- for 3 Weeks' Teaching at 6d					1s	6d
11	To Mr Main for a Year's Shaving &c. due the 5th					17s	
	Received of him a bill		6s	6d			
	To Mary Redhoof a Month's Nursing due 9th					12s	
12	Of Mr Bilsby Junior, Bicker, a bill	£1	4s				
13	1 Yard of Irish Cloth 2s. Thread 2d for Shirts						
	Mending					2s	2d
	3 Strike of Bran 2s for the Horse					2s	
15	The late Mrs Godley's bill, Bicker		16s	6d			
	Of Mr C. Trimnel a bill £1 12s 6d. Present more						
	9s 6d.	£2	2s				
	The weekly bill 14s 8½d.					14s	8½d
17	Of J. Pigott for a Cow & Calf (late Mrs Flinders's)	£8	5s				
19	To Messrs Otters, Druggists, Lincoln, in full[259]				£4	17s	6d
20	To Mrs Tunnard for attending my wife					10s	6d
21	1¾ Yard of Plaid for Susanna's Bed gown					1s	9d
	Carriage of Druggs from F. & Wilson, 6 Stone & ½					4s	10d
	Of Mr Lumby for 3 Grates at Mrs F. house	£1	7s	9d			
22	Of Wm Holbourn, Gosberton Risgate, a bill		19s				
	Retail &c. 17s 6d. Weekly bill 17s 3½d.		17s	6d		17s	3½d
24	Aux. Porcin.[260] 7lb, 2s 11d. Sugar 5lb at 7d, 2s 11d.					5s	10d
26	Of Mr Harvey at the Cow a bill	£2	6s				
	To -ditto- a bill for Malt, Hops & Rum				£2	3s	
	To -ditto- for the Chaise 2 Days to Bolingbrooke				£1	9s	
	Other expences of the Journey					11s	8d
	To Mrs Emmerson for Seven Shirts Mending						
	& other things					1s	7d
	Cera flava[261] 1lb at Mr Hurst's					1s	8d
	£13 10s 2¾d	**£45**	**2s**	**8d**	**£31**	**12s**	**5¼d**

---

259   See Burnby, 58 n.54.
260   See n.130 above.
261   See n.63 above.

My Dear Wife's Death (March 23)

On Sat. March 15, I got a line from Mr Ward,[262] informing me that my dear wife was much worse. I set off immediately and found her bad indeed! I was no way certain she knew me – greatly emaciated, & almost incapable of taking sustenance. I left her on Sunday with little hopes of recovery, having 1st called in Dr Hairby[263] – but alas to no purpose. He said he had seen similar cases – that they sometimes suddenly recovered. I did not see the Dr but Mr Ward said he did not suppose her in any immediate danger, he wrote a prescription of some Nervous & Emmenagogue[264] Medicines which Mr W. brought me on the Tuesday Evening the 18th (having business at Spalding) & he took the [f.63v] Medicines with him on the Wed. Morning, giving me some little hope that they thought her somewhat better – but on Sunday March the 23d the fatal Messenger came in the afternoon that she died very early that Morning. My distress may be better conceived than wrote, at loseing the dearest & most valued friend I had on Earth but I must endeavour to resign myself to the Providence of God. I went over on the Monday Morning the 24th to perform the last sad office which was done on Tuesday Evening the 25 in a decent but not pompous manner, agreable to the wishes of her friends. My situation is truly deplorable and unhappy on my own account, my comfort being gone, but doubly so on account of my 5 Children, two very small and out at nurse. Mr Ward returned home with me on Wed. the 26 & left me next day. My tears are plentifully shed each day, and when I shall regain any peace I cannot tell. I have wrote to my Brother, desiring to have Henny's assistance which I hope may be of use to me. This world has now no charms left for me, there appears nothing for me but care & trouble. However God is infinitely Wise and Good and to him I resign myself and all my concerns. March 31. 83.[265]

March 1783: 3rd Month, 31 Days

		Received			Paid		
Brought over		**£45**	**2s**	**8d**	**£31**	**12s**	**5¼d**
1	To Wm Tooms for Heckling[266] 2 Stone of femble[267]					3s	
	Retail 13s 6d. Weekly bill 13s 9d.		13s	6d		13s	9d
7	Carriage of Druggs from Lincoln					1s	9d
8	Aux. Porcina[268] 6lb at 5d of Mary Castor					2s	6d
	Of Mr Lumby for a Remnant of Hay					14s	
	Retail £1 0s 0d. Weekly bill £1 0s 1d.	£1	0s	0d	£1	0s	1d
9	To Mary Redhoof for a Month's Nursing					12s	
	Gentleman's Magazine for February					1s	
12	To Mrs Chevins for 3 days' work					2s	

---

262 Her brother.

263 William Hairby of Spilsby (MD Glasgow 1779): an apothecary who had qualified as a doctor when in his fifties (Burnby, 57 n.43; Mills, 62).

264 A herbal concoction to stimulate the flow of menstrual blood, or in some cases induce an abortion.

265 In *Family Faculties* Susannah Flinders is described as having dark hair and soft eyes, and being amiable and "clever in housekeeping and managing children" (Galton, *Record of Family Faculties*, 38).

266 Heckling: combing hemp (*OED*).

267 Femble or fimble: the male plant of hemp (*OED*).

268 See n.130 above.

March 1783 (cont.)

		Received			Paid		
	To Eliz. Smith for washing & ironing					2s	
16	Retail 16s 6d. Weekly bill 16s 4¾d.	16s	6d		16s	4¾d	
	Journey to Bolingbrooke cost me					3s	11d
17	Of Mr Caswell, Quadring, a bill	£3					
18	Chalder & ½ of Coals of Mr Clark, Boston, at 25s				£1	17s	6d
	Porterage 1s. Ale 6d. Man 1s. Toll Bar 1s 6d.					4s	
19	To Mr Elverson a bill in full				£4	4s	
	Received of him a bill	£3	9s				
20	Sugar 4 Pound for Shop use					2s	
21	Of Wm Gaunt, Quadring Fen side, a bill	15s	6d				
22	To Wm Smith for Thatching					1s	3d
	Retail &c. 18s. Weekly bill 18s 5½d.	18s				18s	5½d
27	To Messrs Ferneyhough & Wilson				£4	16s	
	To -ditto- for a Year's London Papers				£2	4s	
	My last Fatal Journey to Bolingbrook					2s	11d
	My dear wife's Funeral Expences				£7	19s	
	2 Bottles of Wine 4s 8d. Pound of Biscuits 1s 2d.					5s	10d
28	Of Mrs Baxter, Swineshead, a bill	5s					
29	To Ed. Fox for 6 Strike of Oats					12s	6d
	Of J. Keil, Donington, a bill	11s	6d				
	Retail &c. 14s 6d. Weekly bill 14s 7½d.	14s	6d			14s	7½d
31	Of Mr Ashworth, Quadring Eaudike, a bill	16s	6d				
	Cera flava[269] 1lb, 1s 8d					1s	8d
	Bad 17s 11d	**£58**	**16s**	**8d**	**£59**	**14s**	**7d**

[f.64]

April 1783: 4th Month, 30 Days

		Received			Paid		
Brought over		**£58**	**16s**	**8d**	**£59**	**14s**	**7d**
2	Black Jersey 5½oz. at 4d					1s	10d
	Silesia Cloth[270] ¾ Yard (Shop use)					9d	
5	Of Mrs Pattison a bill	7s					
	Retail &c. 17s. Weekly bill 16s 10½d.	17s				16s	10½d
7	Of Mr Fant, Swineshead, a bill	12s	6d				
	Of Mr Roberds, Gosberton Risgate (a Labour)	£1	1s				
	To Mary Redhoof a Month's Nursing due 6th					12s	
	Of Frances Jackson, Gosberton Cheal, a bill	15s					
9	Gentleman's Magazine for March					1s	
10	Of J. Leatherland, Donington North Ing, a bill	11s					
	To Eliz. Smith for Washing & Ironing					2s	
12	Of Thos Watkin, Bicker, a bill	11s					
	Retail &c. 18s. Weekly bill 18s 3d.	18s				18s	3d
13	Of Mr Taylor, Donington North Ing	£1	19s				
16	Of — Hancock, Northorp (a Labour)	15s					
	To Mary Leah Earnest Money 2s 6d (Wages £3 5s)					2s	6d
	Black Jersey 6½oz. at 2d for Matthew's Stockings					1s	1d
18	Of — Percival Junior, Donington, a bill	5s					
19	Of Mr Hodson, Gosberton Westrop, a bill	12s	6d				
	Of Mr Holbourn, Horfleet, a bill	7s	6d				

[269] See n.63 above.
[270] Fine linen or cotton fabric, originally made in Silesia (*OED*).

April 1783 (cont.)	Received			Paid		
The Salary for Bicker Poor of Mr Torks	£4	4s				
Retail &c. £1 2s 6d. Weekly bill £1 2s 8d.	£1	2s	6d	£1	2s	8d
20 Of Matthew Reynolds, Bicker, a bill		18s				
21 Of Wm Brewster, Donington, a bill		14s				
1 Pound Femble[271] Spining 8d. Communion						
Money 6d.					1s	2d
Of Thos Mathers, Donington, a bill		6s				
Towards Carriage of the London Paper 2s.						
A Letter 7d.					2s	7d
Betsy & Susan 9 Weeks' Schooling at Mrs E.					4s	2d
22 Paid for 3 Chimneys Sweeping					2s	
Spent at the Cow at the Easter meeting					1s	4d
26 Of Thos Cook, Quadring, in part	£1	11s	6d			
Half a Year's Tithe of my Ing Land					4s	1½d
Retail &c. 14s 6d. Weekly bill 14s 8d.		14s	6d		14s	8d
To Mr Parker, Joiner, a bill					4s	3d
28 Of Mr Shilcock towards the London Paper		10s	6d			
29 Window Money ½ Year, 8s 6d. Land Tax ¼ Year,						
3s. House Tax 1s 3d.					12s	9d
Half a Year's Window Money of the other House					7s	
£12 3s 7d	**£78**	**9s**	**2d**	**£66**	**5s**	**7d**

Wm Flinders's Apprenticeship,[272] April 22[273]

I have to note that we have got him Apprenticed to Mr Jennings, Ironmonger at Spalding, the Charity giving their £10 and we are to give also £10 more on his being bound. The Indentures are not to take place as yet, in order that he may be of age before his time of serving is out. He is to be washed & mended at his own expence. I am glad, this affair is concluded on.

My Neice

Sat. May 3d. After long expectation, my Neice arrived & to my surprize my Brother along with her. He left us the Wed. following. I am sorry to remark that Odiam does not answer as yet. I hope Henny will be some consolation to me under my great distress – but God knows I am at times yet miserably unhappy. June 3.

---

271 See n.266 above.
272 MS 'Apprentiship'.
273 William, a son from Flinders's father's second marriage, was born in 1770 (Burnby, 51). He is perhaps to be identified with the man mentioned in the *Stamford Mercury* on 29 September 1809: "Whereas, I, John **DAY** of Boston in the county of Lincoln, apprentice to Mr William **FLINDERS** of the same place, ironmonger, have without any just cause propagated a Report against Robert **HOOD**, Journeyman, with the said Mr William **FLINDERS,** to the great injury of his Character and to the principles of a man, for which the said Robert **HOOD** hath threatened to follow the law on me for the same; but in consideration of my asking him Pardon, and declaring to the public by this advertisement that the Report is totally false, and that I had no just reason for the same and paying all expenses, agreed to drop all proceedings . . ."

[f.64v]
May 1783: 5th Month, 31 Days

		Received			Paid		
Brought over		**£78**	**9s**	**2d**	**£66**	**5s**	**7d**
	To Mrs Chevins for Gowns making and work					2s	2d
1	Of John Thompson, Ostler, a bill		7s	6d			
3	To Mrs Tunnard for Knitting					1s	10d
	Retail &c. 14s. Weekly bill 14s 0½d.		14s			14s	0½d
4	To Mary Redhoof a Month's Nursing					12s	
	Gentleman's Magazine for April					1s	
5	Of Mrs Taylor, Heckington (a Labour)	£1	1s				
	Of J. Green, Donington, a bill		5s	6d			
7	Paid towards my Neice's Journey				£2	2s	
8	Of H. Stimson, Bicker, a bill		14s				
10	Of Mary Day, Donington (a Labour)		10s	6d			
	Of Mrs Brown, Horfleet, a bill	£2	14s				
	Retail &c. £1 7s. Weekly bill £1 7s 2¾d.	£1	7s		£1	7s	2¾d
12	Carriage of a Trunk with Clothes from London					4s	6d
	To J. Bettison half a Year's Wages				£1	10s	
	To Mary Leah half a Year's Wages				£1	10s	
	Of Mr Harvey, Draper, a bill	£1	6s	6d			
13	Of Mr Green's Servant Maid a bill		5s	6d			
14	To Messrs Robinson & Pike in full				£2	19s	
15	Of Captain Nettleton a bill	£1	14s				
16	Of Mr Johnson's Maid a bill		5s	6d			
17	Bill for Grocery at Mr Hunt's					4s	7½d
	Retail &c. 17s. Weekly bill 17s 3¼d.		17s			17s	3¼d
18	Of Mary Castor a bill		10s				
20	Of Wm Edinborough, Caythorp, a bill		18s				
21	Loin of Beef 2 Stone for the Fair					9s	
	Rum a Quart 3s. Red Wine a Pint 1s 2d.					4s	2d
24	Of Mr Pillings, Bicker, a bill	£1	16s	0d			
	Retail &c. £1 4s 0d. Weekly bill £1 4s 3d.	£1	4s		£1	4s	3d
26	Of Mr Crampton, Northorp, a bill	£1	4s				
	Of Mr Indall, Burtoft, a bill	£2	7s				
	Of Mr Wingad, Quadring Eaudike, a bill		17s				
	Of Mr Allen, Swineshead, a bill	£1	3s				
	Of J. Philips, Gosberton Risgate		6s	6d			
	Of Mrs Jackson, Swineshead Fen Houses, a bill		18s				
	Of Wm Cox, Donington (a Labour)		10s	6d			
	Of Mr Matthews, Bicker, a bill		5s	6d			
	Of Mr Bucknell, Wigtoft, a bill		11s				
	Of Samuel Jefford, Swineshead, a bill		8s				
	Of Mr Harrison, Fosdike, a bill	£1	16s	0d			
	Of Mr Ashwell, Gosberton Risgate, a bill		10s	6d			
	Of Thos Smith, Frampton, a Year's Interest due the 4th	£7	10s				
	Of Thos West's Man, Wigtoft, a bill		6s				
31	Of J. Bettison a bill in part		10s	6d			
	Retail &c. 12s 6d. Weekly bill 12s 10¾d.		12s	6d		12s	10¾d
£33 3s 7¼d		**£114**	**15s**	**2d**	**£81**	**1s**	**6¼d**

Inoculation

The Small Pox having appeared in this Parish, I have Inoculated Susan & our Servant Maid & Boy. They have (thank God) passed thro' very well, favourably & to satisfaction. I have more in hand. The 2 young Children being at Nurse I do not intend to inoculate them, at least at present.

[f.65]
June 1783: 6th Month, 30 Days

		Received			Paid		
Brought over		£114 15s	2d		£81	1s	6¾d
1	To Mary Redhoof a Month's Nursing					12s	
3	Of James Nunnery, Blacksmith, a bill	7s					
	Of J. Newton, Shoemaker, a bill	11s	6d				
	Paid to him a bill for Shoes and Mending					9s	
	Half a Year's Rent due to Wm Flinders April 5th				£3	10s	
	To Henry Wills towards the loss of his Cow					1s	
4	Of Mr Carby, Hale Fen (a Labour)	£1 1s					
5	Of Mr Torrinton, Northorp, a bill	£1 3s	6d				
	Paid him for a Load of Straw					10s	
6	To J. Cook, Taylor, a bill in full				£1	7s	7d
	Received of him a bill	9s					
	To Mr Harvey Church Assessment £12 10s at 3d					3s	1½d
7	To Mr Hunt, Draper, a bill in full				£3	8s	5d
	Received of him a bill	£1 2s	8d				
	Interest of Mr Trimnell of £100 for 14 Months	£5 16s	8d				
	Carriage of Druggs from Robinson & Co					3s	9d
	Spent at the Bull with Mr Greenberry &c.					2s	
	Retail &c. 19s. Weekly bill 18s 11d.	19s				18s	11d
8	Gentleman's Magazine for May					1s	
9	To J. Wells, Shoemaker, a bill in full					11s	
11	To Mr Harvey, Draper, a bill in full				£8	1s	11d
	Received of Mr Harvey the ½ Year's Parish Bill to Easter	£7 10s	7d				
	To -do- a Year's Poor Assessment £12 10s at 13d					13s	6½d
12	Grains & Yeast sold for 2s. Brewing paid 2s 6d.	2s				2s	6d
13	Bees Wax 2lb 2oz at 20d of Mr Hunt					3s	6d
14	Paid for Gardening to a Man at Hale					2s	
	Retail &c. £1 1s 0d. Weekly bill £1 1s 1¼d.	£1 1s			£1	1s	1¼d
15	Of Joseph Haw, Northorp (a Labour)	15s					
16	A Brown Heifer bought of Wm Bouldram				£5	14s	6d
	Betsey's Schooling 7 Weeks 2s 4d. Susan's 4 -do- 8d.					3s	
	Half an Irish Ticket[274] with Mr Gleed				£2	12s	8d
19	Of Mr Gilding, Wigtoft, in part	£3 3s					
	Two Hats dressing and Lining					2s	
21	Of Mr Wm Parker, Donington, a bill	£1 7s	6d				
	Retail &c. £1 2s 0d. Weekly bill £1 2s 3½d.	£1 2s			£1	2s	3½d
22	Of Mary Tindall a bill	15s					
	Of Mr Sharp, Horfleet (a Labour)	£1 1s					

274 The Irish Lottery of 1783: the draw took place between 24 June and 25 July (C. L. Ewen, *Lotteries and Sweepstakes* (London, 1932), 340).

June 1783 (cont.)	Received			Paid		
	Insurance Money & paying				7s	2d
23	To Daniel Shays a bill in full	£1	1s	3d[275]		
	Received of him a bill in full				£1	3s 8d[276]
26	Remainder of Mr Gilding's account, Wigtoft	£2	2s			
	Of Mr Samuel Sewerds, Donington, a bill	£1	12s			
28	Sold the Spotted Heifer to Mr Green for	£6	12s			
	Sold the Red Cow's Calf to Mr Pycroft for		12s			
	Bought a 5 year old Horse of Mr Ashworth				£10	12s 6d
	Received of him a bill	£1	11s	6d		
	Retail &c. 16s 6d. Weekly bill 16s 10¼d.		16s	6d		16s 10¼d
29	Of Benjamin Wright a bill		7s	6d		
	To Mary Redhoof a Month's Nursing					12s
	Sold my Chestnut Horse at Spalding for (neat)	£7	2s			
	£38 8s 9¼d	**£164**	**19s**	**4d**	**£126**	**10s 6¾d**

[f.65v]
Money Matters
I have to note an awkward circumstance which has just ocurred to me. In 1772 my Father bought 8 acres of Land in the Fen of Langley Edwards for £200, and Mortgaged it for £150 to Mr Ed. Greenberry of Folkingham, which mortgage & Bond he got me also to sign, assuring me it was conveyed to him and me jointly, and that he would leave it to me in his Will, but alas he forgot, and the conveyance to me was only as trustee, and gave me no property. Mr G—s interest not being punctually paid since my Father's death, Mrs F. desired him to take the Land, which he accordingly did for 2 Years. I thought no more about any trouble concerning it, but a few Months ago Mr Smith his Attorney told me that I must pay off the Mortgage and interest unpaid & take the Land – with which I have been obliged to comply. Accordingly, Mr Gleed has made me an Asignment of Mr G—s Mortgage and we settled the matter at the Bull on Sat. June 7th. The Mortgage and Interest is £158 0s 6d which with the expence of the Writing I imagine will be about £160. I have let the Land to James Clark for £8 8s per Annum. The Property is Wm Flinders's when at Age, paying of this Mortgage. The most disagreable circumstance is the Mortgage was only at 4½ per Cent. I raised the Money by Mr Trimnell taking in his Bond which with my last year's savings were sufficient. I hope the Land will bear the Rent now let at with proper care.

Mrs Langley's Death
I have to remark that poor Mrs L. my late dear wife's mother departed this Life on Sunday June 15, exactly 12 Weeks after her Daughter; indeed when I was over, from her Age & Infirmities I did not expect her time would be long. I sincerely hope in God, they are both in Happiness together! I am yet oftimes exceedingly distressed at my great & irreparable Loss! I must submit! July 8.

New Horse
I bought a new Horse of Mr J. Ashworth on Sat. June 28, having had him some little time on trial – 5 Year old, Light Bay Black list down the back – cut tail –

---

[275] Entered in the receipts column in error.
[276] Entered in the payments column in error.

Blaze in the face – Black Legs. 14 hands high, small tear in the far under eye Lid, as far as I have proved him. I like him well: a much handsomer one than the old one, price £10 12s 6d. J. Tunnard sold my old one at Spalding Fair, on Monday June 30, for something above £7, which is a very good price, the age (9) & aukwardness of him considered.

Henny's Journey
On Sund. Jun. 29, my Neice made a Journey to Spalding, intending to be there a fortnight among her Friends, during the Races &c. She returned on Sat. July 12.

Health
I have begun somewhat of a course of Medication this Month in hopes (thro' a blessing) to escape the Autumnal Intermittent and take off those Nervous Lownesses I am but too subject to in the Summer especially. As preparative have taken 2 doses Pulv. Jal.[277] which operated well and, as I have too long neglected that salutary remedy cold bathing, have contrived a temporary cold Bath, viz. a large Brewing Vessel, into which I go most days & find it very comfortable & refreshing, & I think it braces me much. As I proceed in this plan, shall take a little more Physic – and as the Season advances – some Vin. Rub.[278] & Cortex & continue the Bath. Jul. 28. 83.

[f.66]
July 1783: 7th Month, 31 Days

		Received			Paid		
Brought over		**£164**	**19s**	**4d**	**£126**	**10s**	**6¾d**
2	Of Mr David Clifton by bill	£2					
	Of Mrs Hargrave, Swineshead, in part		5s	6d			
3	4 Grose of Phial Corks 1s 2d. Carriage 2d.					1s	4d
	Of J. Naylor, Donington Northorp, a bill		19s				
	A New Saddle £1 7s 6d & Cloth 4s 6d of J. Straps				£1	12s	0d
4	Honey 13 Pound 6s 6d. Recd of R. Codling 3s.		3s			6s	6d
	Paid for a Scarf & 2 Pair of Gloves for Mr & Mrs Carr					8s	
5	The Old Saddle Repairing					3s	6d
	To J. Kendall for mowing the 2 Acre					5s	
	Retail &c. 15s. Weekly bill 15s 3½d.		15s			15s	3½d
6	Gentleman's Magazine for June					1s	
7	Of Mrs Lamb, Quadring, a bill		12s				
11	To Ed. Sudbury for a Pair of Boots				£1	1s	0d
	Received of him (a Labour)		15s				
12	Retail &c. 18s 6d. Weekly bill 18s 5½d.		18s	6d		18s	5½d
13	Of J. Tebb, Blacksmith (a Labour)		10s	6d			
14	Of Henry Wells, Donington, a bill	£1	3s	2d			
	To him for Oats 14s. A Milk Score 11s 10d.				£1	5s	10d
	Of Mr Hunt's Maid for Inoculating		7s	6d			
15	Of Wm Lyman a bill		12s				
16	Of Wm Tooley at the Cow (Inoculating)		7s	6d			
18	Pair of Beaver Gloves of Mr Hunt					1s	6d

277 *Pulvis jalapae*: powder of jalap (see n.37 above). A cathartic.
278 Red wine or port (*Vinum rubrum Portingallicum*).

July 1783 (cont.)

		Received			Paid		
19	Carriage of Druggs from London					2s	3d
	Retail &c. 17s. Weekly bill 17s 1d.	17s				17s	1d
	Box from Lynn 1s 5d. Letter 7d.					2s	
21	Journey to Spilsby					5s	7d
	To Mr Franklin a bill for Coat & Waistcoat				£2	8s	
22	Composition Money to the Boston Road					1s	6d
26	Of Mrs Vessey, Gosberton, a bill	16s					
	Of Mr Allen, Gosberton, a bill	£2	12s				
	Of Mr Ladd, Shoemaker, Gosberton, a bill	10s	6d				
	Retail &c. 16s. Weekly bill 16s 2½d.	16s				16s	2½d
	Of Joseph Kirkbride, Donington, a bill	8s	6d				
	Lottery Money with the Mountebanks					1s	6d
28	A new Cloaths Brush 1s 6d. Month's Nursing 12s.					13s	6d
29	¼ Land Tax 3s. Plaid 1s 10d for the Children.					4s	10d
	£41 5s 6¾d	**£180**	**8s**	**0d**	**£139**	**2s**	**5¼d**

Journey to S——y[279]

I have now to Note a circumstance will perhaps appear somewhat odd in my records, after the real and extraordinary Grief which I have manifested for my late valuable partner & whom I· shall regret to my latest hour. As a continual grieving can be of no avail, but injurious to me, I begin to be not without thoughts of a 2^d Marriage. Accordingly I have pitched on the amiable Mrs E. – late Miss E.W.[280] of this place – but since her Widowhood at her Sisters at S——y. Accordingly I made a Journey there on Sunday July 20 (having previously exchanged[281] a few Letters with her by which I was rather assured of an agreable reception). I met with the most friendly treatment, and indeed had a most delightfull visit, fully to my satisfaction. It appears (under the good Providence of God) that an union may take place, perhaps in the Winter or Spring. My Brother J.W.[282] kindly went from Bolingbrook with me & introduced me to the Family. I brought a suit of Cloaths home with me & returned on Monday July 21. Aug. 9: 83.

[f.66v]

August 1783: 8th Month, 31 Days

		Received			Paid		
Brought over		**£180**	**8s**	**0d**	**£139**	**2s**	**5¼d**
	The Salary for Quadring Poor of Mr Duckett	£4	4s				
2	To Mr Shaw for repairing and cleaning a Watch					4s	
	Retail &c. 18s. Weekly bill 18s 0¼d.	18s				18s	0¼d
3	Gent. Mag. July 1s. Writing Paper 11d.					1s	11d
5	Gardening 1s. Of David Read, Swineshead, a bill 6s.	6s				1s	
7	To Mr Brotherton, Brazier, a bill					6s	8d
	Of R. Kitchen, Donington Northorp, a bill	10s	6d				
	Sugar Shop use 2s 1d. Of Mr Bowles's Maid	7s	6d			2s	1d

---

279 Spilsby.
280 Elizabeth Ellis née Weeks.
281 MS 'exhanged'.
282 Presumably John Ward, a brother of his late wife.

August 1783 (cont.)	Received			Paid		
8 Of Mr Hodge, Swineshead, in part		7s				
Of Mr Morley, Bicker, a bill	£1	9s				
9 To Mr Gunthorp a bill for meat				£1	6s	
Received of him a bill		6s				
To Mr Albin for printing 500 Godfrey Papers					5s	6d
Of Mrs Brown, Horfleet, a bill	£1	10s				
Retail &c. 16s 6d. Weekly bill 16s 4¼d.		16s	6d		16s	4¼d
10 Of J. Dickinson, Bicker, in part		6s				
11 Of J. Percival, Gosberton Risgate, a bill		6s				
12 Of David Gilding Junior, Wigtoft, a bill		6s				
16 Of Mr Bell, Wigtoft, a bill		19s				
Retail &c. £1 2s. Weekly bill £1 2s 3¾d.	£1	2s		£1	2s	3¾d
17 Of Benjamin Blackwell a bill		12s				
The late Jane Ketton's bill, Quadring Eaudike		19s				
Remainder of J. Berry's bill		9s	6d			
Five Critical Reviews					5s	
18 Of Mr Pycroft for a Calf		12s				
A Silk Purse 2s 6d. Cotton Stocking 3s of J.G's.					5s	6d
19 My 2d Journey to S——-y					5s	4d
To Mr F. a bill for Shirting Cloth				£1	7s	
23 Of Mr B. Farrer, Gosberton	£1	1s	10d			
Weekly bill 16s 7¾d. Retail 16s 6d.		16s	6d		16s	7¾d
24 Of John Coy, Taylor, in part		10s	6d			
Of J. Chevins, Gosberton, a bill		5s	6d			
25 Of Luke Tebb, Northorp (a Labour)		15s				
26 To Messrs Otters, Druggists, Lincoln[283]				£1	16s	
To M. Redhoof a Month's Nursing due 24th					12s	
Received of her a bill		11s	6d			
28 Two Metts of Coals of J. Wells					4s	
29 Remainder of T. Cook's bill, Quadring	£1	7s	6d			
30 Retail &c. £1 0s 0d. Weekly bill £1 0s 0¾d.	£1	0s	0d	£1	0s	0¾d
£52 4s 6d **Carried over**	**£203**	**2s**	**4d**	**£150**	**17s**	**10d**

2d Journey to S——y, Aug: 18. 19. 83

I made my 2d Journey to S., and have the pleasure to note that things go on in that quarter as well as I can wish. I set off[284] from home about 1 o'clock, got tea at Stickney – to S. by 7. Had a most delightfull Evening & Morning of the 19th. As I came home, was taken so ill with a Colic as to render riding exceeding painfull. I reached home about 11 o'clock with very great difficulty indeed! I was poorly all that week with the Autumnal Fever, but by an Emetic & Bark[285] am now thank God very well. September 8. 83.

Samuel's Baptism, September 3. 1783

We baptized Samuel, Mr Wm Ward and my self as Deputy for my Brother & my Neice Henny being Sponsors. We made no feast nor asked any but Mrs Ward, Mr S.W. came by chance. September 8. 83.

---

283 See n.259 above.
284 MS 'of'.
285 See n.194 above.

[f.67]
September 1783: 9th Month, 30 Days

		Received			Paid		
Brought over		**£203**	**2s**	**4d**	**£150**	**17s**	**10d**
1	Of Robert Kirk, Bicker, a bill		8s				
	Of Richard Coats Junior (a Labour)		10s	6d			
2	A Fan for a present to					9s	
3	To M. Redhoof 2s. Harden[286] 2s. Thread 2d						
	(John's Bed)					4s	2d
6	Bees Wax 4lb 7oz at 18d, 6s 7½d. Writing Paper						
	10d.					7s	5½d
	Retail &c. £1 6s 0d. Weekly bill £1 6s 2½d.	£1	6s		£1	6s	2½d
	John's Shoes 1s 4d. Phial Corks & Carriage 11d.					2s	3d
7	The late J. Watson's bill of Bicker		8s	6d			
8	Of H. Cook, Donington, in part		10s	6d			
	1½ Chalder of Coals £1 13s. Expenses 4s.				£1	17s	
9	Of James Johnson a bill		5s				
	Of John Watkin, Horfleet, in part	£1	1s	0d			
12	Rum one Quart 3s. Red Wine 1s 9d.					3s	9d[287]
13	Retail &c. £1 1s. Weekly bill £1 0s 11d.	£1	1s		£1	0s	11d
14	Of Thomas Stokes a bill		12s	6d			
15	To Messrs Ferneyhough & Wilson in full				£8	10s	
	My 3d Journey to S——y					5s	
19	My Share of Irish prize money[288]	£2	3s				
	Share of 4 Quarters of Ticketts, English						
	Lottery 83[289]				£3	19s	
	Of Mr Brand, Hale Bar, a bill	£1	2s	6d			
20	Of Mr Thos Wells, Swineshead Fen Houses	£2	2s				
	Retail &c. 19s. Weekly bill 19s 2d.		19s			19s	2d
21	To Mary Redhoof a Month's Nursing					12s	
22	Of Edward Laykins a bill	£1	12s				
	Paid to him a bill in full				£1	4s	4d
26	To Mr Bouldram for a Quarter of Oats					18s	
	To -ditto- for 2 Cows Bulling 3s. Of him a bill		8s			3s	
	To Daniel Shays a bill in full					14s	
	To Ed. Fox for 4 Gallons of Ale at 1s 4d					5s	6d
27	Of Mr Bowers, Wigtoft, in part	£3	3s				
	Altering a Gold Ring at Spalding					1s	
	Retail &c. 19s. Weekly bill 19s 3½d.		19s			19s	3½d
28	Remainder of Widow Ward's bill, Gosberton		5s				
30	Of Mrs Turpin a bill		6s				
	£47 5s 11½d		**£222**	**4s**	**10d**	**£174**	**18s**	**10½d**

Purchase (of Captain Foggon), September 12 1783

I agreed with Mr Foggon this day for the Purchase of his 3d part of the House and Homestead next me in tenure of Isaac Lumby, and the Shop in Tenure of N. Gunthorp. The Purchase money is £77 10s 0d to be paid, and to enter on the same

---

286 See n.80 above.
287 As in MS: error in calculation.
288 See n.274 above.
289 For the 1783 Lottery, see Ewen, *Lotteries and Sweepstakes*, 206.

at Lady Day next ensuing. I drew up a little agreement with a forfeit of £5 and paid a Guinea in part to bind the agreement. It is freehold and at present Letts for something above £4; and as it is convenient and good Land, I hope it is not too dear, and as the other 2 parts will be sold when Wm Flinders is at age if it please God I live, possibly I may sometime have the whole. In order to pay this at Lady Day I have given Mr S. Ward notice to pay me £50 at that time and the rest I hope I shall be able to spare. As to the writings we are to pay equal shares. October 11.

[f.67v]
3d Journey to S., Sunday September 14. Monday 15
Sunday September 14. Having finished my Morning Business, I set of for S. about 11, dined at Swineshead Abbey and got to S. about 6 in the Evening, when I had the mortification to find the Family and Mrs E. on a visit at Mr Kirkham's at Hornby – on which I immediately set of for that place (4 miles) tho' rainy and almost dark. She in the most obliging manner returned with me to S. and we had as usual a most agreable Evening. We did not go to rest untill 4 o clock: had a very agreable walk on the Monday Morning. I believe almost every thing with regard to our Nuptials are settled, and I hope with the Divine Permission we shall compleat a happy union in the Month of December, the exact day I cannot yet note. I left S. after dinner and did not stop untill I came to the Abbey, where I drank Tea, and got home in good time, thank God in Health. I lost a Labour. We continue writing regularly alternately every week. October 11. 83.

Mr H[ursthouse]'s Marriage, Monday September 22.[290]
Mr Hursthouse being to be married as this day, requested my Neice's attendance on the Wed. preceeding. She went by the Coach and returned home to me on Friday the 26, after having had the principal management of the Nuptial Ceremonies, with a great deal of Company. It is a Mrs Harnew, a young Widow with one Child, a good fortune, and very fit match; he says he is very happy. I am sorry to note that Henny has brought home with her a quartan Ague, but hope she won't keep it long. October 11. 83.

House Improvements, 1783
I have to note that I have got the lumber Chamber over our common sitting room fitted up for a lodging chamber for the Children, having ceiled it, bricked up the old door, and made a new one out of my Chamber, put in a better Window, and made a new Closet, it will now do for 2 Beds very well. I have also got the Best Chamber papered, 2 new Hearth Stones, & Fire Screens &c. &c. and some lesser improvements previous to my intended Nuptials. By noting these things I would by no means have it understood, that I have forgot my ever dear departed friend and wife. God knows I have yet many bitter hours on her account, and am not without some fears, that it will be impossible for me ever to be so happy as I have been, but what can I do. I find my life uncomfortable and hope in the Society of the agreable Woman I have chosen in some degree at least to regain my former happy state. I imagine the improvements this Summer will cost me about £10. October 11.

---

[290] John Hursthouse married Sarah Harnew at Tydd St Mary on 22 September 1783 (Parish Register).

Th. October 16. Mr Hursthouse and his new Lady paid us a Visit and left us the following Morning after Breakfast.

Small Pox
I have to remark my Son John's Recovery from the Small Pox in the natural way at Nurse Tunnard's; he had a fine sort, and favourable quantity. I heartily wish this may so alter his constitution as to render him more healthy. My son Samuel is now ill of the same disorder, and has a most favourable and distinct eruption. Nov. 25. 83.

Journeys
On Wed. the 5th I made my 4th Journey to S. and had a most agreable Visit. I returned the next day. On Th. 20 I went over again and passed some most agreable hours; returned on Friday Evening – days being short. I set off from S. at 12. With God's Blessing I hope this is my last Journey but one, which is intended to be on Monday December 1, & the next day with the Divine Permission we intend to be United. Nov. 25. 83.

[f.68]
October 1783: 10th Month, 31 Days

		Received			Paid		
Brought over		£222	4s	10d	£174	18s	10½d
1	Two Chamber Locks of Mr Morgan, Spalding					6s	
2	Of Eliz. Smith 7s 6d. To her for Washing 1s.		7s	6d		1s	
4	Of John Stukeley, Donington, a bill		15s				
	Retail &c. £1 7s 6d. Weekly bill £1 7s 6d.	£1	7s	6d	£1	7s	6d
5	Of Thos Higgs, Northorp, a bill		11s				
9	To Ed. Sudbury for a pair of Shoes					6s	
10	Carriage of Druggs from London					6s	9d
	Of Jos. Wright Junior a Labour		10s	6d			
11	Two Years' Out Rent at the Wikes Court					16s	10d
	Of Henry Torks, Bicker, a bill		7s				
	Retail &c. £1 1s 6d. Weekly bill £1 1s 4½d.	£1	1s	6d	£1	1s	4½d
13	Critical Review for September, 1s.					1s	
16	Of Mr Crane, Quadring, a bill	£2	4s				
17	Of John Pepper, Gosberton Risgate, a bill		5s				
	To Francis Wilson for 2 Hearth Stones					5s	6d
	Of Mr Harrison, Bicker, a bill		6s				
	Of Mrs Buff a bill		5s	6d			
	Of Mr Elam, Swineshead, a bill	£1	3s				
	Of Mr Dowse, Burtoft, a bill	£1	7s	6d			
	Of John Garner, Bicker, a bill		10s				
	Of Charles Fever, Horfleet, in part		13s	6d			
	Of Daniel Christian, Bicker (a Labour)	£1	1s				
18	Of Mr Herd, Shopkeeper, Gosberton Risgate	£1	1s				
	Retail &c. £1 6s 6d. Weekly bill £1 6s 3¼d.	£1	6s	6d	£1	6s	3½d[291]
19	To Mr Birks for a Stone for my late dear wife,						
	£3 13s 6d. Carriage to Bolingbrooke &c. 5s.				£3	18s	6d
20	To Mrs Emmerson for teaching the Children					7s	6d
	Of Mrs Dixon Junior (a Labour)		15s				

[291] Totals do not agree in MS.

October 1783 (cont.)	Received		Paid		
21 Of Thos Olsop, Shoemaker, in part	10s	6d			
Of Mr Thos Tenny by bills	£3 10s	6d			
22 To Mary Redhoof a Month's Nursing, due 19th				12s	
Of Miss Jaques, Donington, a bill	19s				
25 To Wm Harrison a bill for Meat			£1	1s	6d
Received of him for Inoculation	10s	6d			
Retail &c. £1 0s 0d. Weekly bill £1 0s 0¼d.	£1		£1	0s	0¼d
Half a Year's Tithe of the Ing Land				4s	1½d
Of Mr Root, Swineshead, a bill	£1 15s				
29 Window Money 8s 6d. Land Tax 3s. House -do- 1s 3d.				12s	9d
Plaid for the Children 1s 6d. A Glass Salt 1s.				2s	6d
30 A New Bridle of J. Strapps				6s	
£57 6s 3¾d	£246	8s 4d	£189	2s	0¼d

Marriage, December 2. 1783

On Monday December 1 I went to Spilsby in order to be united to my amiable Friend, having previously procured a Licence of Mr Powell. I got to S. about 3½ in the afternoon, having a thick misty day; we were stirring pretty early in the Morning on account of the ceremony being to be performed before Breakfast.[292] Mr Franklin & myself waited on Mr Vessey (the Clergyman)[293] that Evening to inform him and request his Company to Breakfast. I should have premised that Miss Shepherd had been at S. almost a week to attend my wife thro' this important affair & to attend her home & has thro' [f.68v] the whole behaved with the greatest Friendship; we got thro' the ceremony very well, & set off about 10 for Boston, my Wife, Mrs Franklin and Miss S. in the Chaise, Mr Franklin & Myself on Horseback. We got to Boston about 2, and dined at the White Hart (having previously bespoke a dinner the day before, and invited Dr Knolton who kindly attended). We got off from Boston about 3½ and got home at 5½, the moon favouring us. Mr F. left us the following Morning but Mrs F. staid with us until Monday the 8th. We had Company on Sunday the 7th, Monday the 8th & Tuesday 9th and we have been a good deal harrassed in returning our Visits but we have now almost got thro' at which we are very glad. Jan. 1. 1784.

November 1783: 11th Month, 30 Days

	Received		Paid		
Brought over	£246	8s 4d	£189	2s	0¼d
1 Of John Lammin, Donington, a bill		15s 6d			
Retail &c. £1 3s 0d. Weekly bill £1 3s 0¼d.	£1	3s 0d	£1	3s	0¼d
A Bed Cord 1s. Betsy & Susan's Feast Money 1s.				2s	
Of John Brown, Donington Fenn, in part	£1	4s			
Paid to J. Tunnard for 42 Weeks Board of my Son John at 2s (from Jan.15 to Nov.5.83)			£4	4s	
Of -ditto- 1½ Year's Rent of the Pasture due Oct.10	£3	3s			
2 Of J. Taylor at Mrs Sudbury's, Hale Fen		5s 6d			
3 Of Wm Leverton, Gosberton Risgate, a bill	£1	2s 6d			

292 By Canon 62 of the Church of England, marriages were to be solemnised only between 8 and 12 in the forenoon.
293 Richard Vesey (d.1785), Curate of Spilsby where he resided (LAO, LC31, pp.99, 119).

November 1783 (cont.)

		Received			Paid		
	Of Mr Wm Gee, Hale Fen, a bill	£1	4s				
6	Journey to Spilsby (the 4th time)					5s	2d
	Mr Johnson's Man's bill	£1	1s	6d			
	To Mr Franklin for Shirting Cloth & Muslin				£2	5s	
	Matthew's Scholar Feast Money					2s	6d
	Brewing 2s 6d. Rec'd by yeast 1s 6d.		1s	6d		2s	6d
7	The late Wm Wheatly's bill		10s	6d			
8	Retail &c. 16s. Weekly bill 16s.		16s			16s	
10	Of T. Gunn a bill 5s. Critical Review Aug. 1s.		5s			1s	
14	Of Mr Watson, Gosberton Risgate, a Labour	£1	1s	0d			
	To Messrs Robinson & Pike in full				£3	11s	
15	Red & White Wine 5s 3d. Rasor Strap & Carriage 1s 2d.					6s	5d
	Of Mr Trimnell's Man (Inoculation)		7s	6d			
	Retail &c. £1 5s 0d. Weekly bill £1 5s 0½d.	£1	5s		£1	5s	0½d
	Rum one Quart of Mr Harvey					3s	
16	To Mary Redhoof a Month's Nursing					12s	
18	Of Rebecca Gray a bill		13s	6d			
19	Of Mr Turnhill a bill		9s	6d			
20	Of Mr S. Ward a Year's Interest due June 11	£7	10s				
	To him a Fee for Dr Hairby of Spilsby				£1	1s	0d
21	My 5th Journey to Spilsby					5s	3d
22	Of John Jackson, Bicker, a bill		6s	6d			
	Retail &c. 18s. Weekly bill 18s 2½d.		18s			18s	2½d
23	Critical Review October 1s. Worstead 8d.					1s	8d
25	Of Mr Jackson, Swineshead, a bill		19s	6d			
	Plaid & Flannell 1¼ Yard each for Samuel					2s	8½d
26	Of Michael Grant, Baker, a bill		14s	6d			
27	To Mr Gardiner a bill for Flowered Paper					15s	2d
	Carving Knife & Fork 2s 9d. Lemons 10d. Corks & Carriage 1s 3d.					4s	10d
28	Of Mr Kirk's Daughter, Bicker, a bill		13s				
29	Retail &c. £1 13s 6d. Weekly bill £1 13s 7d.	£1	13s	6d	£1	13s	7d.
	£65 8s 9d	**£274**	**11s**	**10d**	**£209**	**3s**	**1d**

[f.69]

December 1783: 12th Month, 31 Days

		Received			Paid		
Brought over		**£274**	**11s**	**10d**	**£209**	**3s**	**1d**
4	Of Wm Tooley at the Cow a bill		8s				
6	Carriage of druggs from London					6s	10d
	Lost at Cards on the 5th at home					2s	
	Retail &c. £1 16s 0½d. Weekly bill £1 16s 1½d.	£1	16s		£1	16s	1½d[294]
8	Of Mrs Battey, Bicker, a bill		11s	6d			
	Bottles 2s 4d. -Ditto- 1s 6d. A Hankerchief 1s 3d.					5s	1d
11	Of Mr Torks, Bicker, a bill		18s				
	To my Wife				£1	1s	0d
	The whole of our Marriage Expences				£8	13s	2d
12	To Mr Lowe for 8½ Stone of Pork at 4s 6d				£1	18s	
	Received of him a bill £1 1s 0d. Brewing 2s.	£1	3s				

[294] Totals do not agree in MS.

December 1783 (cont.)		Received			Paid		
	Carriage of my Wife's Furniture from Spilsby				£1	11s	6d
13	Weekly bill £1 7s 9 ½d. Retail £1 7s 6d.	£1	7s	6d	£1	7s	9½d
15	To Mr Parker, Joiner, a bill in full				£4	13s	6d
	To Mary Redhoof a Month's Nursing					12s	
16	Worstead for Boot Stockings 8 oz.					1s	4d
17	Of El. Smith 5s. To her for Washings &c. 5s.		5s			5s	
	Of James Nunnery, Blacksmith, a bill	£1	18s				
	To him a bill					7s	
	To J. Strapps a bill 1s 8d. Earnest to J. Hides 1s.					2s	8d
20	Of Thos Risebrook 7s. Of Wm Walker 5s Swineshead		12s				
	Of Mr Jackson's Maid, Swineshead, a bill		11s	6d			
	Retail &c. £1 14s 0d. Weekly bill £1 14s 4½d.	£1	14s		£1	14s	4½d
	1½ Chalder of Coals at 23s, £1 14s 6d. Expences 4s.				£1	18s	6d
21	Critical Review for November					1s	
27	Of Mr Wm Crosby, Gosberton Risgate, a bill		12s	6d			
	Of Mr Matthews, Bicker, a bill	£1	4s				
	Retail &c. £1 5s 0d. Weekly bill £1 5s 2½d.	£1	5s		£1	5s	2½d
28	Of George Fairbanks, Gosberton Westrop (a Labour)	£1	1s				
31	A Shaving Box and Brush					1s	
	Overplus Money from the Retail	£5	5s				
	A Machine called a Wash Maid of Mr Parker				£1	2s	
	£56 15s 8d	**£295**	**3s**	**10d**	**£238**	**8s**	**2d**

Total gained in 1783	£56 15s 8d
Total gained by Twelve Years' Business	£754 1s 2d
Total gained in Thirteen Years	£810 16s 10d

Conclusion of the Year 1783

At the termination of the last year I was in the utmost and most poignant distress, and soon after lost one of the best of Women. I now remark with all gratitude to Divine Mercy that I am in a much better situation, having again the comfort of a kind and Bosam friend. I can with truth assert, that every reasonable prospect of Happiness in a 2d Marriage I do experience as far as a Month can make me a judge – and have not the least doubt of its continuance, from the amiable disposition and goodness of my dearest friend and Wife. This has been a Year of most uncommon expence, but thro' a kind providence I have been enabled to lay by £56 15s 8d. May the Almighty bless us together with Life & Health to bring up our little Family. Jan. 1. 84.

[f.69v]
January 1784: 1st Month, 31 Days

		Received			Paid		
3	Retail &c. £1 2s 0d. Weekly bill £1 2s 2½d.	£1	2s		£1	2s	2½d
5	Of Mr Jarvis, Bicker, a bill	£6	6s	0d			
	Betsey and Susan: 9 Weeks' Schooling					4s	6d
	Cost us during the stay of some Comedians					4s	
9	Of Mr Johnson, Donington (due to my Wife)	£5					
10	Of James Watson, Bicker, for Inoculation		7s	6d			
	Of Richard Leake, Donington, a bill		14s				

January 1784 (cont.)	Received	Paid
Of Humphrey Stimson, Bicker, a bill	9s	
To Mr Shaw for cleaning the Clock		2s 6d
Aux. Porcina[295] 10lb. 3s 4d. Cera flava[296] 2lb. 3s.		6s 4d
Retail &c. 19s 6d. Weekly bill 19s 4¾d.	19s 6d	19s 4¾d
12 Of Mr Leather, Excise Officer, Donington, a bill	11s	
Critical Review for December 1s. A Brush 18d.		2s 6d
To Mary Redhoof a Month's Nursing		12s
13 To Captain Foggon a Year's Rent due Oct. 10. 1783		£3 10s
To John Strapps, Sadler, a bill		12s
To Mrs Pakey for 5 Stone of Flower		10s 3d
15 Of Mr Kirk, Bicker, a bill	£1 15s	
17 Retail &c. 16s. Weekly bill 16s 1d.	16s	16s 1d
19 Of Mr Bartol, Gosberton, a bill	£3 12s	
Of Mr Percival, Blacksmith, Quadring, a bill	10s	
Of Henry Wells for 2 Stone of Com. Cheese	6s 6d	
To Thos Holland, Gosberton, in Charity 1s.		1s
22 To Wm Boldram for 10 Strike of Oats		£1 1s 10½d
23 To Mr Torry, Glazier, a bill in full		£3 4s 6d
Received of him a bill	£2 3s 6d	
24 Of Mr Jackson, Donington North Ing, a bill	£1 3s	
Retail &c. 16s. Weekly bill 16s 2½d.	16s	16s 2½d
26 To J. Wells, Shoemaker, a bill for Matthew		9s 4d
A quarter's Land Tax		3s
Aux. Porcina[297] 12lb. 5s. 15½ doz. Bottles 5s 5½d.		10s 5½d
29 Of Thos Allen, Shoemaker, Donington, a bill	16s	
To him for 2 Pair of Shoes for Betsey		5s
Of Mr David Pike, Donington, a bill	13s	
To Mr Hunt a bill for Matthew		£1 7s 6d
30 Of Mr Gleed, Attorney, by bills	£3 12s 3d	
Paid to him a bill		£1 19s 8d
31 Of Mrs Shepherd a bill	17s	
Of Mr Palmer, Quadring, £2 4s 6d. Paid for Hog's Lard, 2s 6d.	£2 4s 6d	2s 6d
Retail &c. £1 1s 6d. Weekly bill £1 1s 2½d.	£1 1s 6d	£1 1s 2½d
£15 11s 2¾d **Carried over**	£35 15s 3d	£20 4s 0¼d

Henny's Visit

Jan. 6. 1784. Henny[298] made a Visit to Spilsby & Croft and is not yet returned. Am very sorry to remark that by letters from Hampshire our friends do very indifferently there, & my Brother talks of a remove again into Lincolnshire this Spring. Feb. 12. 1784.

Long continued Frost

I have to note the intense coldness of the Weather. The frost has continued 8 Weeks & still likely to stay, with frequent severe winds and much Snow. On Th. Feb. 12. the air was intensely cold; I put a half pint glass of water in the air, in 15

---

[295] See n.130 above.
[296] See n.63 above.
[297] See n.130 above.
[298] Flinders's niece.

Minutes it bore 3s 6d, in 30 Minutes a Crown Peice, in 45 Minutes 6½ oz. & in one hour a Pound Weight. The Poor are much distressed; 'tis generally allowed the weather is severer than in the great Frost 39-40.[299] Feb. 13. 84.

[f.70]
February 1784: 2nd Month, 29 Days

		Received			Paid		
	Brought over	**£35**	**15s**	**3d**	**£20**	**4s**	**0¼d**
	The late Mrs Wilton's bill of Mr D. Pike	£4	12s				
1	Of Mr J. Ward for joist[300] of 6 Sheep per 12 Weeks		18s				
	Of him a Physic bill		4s				
2	Rum one Quart 3s. Lemons ½ Dozen 1s.					4s	
4	Subscription to Donington Association					5s	
7	Of Mrs Battey, Bicker (a Labour)	£1	1s				
	Carriage of Druggs from London (2 Stone)					1s	6d
	Retail &c. £1 6s 0d. Weekly bill £1 5s 10½d.	£1	6s	0d	£1	5s	10½d
	To Mr Main for a Year's Shaving &c. due the 5th Inst.					17s	
	To J. Wells for Shoes Soling &c.					2s	
8	To Mary Redhoof a Month's Nursing					12s	
	Crit. Review Jan. 1s. Bottles 1s 4½d.					2s	4½d
11	Towards the Charitable Contribution for the Poor					5s	
12	Corks 1s 4½d. Sugar Shop use 2s 1d.					3s	5½d
14	Of Captain Nettleton, Swineshead, a bill	£2	12s				
	Of Thos Wright, Donington, a bill		5s				
	Six Pounds of Hemp Spining at 7d					3s	6d
	Retail &c. 16s 6d. Weekly bill 16s 6½d.		16s	6d		16s	6½d
19	Of Mr Blissett (Lingar House) a bill		8s	4d			
21	To John Wells 9 Months Wages				£1	2s	6d
	Of Mr Marsh, Quadring, a bill	£2	14s				
	Retail &c. £1 0s 0d. Weekly bill £1 0s 3¾d.	£1			£1	0s	3¾d
25	To Mr Hunt a bill in full				£2	13s	
	Received of him a bill		13s				
26	Of T. Madders the late Mr Tollet's bill		11s	8d			
	Of Francis Cubley, Donington Eaudike (a Labour)	£1	1s				
27	Paid Mr Lumby for 14½ of Hog's Leaf[301] at 4½					5s	5d
28	To Mr Harvey, Draper, a bill in full				£3	12s	6d
	Of J. Cook, Taylor, a bill		19s	4d			
	Paid to him a bill in full					8s	1d
	Retail &c. £1 1s 6d. Weekly bill £1 1s 8d.	£1	1s	6d	£1	1s	8d
	£20 12s 10d	**£55**	**18s**	**7d**	**£35**	**5s**	**9d**

My Neice

I may remark that the extreme severe weather & the impassibility of the Roads prevented my Neice from returning from Croft untill the middle of March when

---

[299] 1739/40 is believed to have been one of the coldest winters – possibly the coldest – in recorded history. At the time Flinders wrote this Britain was experiencing two successive extremely cold winters, with the Thames freezing over. There were numerous other notably cold winters during Flinders's lifetime, and the whole period from around 1450–1850 has been called the "Little Ice Age" (see D. Wheeler and J. Mayes, *Regional Climate of the British Isles* (1997), 291).

[300] See n.224 above.

[301] Leaf: the layer of fat round the kidneys of a pig (*OED*).

my Uncle H. brought her through & staid with us a Night, and she left us for alto-gether on Sunday April 18, intending to continue[302] at Spalding about a Month, and then to return to Greenwich with Mr & Mrs Gardiner & perhaps my Brother, who it seems is shortly to come down. The present plan is to remove from Odiam to Greenwich, to attempt a Girls' Boarding School – & Physic. I pray God it may answer, and that they may at length get fixed somewhere where Bread may be obtained & not continue in this distressed & most disagreable way. I believe Henny has cost me about £8 since being with me. It seems John is just returned from America, I hope in a good situation. Am glad to hear his character stands fair, & that he is not far from being a Lieutenant, that he has all his Wages and some prize money to receive. I wish it may be considerable for his own & Parents sake. I believe Mr G. is raising supplies on the Weston Land, I dare say they are indispensably necessary. May 4. 84.

[f.70v]
March 1784: 3rd Month, 31 Days

		Received			Paid		
Brought over		**£55**	**18s**	**7d**	**£35**	**5s**	**9d**
1	1½ Chalder of Coals at 22s, £1 13s 0d. Expences 4s.				£1	17s	
2	Of Mr Fant (Baker), Swineshead (a Labour)	£1	1s				
5	Of John Staples, Gosberton (a Labour)	£1	1s				
6	Two Hankerchiefs of Mr Harvey					3s	6d
	Retail &c. 17s 0d. Weekly bill 17s 1d.		17s			17s	1d
7	To Mary Redhoof a Month's Nursing					12s	
	Of Thos Fant (Baker), Swineshead, a bill		5s				
9	Of Mrs Bucknell, Donington, a bill	£1	2s				
	Paid to her for a sack of Oats					9s	
10	To Mr Torry for Pump repairing					2s	6d
11	To Mrs Pakey for 5 Stone of Flower					10s	3d
12	Of John Green, Donington, in part	£1	1s				
	Of Thos Percival, Blacksmith, a bill		4s	11d			
	Paid to him a bill in full					5s	1d
	Of Mr Shilcock a bill	£2	3s				
13	Retail &c. 19s 6d. Weekly bill 19s 8½d.		19s	6d		19s	8½d
14	Of Mary Tindall a bill		16s				
15	Of J. Bilsby Junior, Bicker, a bill	£1	4s	6d			
16	To Messrs Otters, Lincoln, Druggists				£1	2s	6d
19	Of Motteram, Donington Eaudike, a bill		13s	6d			
20	Retail &c. £1 6s 0d. Weekly bill £1 6s 1½d.	£1	6s		£1	6s	1½d
22	Bees Wax 1lb, 1s 6d. Hog's Lard 6 Pound 2s 6d.					4s	
24	To John Mitchell for 2 Carts of Hay & Carriage				£1	7s	
	Received of him a bill		14s				
25	A Lock for the Coal House Door					2s	
	Of Mr Lumby a bill	£1	3s	6d			
	Of Mr Lumby a Year's Rent due this day	£6	16s	6d			
	To him towards Ditching 3s. Fencing 1s. For Hay 2s.					6s	
	To Wm Flinders a Year's Rent will be due April 5th				£7		
26	Carriage of Druggs from Lincoln					2s	7d

---

302 MS 'contine'.

March 1784 (cont.)	Received	Paid
5 Pounds Sugar Shop use 2s 1d. Paid for Phials 2s 6d.		4s 7d
27 Retail &c. £1 5s 6d. Weekly bill £1 5s 6d.	£1 5s 6d	£1 5s 6d
£24 10s 3½d	**£78 12s 6d**	**£54 2s 2½d**

Health

Am sorry to remark that my wife has been in a very poor state of Health for many weeks, excessive dangerous about a week. Dr K. has been 3 times – begun with a profluvium Mensium,[303] of some weeks' continuance which brought her very low, attended with pain, bad cough &c. I thank God I can now remark that she is greatly better, eats & sleeps well, gets about Business; her Cough is the worst Symptom[304] that remains – but am in hopes that will wear of. I may add that I have been very poorley a week myself, had two Fitts of a Tertian,[305] with a bad sore Mouth, but by an Emetic & Bark[306] am thank God well & have been so about a fortnight. May 19. 84.

Brother

My Brother has been down into Lincolnshire, & came from Spalding, & staid one night with us. He came on Th. May 13 & left us on the 14th & went for London that day. They are to open a School at Greenwich (not having agreed with Mrs Williamson) at Midsummer. I pray God this scheme may answer.

My Wife's Journey to Spilsby

My Wife I thank God being well recovered, she along with Matthew made a Journey to Spilsby on Friday June 4 and returned on Sat. 12. One of Mr Franklin's Daughters came back with her to stay awhile. June.[307]

[f.71]
April 1784: 4th Month, 30 Days

	Received	Paid
Brought over	£78 12s 6d	£54 2s 2½d
1 Of Mrs Torry, Gosberton, a bill	7s 6d	
3 Of Mr Millington a bill	£4 15s 6d	
Of Mr Ashwell, Gosberton, a bill	16s	
To Edward Gibson a bill in full		£2 8s 11d
Received of him a bill	£2 3s 6d	
Retail &c. 13s 6d. Weekly bill 13s 5½d.	13s 6d	13s 5½d
4 A Magazine 6d. Stamps for Receipts 1s.		1s 6d
To Mary Redhoof a Month's Nursing		12s
8 To Mary Leah Earnest Money (Wages £3 5s)		2s 6d
10 Of Mr Fletcher, Horfleet, a bill	5s 9d	
Of Mr Fant, Swineshead, a bill	13s	
Of J. Philips, Gosberton, a bill	7s	
Of Mr Limbird, Bicker, a bill	14s	

---

303 Excessive or heavy menstruation.
304 MS 'Sympton'.
305 An intermittent fever whose paroxysm recurs every third day (*OED*).
306 See n.194 above.
307 Remainder of date lost.

April 1784 (cont.)

		Received			Paid		
	Of Mr Garner, Gosberton Risgate, a bill	£1	17s				
	Of Mr Barnett, Bricklayer, a bill	£1	1s	5d			
	Paid to him a bill				£1	19s	5d
	To M. Grant for brewing 2s 6d. Yeast & Grains 1s 6d.		1s	6d		2s	6d
	Retail &c. £1 4s 0d. Weekly bill £1 4s 0d.	£1	4s		£1	4s	
	Paid to my Wife				£1	1s	
12	To Ann Towns for Spining 6 Pound of Hemp					3s	6d
13	Of Revd Mr Ferne, Wigtoft, the Maid's bill	£1	0s	6d			
	Of Mrs Pattison, Donington, a bill	£1	10s				
	A Wire Cinder Riddle of Mr Jennings 2s 9d & Carriage 2d					2s	11d
	To my Neice at various times during the Year				£5	10s	6d
15	Sold the Red Cow to Mr Shilcock for	£6	14s				
	To John Elsom Earnest Money 1s 6d (Wages 40s)					1s	6d
	To John Mitchell for Hay					12s	6d
16	Of Robert Jackson, Bicker, a bill		9s				
17	Retail &c. £1 2s 6d. Weekly bill £1 2s 4d.	£1	2s	6d	£1	2s	4d
	A Pair of Stays for Bettsey of Mr Brighton					7s	
19	Bettsey & Susan: 15 Weeks' Schooling at 5d					6s	3d
24	To Mr Harvey at the Cow a bill in full				£1	18s	
	Received of him a bill		4s				
	To John Strapps for Horse Hire to Spalding					2s	
	Retail &c. 16s 6d. Weekly bill 16s 5½d.		16s	6d		16s	5½d
26	Window Money ½ Year 8s 6d. Land Tax ½ Year 3s. House Tax 1s 3d.					12s	9d
28	Of Mrs Page, Gosberton, 5s. Of Mrs Vessy's Maid, Gosberton, 5s.		10s				
	Of J. Cole, Donington, in part, 9s. To -ditto- for Susan's Shoes, 2s.		9s			2s	
30	Of Wm Smith Junior in part		5s				
	£32 7s 5½d	**£106**	**12s**	**8d**	**£74**	**5s**	**2½d**

Son John

On Mon. June 14, we took home my Son John from Nurse. He is above 3 years old, & has, since having the small Pox, been much more healthy and is a fine boy. He has behaved much better than we expected. This has been a very expensive Child, both before & since his Dear Mother's Death.

Purchase concluded

On Sat. June 19 I paid to Captain Foggon £92 10s, having given him an additional £15 for the third of the three Cottages over the way. I sincerely thank God for this addition to my property & hope it may be usefull for my poor Children.

[f.71v]

May 1784: 5th Month, 31 Days

		Received			Paid		
	Brought over	**£106**	**12s**	**8d**	**£74**	**5s**	**2½d**
1	Recd. the ¼ of a ¼ of a £20 Prize	£1	5s				
	Remainder of T. Audis's bill late of Swineshead		14s				
	Retail &c. £1 0s 6d. Weekly bill £1 0s 5½d.	£1	0s	6d	£1	0s	5½d

May 1784 (cont.)		Received			Paid		
	No 1 of Walpole's British Traveller[308]						6d
	Mr Powell's half year's Tithe					4s	1½d
5	To Ann Uffindale for Spining 6 Pound Hemp					3s	6d
	Two Gallons & 3 Pints of Rum at 12s 6d				£1	9s	8d
7	Carriage of Druggs from London					1s	1d
	Of Mr Goodwin a bill	£2	5s				
	6 Dozen of Gally-pots[309] of Mr Knight					3s	
8	No 2, 3, 4 of the British Traveller					1s	6d
	Of Mr Taylor, North Ing, a bill		5s				
	Retail &c. 19s. Weekly bill 19s 1½d.		19s			19s	1½d
	Bees Wax 1lb: 1s 8d. Magazine 6d.					2s	2d
9	Of Thos Bee, Bicker Gauntlet, a bill		5s	6d			
10	To Captain Foggon ½ Year's Rent due April 5th				£1	15s	
	1½ Chalder of Coals £1 14s 6d. Expences 4s.				£1	18s	6d
11	Sugar 1½ Pound Shop use 11d. A Tin Broiler 14d.					2s	1d
14	Of a Young Woman for Inoculation		7s	6d			
	To Mr Wilson, Druggist, in full				£7	3s	
	To Mary Leah a Year's Wages				£3	5s	
15	Retail &c. £1 0s 6d. Weekly bill £1 0s 8d.	£1	0s	6d	£1	0s	8d
20	To Messrs Robinson & Pike in full				£6	14s	
	A Kettle and Lamp Repairing					1s	9d
22	Retail &c. 16s. Weekly bill 15s 9¾d.		16s			15s	9¾d
24	A New Pump Buckett of Mr Torry					2s	6d
25	Of Wm Fairbanks, Gosberton Westrop, a bill	£1	2s				
	To John Elsom Wages due before May 12th					7s	6d
26	Of Mr Petchill Senior, Gosberton Risgate, a bill		7s				
	Of Jos. Robinson, Gosberton, a bill		10s				
	Of Mr Petchill Junior, Gosberton	£1	8s	6d			
	Of Mr Allen's Servant, Gosberton, a bill		7s				
	Of Mr Hanley, Shoemaker, a bill		10s	4d			
	A Year's Rent of James Clark due April 5th	£8	8s				
	Allowed him for Ditching				£1	5s	8d
	Of Thos Smith, Frampton, a Year's Interest due the 4th	£7	10s				
	Of Mr Allcock, Gosberton, a Labour	£1	1s				
	Of Wm Allvey, Quadring Fen, a bill		7s	6d			
	Bicker Parish bill of Mr Parker	£4	11s	6d			
	Of Mr Parker a bill (Bicker)		18s				
	Of Thos Roberts, Gosberton Risgate, a bill		9s	6d			
27	To J. Lamiman a bill for Quick & Work					11s	9d
29	Of David Read, Swineshead, a bill		5s	6d			
	Retail &c. £1 5s 0d. Weekly bill £1 5s 1½d.	£1	5s		£1	5s	1½d
31	Bettsey and Susan 5 Weeks' Schooling at 7d					2s	11d
	My wife going to the Assembly the 27th					2s	6d
	Of Mr Charles Trimnell, Bicker Fenn		5s				
	Paid for Phials during the Month					3s	3d
£39 9s 1¾d	**Carried over**	**£144**	**16s**	**6d**	**£105**	**7s**	**4¼d**

---

[308] *The new British traveller; or, a complete modern universal display of Great-Britain and Ireland: . . . The whole published under the immediate inspection of George Augustus Walpoole, . . . Embellished with upwards of one hundred and fifty . . . views . . .* (London, 1784). Published in 60 parts (ESTC).
[309] See n.179 above.

Samuel came from Nurse, Wed. June 30. 84

I have to note my youngest child Samuel came from Nurse – he has just begun to go alone. I have now all my 5 Children with me, this causes a considerable additional Trouble but is not so much as expected and saves me 5s 6d per Week in my Pockett. July 13. 1784

[f.72]

June 1784: 6th Month, 30 Days

		Received			Paid		
	Brought over	£144	16s	6d	£105	7s	4¼d
1	Of Charles Thompson, Gosberton Risgate, a bill		14s				
	Horse Triming by Wm Oliver 6d						6d
4	To Eliz. Wells for Spining 9 Pound of Hemp at 7d					5s	3d
	Of Mr Jennings, Bicker Gauntlet, a bill	£2	8s				
	Cash paid to my Wife on going to Spilsby				£3	13s	6d
5	Of Mr John Lee a bill in full	£3	5s	10d			
	Paid to him a bill in full				£3	4s	10d
	Carriage of Druggs from London					10s	5d
	Nos 5, 6, 7, 8 of the British Traveller					2s	
	Of Mr Holbourn, Horfleet, by bills		13s	6d			
	Retail &c. 18s. Weekly bill 18s 1¼d.		18s			18s	1¼d
7	Of John Sutton, Donington, a Labour		10s	6d			
9	Of Mr Garner's Man, Gosberton Risgate, a bill		17s				
12	Retail &c. 14s 6d. Weekly bill 14s 5½d.		14s			14s	5½d
14	To J. Tunnard for Boarding Jackey 8 Months				£4		
	Of -do- ½ Year's Rent of the Pasture due Lady Day last	£1	1s				
	Of Mr Franklin for a Mahogany Card Table		18s	6d			
	Paid him for a Joiner Packing the Furniture					6s[310]	
	3 Yards ¾ of Shalloon[311] at 20d of -do-					6s	[3d]
	To my Wife in Cash				£1	1s —	
18	The Salary for Wigtoft Poor from Easter 83 to -do- 84	£4	4s				
	Pair of Gloves of J. Cew 1s 6d. Bellows Mending 1s.					2s	[6d]
19	Retail &c. £1 2s 0d. Weekly bill £1 2s 1½d.	£1	2s		£1	2s	[1½d]
	Spent at the Cow 1s 6d. John's Entrance at School 1s.					2s	[6d]
23	One Year's Insurance Money					7s —	
26	Retail &c. £1 2s 6d. Weekly bill £1 2s 6d.	£1	2s	6d	£1	2s	[6d]
28	Of Wm Blancher, Gosberton, a bill		6s				
	Four Grose of Phial Corks 1s. Carriage 2d.					1s	[2d]
29	Remainder of Wm Smith's (Junior) bill		5s	6d			
30	Of Mrs Cook, Quadring, in part	£1	1s				
	A Cornelian[312] Seal of a Jew					— —	
	Paid for Phials in June					— —	
	£41 6s 2½d Carried over	£164	18s	4d	£123	[12s	1½d]

---

310 From this point, the edge of the page is torn away, leaving the pence column missing.
311 Shalloon: closely woven woollen material (*OED*).
312 Cornelian: semi-transparent quartz of a deep dull red (*OED*).

Journey to Tidd[313]

Th. July 1. Myself and Son Matthew went to Tidd to … Mr and Mrs Hursthouse. We went by the Reservoir, … is a saving of 4 Miles, came to Mr Decamps's at Fleet … and to Tidd by Tea, staid with him untill Friday 3 o'clock … came to Mr Decamps to Tea & home by the same road by … it happened rather unlucky Mr H. had company both days … was much affected on the Friday at the distressing … that the last time I was at Tidd I had my late dearest … with me, & the late good Mrs H. was there also alive: 4 … N.B. Matthew went on a borrowed Poney & performed tolerab[ly] …

Dr Peckwell

Sund: Aug: 29 I went in Company with Mr Gleed to … the celebrated Dr Peckwell preach.[314] We were just in time … the service at Great Hale[315] where he did the whole duty … We dined at Mrs Arnalls at Heckington then went to …-phringham[316] to hear another Sermon from him. I was [?not] … disappointed. He preaches extempore & with much eloquence … – and as to his tenets I have lately thought much [?more] favourably of them as consonant to Scripture than fo[rmerly] …

[f.72v]
July 1784: 7th Month, 31 Days

		Received			Paid		
Brought over		£164	18s	4d	£123	12s	1½d
1	Of J. Harvey (Labourer) a Labour		10s	6d			
2	Of James Clifton, Quadring Eaudike, a bill	£1	6s	6d			
	To Mr Hollingworth, Lynn (by Mr Hursthouse)					14s	9d
	To Mr Marshall, Lynn (by Mr Hursthouse)				£1	19s	
	Expences of a Journey to Tidd					5s	2d
3	Of John Chevins, Gosberton (a Labour)	£1	1s	0d			
	No 9, 10, 11, 12 of the British Traveller					2s	
	Of John Beecroft Junior, Donington, in part		10s	6d			
	Of Mr Carnal, Swineshead, a bill	£1	15s	6d			
	Retail &c. 14s 6d. Weekly bill 14s 3½d.		14s	6d		14s	3½d
4	Of Rebecca Fairweather, Donington, a bill		11s	6d			
	Of Samuel Ashton a bill		19s				
5	To Mrs Pakey for 5 Stone of Flower					10s	2½d
	To Mary Redhoof for 3 Months' Nursing				£1	16s	
	To -ditto- for 3 Days' -ditto-					1s	6d
6	Cash taken from the Retail Money	£5	5s				
	To Mr Lumby for a Cow (an Inn calver)				£7	15s	
8	Of J. Kendall a bill	£1	4s	6d			
10	To Mr J. Ward 2 Years' Drainage Tax due at Lady Day of the Ing Land 5ac.3r.8p. at 1s 3d per Acre 7s 3d per Year					14s	6d

[313] The right edge of the page is torn away, leaving the text of this paragraph and the next incomplete.
[314] Dr Henry Peckwell (1747–87), Anglican clergyman and a popular Methodist preacher, who studied medicine and established a foundation called The Sick Man's Friend to provide medical care to the poor. He was Rector of Bloxholm with Digby near Sleaford from 1782 until his death (*ODNB*).
[315] Around 10 miles north west of Donington.
[316] Possibly Helpringham, immediately south of Great Hale.

July 1784 (cont.)

	Received			Paid		
A Magazine 6d. Lump Sugar 1½lb: 1s.					1s	6d
Retail &c. £1 4s 6d. Weekly bill £1 4s 7½d.	£1	4s	6d	£1	4s	7½d
Of John Keil, Donington, a Labour		10s	6d			
11[317] To Mr May, Glass Manufacterer, in full[318]				£6	8s	6d
Of Nathaniel[319] the Miller a bill		8s	6d			
To J. Hall for Mowing the Ing 2 Acres					4s	8d
Of Elizabeth Smith a bill		5s				
Of Mr Pycroft for a Calf		12s				
To my Wife in Cash					10s	6d
Of Mr Calf, Gosberton, a bill	£2	2s				
Of Richard Jackson a bill		6s				
Of Mrs Marshall, Quadring, a bill	£2	0s	0d			
Retail &c. 16s 6d. Weekly bill 16s 8d.		16s	6d		16s	8d
Of Wm Green, Bicker Fen	£1					
Of John Bartram a bill		13s	5d			
To Henry Wells for attending &c. the Cow					2s	
Dimothy[320] 1½ Yards at 1s for two Night Caps					1s	6d
Of Mr Caswell, Quadring, a bill	£1	18s				
Of John Hall, Donington, a bill		19s	6d			
To him for 2 Load of Hay £2 5s. For Milk 8s 1½d.				£2	13s	1½d
Retail &c. £1 1s 0d. Weekly bill £1 1s 1½d.	£1	1s	0d	£1	1s	1½d
Of Mr Thos Green, Donington, a bill	£1	17s	6d			
[To] him for two Strike of Oats					4s	3d
[Land] Tax 3s. Bees Wax 1s 6d.					4s	6d
[To] Daniel Shays a bill £1 4s 6d. Of him -do- 15s.		15s		£1	4s	6d
[Of] Mr Torry, Donington, a bill	£2	7s				
[Two] Piggs of J. Cole, Shoemaker				£1	1s	0d
[Of] Wm Hall (in part of £1 16s) £1 1s 0d	£1	1s				
[Of] Mr Turnhill at the Cow a bill		5s				
Retail &c. £1 0s 0d. Weekly bill 19s 9½d.	£1				19s	9½d
[£4]4 16s 5½d **Carried over**	**£199**	**19s**	**3d**	**£155**	**2s**	**9½d**

[f.73]

August 1784: 8th Month, 31[321] Days

		Received			Paid		
	Brought over	**£199**	**19s**	**3d**	**£155**	**2s**	**9½d**
	Paid for Phials in July					2s	5½d
	Of Mr Charles Trimnell, Bicker Fen, a bill	£4	1s	0d			
2	Of Mr Golding in part of the Parish bill	£10	10s				
6	Carriage of Druggs from London					1s	8d
7	4 Nos of the British[322] Traveller 2s					2s	
	Retail &c. 18s 6d. Weekly bill 18s 7d.		18s	6d		18s	7d
8	Of Francis Horn, Donington, a bill		17s				
9	184 Pan Tiles 10s. 10 Ridge -do- 4s 2d. Cow House.					14s	2d
	Of Mr Thomas Green for Arg. Viv.[323] &c.		6s				

---

317 From this point, the left edge of the page is torn away, leaving the date column missing.
318 See n.202 above.
319 Surname left blank in MS.
320 Presumably dimity: a stout cotton fabric (*OED*).
321 MS '30'.
322 MS 'Bristish'.
323 *Argentum vivum*: quicksilver or mercury.

August 1784 (cont.)	Received			Paid		
10 Of Mr Pycroft a bill	£1	19s				
Paid him for Lime ¾ Chalder 9s.						
Carriage of H. Stons. 3s.					12s	
11 Of J. Allen, Swineshead (a Labour)	£1	1s				
Cera flava[324] 1lb: 1s 6d. Cow Bulling 2s.					3s	6d
13 Of Michael Grant, Baker, a bill		11s				
14 Retail &c. 17s. Weekly bill 17s.		17s			17s	
Cera flava 3lb 6oz at 1s 6d					5s	
Of Mr Maidens, Gosberton		10s	6d			
Magazine for July and Supplement					1s	
21 Retail &c. 14s. Weekly bill 14s.		14s			14s	
22 Of John Neale, Swineshead Woad Houses, a						
Labour	£1	1s				
26 Sugar Shop use 2s 1d. Hobbing[325] the Green 2s.					4s	1d
28 To Mrs Pakey for 10 Stone of Flower				£1	1s	0d
Retail &c. 15s. Weekly bill 14s 9d.		15s			14s	9d
30 Of Wm Bell, Wigtoft, a bill	£1	2s				
31 To Messrs Otters, Druggists, in full				£5	10s	
Of John Chamberlain, Blacksmith, a bill	£1	3s	6d			
Phials bought in August					2s	8½d
£58 19s 0½d	**£226**	**5s**	**9d**	**£167**	**6s**	**8½d**

Spilsby Journey

On Sunday September 26, I made a Journey to Spilsby. Mr S. Ward was with me, having lain at our house the preceeding night. The weather proved rainy & unfavourable. We dined at the Red Lion, Boston – got tea at Mr S. Ward's – and got to Mr Franklin's about 8 at night, having the Benefit of the Moon. They were from home but soon returned. We staid the night, & I came off about 10 Monday Morning; dined and got Tea with Dr K. at Boston & home in the Evening. Lost a Labour; generally have that alloy to my pleasure visits, so they must be few indeed, they are not much pleasure to me.

Auction of Books, October 4th &c. &c.

I have to note a circumstance that I never before knew in Donington, viz. an Auctioneer with Books; was in the Town about a week, at the Peacock. I attended several Evenings,[326] and made several purchases, but his collection was not the most brilliant, nor his method the most striking – nor[327] did he part with anything cheap. What I bought were as follow:

Entick's History & Survey of London, 4 Vol., 8vo[328]	12s 0d
Hudibrass[329] 12vo, Bound & Lettered	1s 1d

---

324 See n.63 above.
325 Hob: to cut the high tufts of grass in a pasture, or those missed in ordinary mowing (*OED*).
326 MS 'Evening'.
327 MS 'not'.
328 John Entick (1703?–1773), *A new and accurate history and survey of London, Westminster, Southwark, and places adjacent; containing whatever is most worthy of notice in their ancient and present state* (London, 1766).
329 Samuel Butler (1612–1680) published his satirical poem *Hudibras* between 1663 and 1678. It was reprinted regularly during the eighteenth century.

Doddridge[330] on the N. Testament,[331] 2 Vol., 12vo, Bd & Ld	3s 3d
Lady Montague's Letters,[332] 12vo, Bd & Lettd	2s 0d
Beauties of Dr Watts,[333] 12vo, Bd & Lettd	2s 0d
Gray's Poems,[334] 10d. Blair's Grave,[335] 3d.	1s 1d
Young's Last Day,[336] 3d. A Letter Case, 3d.	3s 0d
	£1 5s 2d

[f.73v]

September 1784: 9th Month, 30 Days

		Received			Paid		
Brought over		**£226**	**5s**	**9d**	**£167**	**6s**	**8½d**
2	Of Mr Pycroft's Man a bill		8s	6d			
4	Retail &c. 15s 6d. Weekly bill 15s 5½d.		15s	6d		15s	5½d
6	Of the Revd Mr Coates a bill		10s	6d			
	Stamps for Receipts 1s. A Magazine 6d.					1s	6d
7	Of Mr Hodge, Blacksmith, Swineshead		8s				
8	Of Mr Nunnery, Blacksmith, a bill		5s	6d			
	Two Nos of the British Traveller					1s	
9	To Wm French towards his loss of a Cow					1s	
	In Charity to an old Man (name J. Flinders)					1s	
10	Carriage of Druggs from Lincoln 5 Stone 5 Pound					1s	9d
	Brewing 2s 6d. By Yeast 11d received			11d		2s	6d
11	Retail &c. £1 1s 0d. Weekly bill £1 1s 1¼d.	£1	1s		£1	1s	1¼d
15	Of Richard Hales, Gosberton, a Labour	£1	1s				
	Of Mr Clark, Glover, a bill	£1	13s				
	Paid to him a bill in full					7s	3d
16	Of Luke Tebb, Northorp, a Labour		15s				
18	Retail &c. 13s. Weekly bill 12s 11d.		13s			12s	11d
21	To Mr Lee for Malt £1 5s 0d. Hops 2½ Pound:						
	4s 2d.				£1	9s	2d
23	Mercur. Sublim. Cor.[337] 1lb of Mr Lane					6s	
	Of John Tunnard for Attending a Vagrant		6s				
25	Of Cook,[338] Gosberton Bank, a bill				£1	4s	6d
	Retail &c. 16s. Weekly bill 16s 2d.		16s			16s	2d
26	Of Mr Trickett, Donington, a bill	£2	11s				
	Of J. Kirkbridge a bill	£1	6s	6d			
27	Journey to Spilsby cost me					4s	6d
	Ather[339] & Phial 6oz at Mr Lane's					1s	2½d

330 MS 'Dodsley'; see also accounts for 4 October 1784 below.
331 Philip Doddridge (1702–1751), *The family expositor: or, a paraphrase and version of the New Testament: with critical notes; and a practical improvement of each section*, 2nd ed. (2v., London, 1745), or 3rd ed. (2v., London, 1756) (ESTC).
332 The letters of Lady Mary Wortley Montagu (1689–1762) were first published in 1763 and were frequently reprinted (ESTC).
333 Isaac Watts (1674–1748), *The beauties of the late Revd Dr Isaac Watts* (London, 1782).
334 The poems of Thomas Gray (1716–1771) were first printed in 1756 and were reprinted in many subsequent editions (ESTC).
335 Robert Blair (1699–1746), *The grave: a poem*, first printed in 1743 (ESTC).
336 Edward Young (1683–1765), *A poem on the last day*, first printed in 1713 (ESTC).
337 *Mercurius corrosivus sublimatus*, or bichloride of mercury (*Supplement*).
338 Christian name left blank in MS.
339 *Æther*.

September 1784 (cont.)		Received			Paid		
29	Of a Man at James Hare's, Quadring Eaudike		5s				
30	Of Mr Baxter, Baker, Swineshead, a bill		17s	6d			
	Worstead 8oz at 2½d					1s	8d
£67 13s 3½d	**Carried over**	**£241**	**4s**	**2d**	**£173**	**10s**	**10½d**

Comedians

I have to remark that in the latter half of October and begining of November we have had a small Company of Comedians with us. I went 3 or 4 times and once or twice was tolerably entertained – tho' the accommodations were but indifferent, being a cold Barn in the Church Street. Saw the Quaker's Wedding[340] & Mayer of Garret[341] very decently done. They came from Tattershall here & left us for Swineshead, but there I hear disentions took place among them & they have seperated. December 28. 84.

My Brother

Have had 2 Letters from my Brother lately, & he gives me some faint hopes of the School succeeding, having at present Six Boarders and hopes of more after the Holidays; but not much hopes in the Physical Line. I sincerely hope in God they may succeed – have sent a Turkey as a Christmas present. December 28. 84.

[f.74]

October 1784: 10th Month, 31 Days

		Received			Paid		
Brought over		**£241**	**4s**	**2d**	**£173**	**10s**	**10½d**
1	Of Jonathan Hanson a bill	£1	2s	6d			
	Of a Woman (late Servant to Mr Green, Bicker)		8s				
2	Retail &c. 14s. Weekly bill 14s 0½d.		14s			14s	0½d
3	A Magazine for September 6d.						6d
4	Of Mary Orry, Donington, for Inoculation		7s	6d			
	Doddridge on the New Testament 2 Vols					3s	3d
	Assosiation Subscription 5s. Spent at[342] Dinner 1s 9d.					6s	9d
6	Gray's Poems 10d. A Letter Case 2s 9d.					3s	7d
	L. Montague's Letters 1s 4d. Hudibrass 1s 10d.					3s	2d
	Beauties of Dr Watts 1s 4d. Two Phamphlets 5d.					1s	9d
9	Entick's Survey &c. of London, 4 Vols, 8vo					12s	
	The abominable Horse Tax for one Year					10s	
10	To Wm Flinders ½ a Year's Rent due this day				£3	10s	
	Cash made of the Fruit in the Orchard	£3	15s	6d			
	To my Wife in Cash				£1	12s	
	Exchange of Watts & Montague for others Bd					1s	6d
	Retail &c. 15s. Weekly bill 15s 3d.		15s			15s	3d
	Of Elsom,[343] Northorp, a Labour		15s				
11	Of Mr Fant, Swineshead, a bill		15s	6d			

---

[340] Richard Wilkinson (fl.1703), *The Quaker's wedding. A comedy. As it is acted at the Theatre-Royal by His Majesty's Servants* (London, 1723) (ESTC).

[341] Samuel Foote (1720–1777), *The Mayor of Garret. A comedy, in two acts. As it is performed at the Theatre-Royal in Drury Lane* (London, 1764 and subsequent editions) (ESTC).

[342] MS '&'.

[343] Christian name left blank in MS.

October 1784 (cont.)

		Received			Paid		
	To Mr Hunt a bill (Trimings for a Coat &c.)					5s	7d
	One Year's Out Rent at the Wikes Court					8s	5d
12	Of Jos. Haw, Northorp, a bill		18s	6d			
16	Of Mr Garner, Donington Fen, a bill	£2	12s	6d			
	Retail &c. £1 14s 0d. Weekly bill £1 13s 11¼d.	£1	14s	0d	£1	13s	11¼d
	Sugar Shop use 2s 1d. Lump Sugar 1½lb: 1s: -do-					3s	1d
17	Of Zebidee Elsom in part		10s	6d			
18	Of J. Bates, Wigtoft, a bill		13s	6d			
	Of Mr Towns, Gosberton Bolney	£1	7s				
	Of Thompson, Kirton (J. Thompson's Father)		8s				
	Of Mr Carby, Hale Fenn, a bill		10s	6d			
	Of Mrs Southern, Swineshead, a bill		9s	6d			
	Of Mrs Reckaby, Kirton Holme, a bill		9s				
	Of James Skeath, Gosberton, a bill		10s	6d			
	Of John Unwin, Gosberton, a bill		12s	6d			
19	Of Mr Burrus, Cooper, in part	£1	1s				
	Of a Gentleman at the Peacock		7s				
	Of Robert Kirk, Bicker, a bill		6s	6d			
	Half a dozen Knives and Forks					4s	
20	Of Mr Lee's Servant Maid a bill		6s	6d			
	Of J. Beecroft Junior, Donington, in part		10s	6d			
	To Mrs Emmerson for Teaching since May 31					13s	10d
22	To Mr Thos Pike a bill for Leading Coals &c.				£4	2s	5d
	Received of him a bill	£3	14s	5d			
23	Of Mr Cook, Quadring, in part		10s	6d			
	Retail &c. 13s. Weekly bill 13s 0½d.		13s			13s	0½d
24	Of Thos Olsop, Donington, a bill in part		10s	6d			
25	Cost us going to the Play					3s	6d
	Window Money ½ Year 8s 6d. House Tax -do-						
	1s 3d. Land Tax ½ Year 3s.					12s	9d
	£77 7s 10½d	**£268**	**13s**	**1d**	**£191**	**5s**	**2½d**

[f.74v]

November 1784: 11th Month, 30 Days

		Received			Paid		
Brought over		**£268**	**13s**	**1d**	**£191**	**5s**	**2½d**
Oct							
27	Two Chalders of Coals £2 4s. Expences 4s 6d.				£2	8s	6d
29	To R. Hall for Leading Manure, 13 Load					11s	
30	Of Mr Green, Bicker, a bill	£4	14s	6d			
	Cost me at the Play on Friday Evening					1s	9d
31	Of J. Ryland, Bicker Fen (a Labour)	£1	1s				
Nov							
1	The Play 1s. Sack of Oats 7s 6d.					8s	6d
3	Matthew's Scholar Feast Money					2s	6d
4	The Play 1s 6d. 4 Nos British Traveller 2s.					3s	6d
6	Of Revd Mr Powell a bill	£7	13s				
	Retail &c. 12s 6d. Weekly bill 12s 3d.		12s	6d		12s	3d
11	Betsey & Susan's Scholar Feast					1s	
13	For attending Quadring Poor ½ a Year	£2	2s				
	To Mr Wilson, Druggist, in full				£9	16s	6d
	Discount allowed 4s 7d. Packages -ditto- 8s 10d.		13s	5d			

October 1784 (cont.)	**Received**		**Paid**		
Weekly bill 14s. Retail &c. 14s 1½d.	14s			14s	1½d [344]
15 Of Thos Higgs, Northorp, a bill	15s	6d			
16 To Mr Robinson, Druggist, in full			£2	16s	6d
To Mr Parker, Joiner, in full			£2	18s	6d
Canthar.[345] 2oz: 1s 8d. Calom. pp.[346] ½ oz: 4d.					
Carriage 2d of Mr Lane				2s	2d
17 To Mrs Pakey for 5 Stone of Flower				10s	9d
20 Retail &c. 18s 6d. Weekly bill 18s 8d.	18s	6d		18s	8d
22 To Edward Laykins a bill in full				15s	
Received of him for Joist &c.[347]	10s				
24 Of Mr Garner's Man, Gosberton, a bill	7s	6d			
Paid for Four Strike of Potatoes				4s	
25 Of John Stukeley, Donington, a bill	11s	6d			
27 To Mr Harvey, Mercer, a bill in full			£5	9s	10d
Of Robert Reading, Quadring Eaudike, a bill	9s				
Retail &c. 14s. Weekly bill 14s.	14s			14s	
30 Paid for Phials in October and November				4s	2d
£69 11s 1d	**£290**	**9s**	**6d**	**£220 18s**	**5d**

Family

I have to remark in regard to my Son Matthew, who is now approaching fast to his 11th Year, that I have not yet sent him out to a Grammer School – tho' I thank God he improves in his Latin very well under my own Tuition. He goes only half days to Mr Whitehead, keeping close to his Latin each afternoon and while he continues so to improve & I can teach him I think I shall not send him; my present intention is not to send him untill 12 Years old & then to give him 2 Years at the best neighbouring School I can. It is now approaching toward 2 Years since it pleased Divine Wisdom in its unfathomable councils to take from me my dearest first partner, and I here acknowledge my gratitude to the same Divine Wisdom in repairing my loss with my present valuable Friend and wife. May Providence bless us with some comfortable Years together to the Nurture & advantage of own [sic] Young ones. Jan. 3. 85.

[f.75]
December 1784: 12th Month, 31 Days

	Received			**Paid**		
Brought over	**£290**	**9s**	**6d**	**£220**	**18s**	**5d**
3 The late Andrew Hodson's bill, Gosberton	£1	14s	6d			
Of Mr Caswell, Donington, a bill		10s				
To Mr Powell for ½ a Year's Tithe					4s	1½d
Worstead 9oz at 2½d: 1s 10½d. Carriage 2d.					2s	0½d
4 Of Mr Wm Gee, Hale Fenn, a Labour	£1	1s				
Carriage of Druggs from Mr Wilson					5s	8d
To James Moon for weaving 36 Yards of Cloth					12s	8d
Retail 17s 6d. Weekly bill 17s 10¼d.		17s	6d		17s	10¼d

---

[344] Totals entered wrongly, as in MS.
[345] Probably *Cantharides*, from *Cantharis*, or Spanish fly, an inflammatory (*Supplement*, 163).
[346] Probably Calomel pills (*Pilulae hydrargyri submuriatis*), a purgative (*Supplement*, 394).
[347] See n.224 above.

December 1784 (cont.)		Received			Paid		
7	Of Mr Caswell, Donington, a bill		7s	6d			
	Of Mr Philips, Gosberton, a bill		13s				
11	The late Wm Mablestone's bill, Bicker		5s				
	Retail &c. 15s. Weekly bill 15s 0½d.		15s			15s	0½d
12	Carriage of a Turkey to London					2s	10d
14	One Sack of Oats of Mrs Emmerson					7s	6d
	To John Sawdbell for killing 2 Swine					2s	
15	Of Mr Rossiter, Helpringham Fen	£1	1s	0d			
	Of Peregrine Moor a bill		8s	6d			
	Paid to him for Shoes Soling					2s	
16	Composition 3 Days to the Highways					1s	
18	Of Mr Rosby, Spalding, his Son's bill		8s	10d			
	Of Mr Jos. Dodd for Winter eat of the Ing Pasture		10s	6d			
	Retail &c. 19s. Weekly bill 19s 3½d.		19s			19s	3½d
22	To Mrs Pakey for 5 Stone of 2d Flower					10s	3d
23	To Mr Gleed 2 Years' Mill Tax (Ing Land)					5s	10d
25	Retail &c. £1 2s 0d. Weekly bill £1 1s 9¼d.	£1	2s		£1	1s	9¼d
27	Of John Tebb, Blacksmith (a Labour)		10s	6d			
	Christmas Boxes 2s 9d. Carriage of Druggs 2s 8d.					5s	5d
31	Of Mr Jarvis, Bicker, a bill	£1	13s	6d			
	Retail &c. 10s. Weekly bill 9s 8¾d.		10s			9s	8¾d
	Children's Clothing bill from May 8th				£5	16s	4½d
	Those Articles I took of Mrs Flinders's now first accounted for				£3	19s	9d
	Cash taken from the Retail	£4	4s	0d			
£70 1s 3¼d	**Total Receipts & Payments**	**£308**	**0s**	**10d**	**£237**	**19s**	**6¾d**

Total gained in 1784	£70	1s	3¼d
Total gained in Thirteen Years	£810	16s	10d
Total gained in 14 Years' Business	£880	18s	1¼d

Conclusion of the Year 1784

With humble gratitude to Divine Providence I remark that myself & remnant of my Family are again entering on a new Year & tho' my expences appear great (not greater than last year) yet thro' a Blessing my receipts have exceeded them by £70, for which I desire to be sincerely gratefull. I have estimated my present annual income by Interest, Rent &c., which with what I have in my own Tenure amounts to £50. May the Good God continue my Health and enable me to continue laying up something for my poor Young ones. Jan. 3. 1785.

[f.77v][348]

Present Annual Income, January 1785

£200	In Mr Walls's hands, Spilsby, Interest due December 2	£10	0s	0d
£160	Rent of the Fen 8 acres due April 5	£8	8s	0d
£150	Mortgage of J. Smith, Frampton, May 4	£7	10s	0d
£100	Bond of Mr Samuel Ward, June 11	£5	0s	0d

---

348 Ff. 75v–77r contain accounts of Flinders's annual income from property and interest for 1786 and 1792, together with his annual receipts and payments from 1771 to 1799 and a note of Lady Day rents received in 1841. These will be printed as an Appendix to Volume II of this edition.

£45	Rent of the 3 Acres Ing Pasture, J. Tunnard, O.L.D.[349]	£2	2s 0d
	{3d Part of Peregrine Moor's Rent, O.L.D.	£0	15s 0d
£20	{3d Part of Wm Reddiff's Rent, O.L.D.	£0	13s 4d
	{3d Part of John Sawdbell's Rent, O.L.D.	£0	11s 0d
£75	{3d Part of Nicholas Gunthorp's Rent, O.L.D.	£0	10s 0d
	{3d Part of the House and Pasture next me Rent	£3	10s 0d
£200	My dwelling House and Homestead Rent	£10	0s 0d
£30	The 2 Acre Ing Pasture Rent	£1	10s 0d
£980		**£50**	**9s 4d**

[349] Old Lady Day, i.e. 5 April (6 April from 1800).